THE FORTUNES OF WANGRIN

THE
FORTUNES
OF
WANGRIN

Amadou Hampaté Bâ

translated by Aina Pavolini Taylor
with an introduction by Abiola Irele
and an afterword by the author

Indiana University Press
BLOOMINGTON AND INDIANAPOLIS

This book is a publication of
Indiana University Press
601 North Morton Street
Bloomington, Indiana 47404-3797 USA

http://www.indiana.edu/~iupress

Telephone orders   800-842-6796
Fax orders   812-855-7931
Orders by e-mail   iuporder@indiana.edu

Library of Congress Cataloging-in-Publication Data

Bâ, Amadou Hampaté.
    [Etrange destin de Wangrin. English]
    The fortunes of Wangrin : the life and times of an
African confidence man / Amadou Hampaté Bâ ; translated
by Aina Pavolini Taylor ; with an introduction by Abiola
Irele and ; an afterward by the author.
        p.   cm.
ISBN 0-253-33429-2 (cloth : alk. paper). —ISBN 0-253-
21226-X (pbk. : alk. paper)
1. Wangrin—Fiction. I. Taylor, Aina Pavolini. II. Title.
PQ3989.2.B2E8813   1999
843—dc21   98-17131

        4   5   05

CONTENTS

INTRODUCTION BY ABIOLA IRELE

Amadou Hampaté Bâ's reputation as an advocate of the African oral tradition and as historian of the continent's precolonial past was well established before the publication of what is now regarded as his master-piece, and indeed, as one of the most significant texts in all of modern African literature: the work translated here under the title *The Fortunes of Wangrin*. Ostensibly a biography of Wangrin, an African interpreter in the service of French administration during the years of its establish-ment in West Africa, this is a compelling reconstruction of the colonial experience, and as such, a social document of great significance. The narrative constructed around the facts of Wangrin's life provides a fasci-nating record of the beginnings of French rule in what used to be known as "le Soudan Français" (the French Sudan), today more commonly re-ferred to as the Sahel. But more important, this book registers the formi-dable impact of this historical process, as it begins to unfold, upon Afri-cans of every class and station in the region.

The work derives its documentary value from what I have called elsewhere its "concrete quality of representation." This quality endows Hampaté Bâ's account with a sense of objectivity that provides the inspi-rational ground for the chronicler's art, displayed here in all its expres-sive vitality. For the factual basis of the account does not preclude a strong emotional tonality that colors the narrative and determines its character as personal testimony. Hampaté Bâ writes here not simply as a detached observer of the events that surrounded the exceptional life he is at pains to record, but as a concerned witness of the unique conjunction of events that marked the violent incursion of the French into the African world.

Perhaps no one was better qualified to provide this testimony than Amadou Hampaté Bâ himself, whose long life was closely interwoven with the very history that he recounts. He was born at the turn of the century in Bandiagara (in present-day Mali), the capital of the precolonial state of Macina, founded only a few decades earlier by the Fulani con-queror El Hadj Omar, who imposed Islam upon the populations through-out the area around the bend of the river Niger. Hampaté Bâ's parents on both sides were closely connected with the ruling elite of the new state and were tragically involved in the drama of its confrontation with the relentless progression of the French colonial enterprise, which put an end to the existence of Macina as an independent state. In the closing years of the nineteenth century, the French completed their conquest of the Sahelian region with the aid of troops led by Colonel Archinard along the Senegal River into the valley of the Niger, into the very heart of the West African savannah. Shortly before the birth of Hampaté Bâ, Macina was overrun and incorporated into the new colony of Soudan, as part of what was later to become Afrique Occidentale Française (AOF). Thus, although claiming descent from a prestigious line of warriors and rulers, Hampaté Bâ came into the world as a French colonial subject.

His childhood was spent largely within the family circle ruled over by his iron-willed mother, Kadidja. After an early education at the Koranic school, he was enrolled in 1912 at the French primary school in Djenné, a city famous as a center of Islamic learning. The school was known as l'école des otages ("the school for hostages"), so-called because, like other schools started at this time by the French in their new colonial empire, it was intended for the children of local notables, as a means of loosening their family ties and cultural links, fostering in them a sense of identification with the French, and thus ensuring (it was hoped) their loyalty to France. Hampaté Bâ began to learn French and to acquire the rudiments of Western education at the school in Djenné. After obtaining his first school certificate, he decided to interrupt his studies in order to rejoin his parents at Bandiagara. At this time he came under the influence of Tierno Bokar, the Sufi religious leader, who began to give him advanced lessons in Arabic and became his life-long spiritual guide. Despite his devotion to the person and the teachings of Tierno Bokar, Hampaté Bâ came to realize that his future lay irrevocably with the new order introduced by the French. He resumed his Western education and in 1918 entered the École Régionale at Bamako. Three years later, he passed the competitive examination for admission to the École Normale de Gorée, in Senegal, for a long time the hothouse of the emerging French African elite. Because his mother objected to his going so far from home, he sought a position within the newly established French administration instead. He was promptly posted to Ouagadougou, in what was then Upper Volta (now Burkina Faso), to begin a career as an African auxiliary in the French colonial civil service.

This career took an auspicious turn when he was recruited in 1942 by Théodore Monod, the eminent French anthropologist, as research assistant at the newly founded Institut Français de l'Afrique Noire (IFAN), in Dakar. With this appointment, Hampaté Bâ began a new life as historian and folklorist. His assignments took him through the length and breadth of French West Africa collecting research material for IFAN, and recording aspects of the oral traditions and cultures of the various populations in the region. He made his first visit to France in 1951 on a UNESCO fellowship, which enabled him to do research at the Musée de l'Homme, the principal institution in France for ethnological studies. He had begun by this time to acquire a reputation throughout French West Africa as a major intellectual figure through his scholarly publications and radio broadcasts on the history and indigenous cultures of the West African savannah. This reputation enabled him to secure sufficient funds in 1958 to found the Institut des Sciences Humaines in Bamako, of which he was named Director. After the independence of Mali in 1960, he formed part of his country's delegation to the UNESCO General Conference, held that year in Paris; it was on this occasion that he made his passionate plea for the preservation of Africa's heritage with the famous statement, "En Afrique, quand un vieillard meurt, c'est une bibliothèque qui brûle" ("In Africa, when an old person dies, it's a library burning down"). In 1962, he became a member of UNESCO's executive council, and in this capacity exerted his influence in determining that organization's orientation and priorities. At his retirement from public life in 1970, he settled in Abidjan, where he set up an informal school in the extensive family compound, complete with private mosque, that he had constructed at Macory, on the outskirts of the city. Here he spent his time writing his memoirs and receiving visitors from all over the world. At his death in 1991, he left behind an impressive output of some twenty books.

This outline of Hampaté Bâ's biography suggests the immediate connection between his own life and career and the material of this book, for he was himself, in a very real sense, an embodiment of the experience that he ascribes to Wangrin. The parallels between Wangrin's career and his own provided a strong foundation on which Hamapté Bâ could build his narrative. What is more, as he has indicated in the two volumes of his autobiography, the two lives touched at certain crucial points. As he tells the story, it was as a child in the early years of the century that he first caught sight of the man who came to be called Wangrin, at a time when, as monitor interpreter at Bandiagara, Wangrin had just begun his own career in the French colonial service. This early meeting not only favored a strong sense of personal identification with his subject when Hampaté Bâ came to write the story of Wangrin's life, but also conditioned the larger-than-life image he presents of his character.

But more important than a personal fascination with Wangrin going back to a childhood memory, the determining factor in the shaping of Hampaté Bâ's narrative was the shared background which bound him to his character. They belonged to a common universe of values, marked by vivid conceptions of individual rank, personal honor, and social obligations, a universe that Hampaté Bâ has reconstituted in this work with an evident sense of attachment, all the stronger for having remained more a thing of memory than a living reality. This was a universe that was governed at the spiritual level by a structure of belief that, in constant tension with Islam, has continued to operate as an active force in the collective existence and apprehension. The power of myth as a conceptual reference for understanding the world and as a guide to individual endeavor gives significance to his constant evocation of the deities associated with the personality of Wangrin—Komo, Sanu, and especially Gongoloma-Sooke, his tutelary god—an evocation that must be read as a celebration of a communal vision and sensibility that Wangrin came so powerfully to embody for him.

It is against this background that the impact of French colonization as described in this book needs to be appraised. In the aftermath of their conquest of the region, the French embarked on what they described as "pacification" of the Sahel. Beginning with the drawing of new administrative and juridical lines around local populations, the massive reorganization of political, social, and economic life undertaken by the French had no other aim than to undo the political and social order, which had been in place in the region for centuries, and to substitute systems of their own making. As recounted by Hampaté Bâ in this work and in his autobiography, the French concentrated their efforts on creating new loyalties by dethroning previous rulers and replacing them with selected individuals, who would be beholden to the colonial authorities. An essential plank of this French policy was the systematic devaluation of traditional beliefs and forms of cultural expression, and the active promotion of what call only be called a French ideology, of which an ideal image of France as a benevolent agent of African promotion was the central reference. It did not matter that this ideology was contradicted by the reality of French colonial policy and practice. The civil service which was rapidly put in place, often administered by former officers of the French army, was essentially an instrument of economic exploitation; if, in the circumstances, it had to assume a formal character based upon an elaborate system of procedures and regulations, its essential function was furthered through the more brutal form of forced labor, with devastating effects upon whole communities throughout the expanse of the territories under French rule in West Africa, as also in the other half of the French colonial empire on the continent—in Equatorial Africa.

The social and moral consequences of the drastic reordering of life undertaken by the French in the Sahel are at the heart of the historical reminiscence contained in *The Fortunes of Wangrin*. The most striking aspect of this process toward a new order was the assault upon the local aristocracy. The realignments which the new system provoked account for the atmosphere of intrigue and the jostling for power that provides the testing ground for Wangrin's project of self-realization as recounted in this book, in which he is presented as an exceptional individual who takes advantage of the moral confusion and cultural misunderstanding generated by the colonial situation for his own self-advancement. The book can be read as the story of a quest—determined, wilful, and even desperate—for self-fulfillment in a world of uncertainty.

In this respect, Wangrin stands out as an individual endowed with a remarkable lucidity, for he is one of the very few among the African population to grasp the import of the new dispensation, the original relation it established between the social order and system of values ushered in by the French, and a new understanding of the individual's standing in the world, manifested henceforth by one's economic success rather than the inheritance of birth and social ties. The story of Wangrin's rise to eminence (and of his eventual decline and fall) thus encapsulates the transition in the Sahel from the self-contained world of a precolonial feudalism to a new political and socioeconomic structure distinguished especially by the denial to Africans of historical initiative.

In the broader cultural perspectives intimated by the work, Wangrin's experience epitomizes the movement from a heritage of life that, for all its limitations, provided an anchor for the self, to an externally imposed and problematic modernity derived from the Western paradigm. It is the narrative uncovering of this fundamental relation between individual fate and the force of events that constitutes Hampaté Bâ's work as an important document of Africa's social history. But if his biography of Wangrin counts as a subcategory of history, it also takes the form of an extended narrative, one in which the *peripeteia* provide the elements of a plot charted along a definite line of development: the single-minded pursuit of a consuming passion, vindicated at first by its apparent triumph, only to be contradicted soon afterward by its tragic undoing. Hampaté Bâ creates a dramatic context for the restless unfolding of Wangrin's life experience, complete with elaborate settings and arresting and colorful dialogue as essential formal components of his narrative presentation. The series of adventures marking his progression is recounted with a verve that reflects the writer's expressive resources. But it is not only the external aspects of Wangrin's life that we witness: we also participate in the evolution of his mental states and are even occasionally provided with insights into his inner life.

Hampaté Bâ's exploration of Wangrin's personality may well appear summary in some important respects, but it is sufficient to establish Wangrin as the quintessential marginal man, burdened with an ambiguity grounded in his existential condition. Wangrin the colonial interpreter, situated in time and place at the meeting point of two disparate languages, is seen to assume the demanding vocation of arbiter between two cultures in conflict, between two antagonistic value systems. The amorality that he displays through most of the story functions as the regulatory principle of his ambition, but it can also be considered a form of response to his stressful situation, an ethos that he assumes as a moral shield, the sign of his resolve to overcome the limitations imposed upon him and, most important, upon his self-conception. Thus, for all the ambiguity of his representation, Wangrin is far from being a pathetic figure; he emerges rather as an energetic, full-blooded character in a strongly articulated narrative.

He exists moreover in a world bustling with movement. *The Fortunes of Wangrin* presents a vast fresco of peoples and manners, sharply delineated and evoked as much in realistic detail as in symbolic terms. The procession of characters that moves through these pages comprises both Africans and Europeans, swirling around the figure of Wangrin in an incessant play of motives and impulses. The story takes its full life from the activity and interactions of these characters: on the African side, the local notables and the ordinary people whose condition as colonized subjects he shares, and on the French side, the administrators whose paths he crosses with dramatic results, notably Count de Villermoz, with whom he engages in a contest of wills that casts him, at least by implication, as a prototype of colonial rebel.

The scope of Hampaté Bâ's representation of Wangrin underlies the heroic dimension of his work, which, as Eileen Julien has rightly observed, is governed by what she discerns as "an epic impulse." This feature of the narrative is overtly reflected in the interventions of the griot Kountenna, who sings Wangrin's praises by reference to the exploits of the great figures of collective memory in the Sahel, the emperors of Mali and Ségou. Wangrin's adventure is situated squarely within the context of modern experience. At the same time, it is evident that, despite the realism of this narrative, Hampaté Bâ's representation of Wangrin's character corresponds to a recognizable figure lodged within the deepest recesses of the African imagination: that of the trickster in the oral tradition. It is not without interest to observe the affinities between this figure and such characters of European folk consciousness as the French Renart and the German Till Eulenspiegel, a type that is given striking literary embodiment in Molière's Scapin. Wangrin's character may thus be said to be grounded in a universal imaginary, a fact that endows his adventure with a symbolic significance, brought home to the reader by the quest theme through which the narrative development of earthly existence is organized. The obvious connection of the journey motif with the quest theme in African initiation tales adds a special dimension to this aspect of Wangrin's experience. It is pertinent in this regard to observe that the tragic grandeur of Wangrin's final years confers a certain meditative quality to his story, which can be interpreted not merely as the unfolding of a singular destiny but also, and perhaps in its most authentic quality, as an allegory of our general human condition.

We are taken, then, in this book well beyond the bounds of a factual account of a life, of the kind we associate with standard biography, or the linear progression of events that we recognize as historical. As a text, *The Fortunes of Wangrin* lies at the intersection between history, considered, in the words of Bernard Baylin, as "correspondence to actuality," on one hand, and, on the other, literature, understood as pure projection of the imagining faculty. As Louis Mink and Hayden White among others have pointed out, the formal relation between the two is constituted by the principles of narrative discourse which imply a concern for relevance and coherence in the telling, in order to impose a meaningful pattern on the impersonal flow of time and the undifferentiated flux of experience. The demands of narrative construction thus determine for both genres not only a common rhetorical ground but also a fundamental imaginative framework. It is in this light that we must consider Hampaté Bâ's insistence upon the veracity of his story. One cannot help but observe that he does himself less than justice in underplaying the literary status of his work, in order to emphasize its purely factual reference. Although its documentary aspect makes for credible history, this history is not directly recounted so much as inferred from the circumstances of Wangrin's experience, for which it serves, from the point of view of the reader's engagement with the text, as largely incidental support. The focus here is placed unambiguously upon the personality of Wangrin, so that the historical reference of the work does not in any way undermine the claim to imaginative significance of its comprehensive representation of Wangrin's life and times. It is not the bare facts that matter, but the narrative strategies that have gone into this representation, and lend it an incomparable human interest. The essential consideration here must surely be not the exactitude of the recollection but the evocative power of the account.

These remarks lead us inevitably to the question of form. Hampaté Bâ, who was an accomplished poet in the Fulani language, also enjoyed the privilege of being a second-language writer in French, placed at the confluence of two linguistic systems and two imaginative traditions. He was endowed with a literary consciousness at the critical interface between African and Western forms of discourse. Although a traditionalist, he understood more than most African writers and intellectuals the need to negotiate a convergence between the singular speech patterns of a formalized orality and the structures of literate expression as determined by print culture. *The Fortunes of Wangrin* illustrates this convergence admirably. The narrative method approximates as nearly as is possible within a written text the performance mode of oral composition and delivery. We are made aware throughout of the interplay and creative tension between the immediacies of speech acts in traditional communities and the conventions of textual production in literate cultures.

Given this quality of the work, and the exceptional vigor that Hampaté Bâ's writing often displays, it was inevitable that *The Fortunes of Wangrin* should have been approached as a novel. But it does not take much reflection to understand that it does not conform to the conception of the Western genre as defined by Ian Watt, for example, with its emphasis on realism and its narrow psychological interest. Samba Dieng's term *conte historique* comes close to suggesting the nature of the work, its integration of the traditional moral fable within a historical narrative. Non-African readers will perhaps be inclined to explain this peculiarity of the work, and its interweaving of the supernatural with a realistic narrative, by reference to the much-abused term "magic realism." The truth, however, is that the variegated character of Hampaté Bâ's work challenges classification. His achievement consists in the creative adaptation of mode to material, reflected here in the complex narrative procedures employed to give expression to the multiple levels of an expansive creative imagination.

Confronted with the singularity of his material, Hampaté Bâ was compelled to recreate the forms of narrative in order to accommodate fully the cultural grounding of his story. The convergence of history, culture, and language in the making of the African text, so much in evidence here, amounts ultimately to the elaboration of a distinctive aesthetic. *The Fortunes of Wangrin* thus provides us with an especially striking example of the relation between theme, language, and expressive mode in African literature. But beyond this formal significance, it points ultimately to the existential import of narrative as a means of ordering experience and of relating to the world.

Abiola Irele
Columbus, Ohio
December 1998

References

Amadou Hampaté Bâ. *L'Empire peul de Macina*. Paris: Mouton, 1955.
————. *Koumen, texte initiatique des pasteurs peul*. Paris: Mouton, 1961.
————. *Kaïdara, récit initiatique peul*. Paris: Julliard, 1969. Collection Classiques Africains.
————. *Aspects de la civilisation africaine*. Paris: Présence Africaine, 1972.
————. *L'Etrange destin de Wangrin*. Paris: 10/18, 1973.
————. *Vie et enseignement de Tierno Bokar, le Sage de Bandiagara*. Paris: Seuil, 1980.
————. *Njeddo Dewal, mère de la calamité*. Abidjan: Nouvelles Editions Africaines, 1985.
————. "The Living Tradition" in Joseph Ki-Zerbo, ed., *UNESCO General History of Africa*, Vol. I, pp. 166–203.
————. *Amkoullel, l'enfant peul*. Paris: Editions Actes du Sud, 1991.
————. *Oui, mon Commandant!* Paris: Editions Actes du Sud, 1994.
Bernard Baylin. *On the Teaching and Writing of History*. Hanover, N.H.: University Press of New England, 1994.
Samba Dieng. "*L'Étrange destin de Wangrin*: Essai d'interpretation" in *Annales de la Faculté des Lettres et Sciences Humaines*. Université de Dakar, No. 15, 1985.
Abiola Irele. "Wangrin: A Study in Ambiguity." Introduction to *The Fortunes of Wangrin*. Ibadan: New Horn Press, 1987. iii-xv.
Eileen Julien. *African Novels and the Question of Orality*. Bloomington: Indiana University Press, 1992.
Louis O. Mink. *Historical Understanding*. Ed. Brian Fay, Eugene O. Golob, and Richard T. Vann. Ithaca: Cornell University Press, 1987.
Ian Watt. *The Rise of the Novel: Studies in Defoe, Richardson, and Fielding*. 1957. Reprint, London: Hogarth, 1987.
Hayden White. *Metahistory: The Historical Imagination in Nineteenth-Century Europe*. Baltimore: The Johns Hopkins University Press, 1973.

FOREWORD

This book is the fulfillment of a promise I made to a man I met in 1912. I was then a twelve-year-old schoolboy, and he worked as interpreter for the Commandant[1] of that area. He became attached to me for two reasons: first, because he was very close to my maternal uncle Hammadun Pate and secondly, because of the large number of stories I collected for him at his prompting.[2]

These stories I had heard from Kullel, who at the time was the greatest raconteur of traditional tales along that loop of the Niger. Kullel lived at the court of my adoptive father, Tidjani Amadu Ali, chief of the Luta province until French occupation brought about the political decline of the Tukulors of Bandiagara.

Fifteen years later I came across the hero of this book once again. He had resigned his job as interpreter and set up in business with what seemed at the time a vast amount of capital for any indigenous African to own. This is how we happened to meet again.

A European businessman had been murdered in Diussola. As he had no heir, the administration and liquidation of his property were put in the hands of the Probate Office, where I was employed at the time. Accordingly, my superior and I went to that town where I was received and sheltered by my uncle's friend. As Malian tradition has it, he considered me and therefore treated me as his own nephew.

We were both exceedingly happy to meet again. Remembering what a fine storyteller I had been in my youth, he felt the need to relate to me in detail his adventurous and tempestuous life.

One day he came up to me and said: "My little Amkullel,[3] in days gone by you were a fine storyteller. Now that you have learned to write, you must take down the story of my life and after my death compose it into a book which will not only amuse but also instruct those who read it. I am asking you explicitly not to mention my real name so as to spare my relatives the risk of feeling superior or inferior. . . . Rather, you will use one of my borrowed names—the one dearest to me, 'Wangrin.'"

Every evening, after dinner, from eight to eleven, and sometimes even twelve, Wangrin would recount episodes from his life. His conversation was accompanied by the strains of a lute, played skillfully and indefatigably by his griot, Dieli Madi. We went on in this way for three whole months. Apart from collecting and noting down carefully a number of tales told by Wangrin himself, later on I had the good fortune of being employed in all of Wangrin's former stations. There, talking with the people who had in one way or another been involved in his adventures, I was able to add to the information already at my disposal.

As for my account of the last years of Wangrin's life, I owe a debt not only to his griot Dieli Madi, who remained faithful to him in the days of his decline as he had been in those of his glory, but also to Romo who, paradoxically, in spite of having been his greatest enemy, had the honor of presiding, with sincere sorrow in his heart, at the funeral of a man with whom he had never for a moment ceased fighting. Finally death proved more effective than strength, ruses, or jealousy, for the sight of Wangrin's remains moved Romo deeply. Before his bier, Romo forgave and asked to be forgiven.

I have faithfully related, then, all that was told to me here and there. Let no one try, then, to look for any kind of thesis, be it political, religious, or other, in the following pages. This is no more than a man's life. But my readers will doubtlessly want to hear a few things about the man whose weird and tumultuous history I am about to recount.

Who was Wangrin? He was a profoundly strange human being with so great a mixture of good qualities and faults that, at a mere glance, it was impossible to describe him, and even less to place him. Wangrin was an eminently intelligent as well as an outstanding man. He was extremely superstitious and from time to time a diehard skeptic. An implacable and sometimes even fierce embezzler when dealing with the rich, he had never stopped being tender-hearted and charitable, and he had always felt an inclination toward helping the poor. His imperturbable self-assurance, leonine daring, and proverbial effrontery were practiced to the detriment of European, Lebanese, and Syrian businessmen, chiefs, and other men who were powerful in his day. But his prowess found its finest expression in his handling of "those gods of the bush," or colonial administrators, who happened to cross his path. Indeed, at that time it was certainly easier to have the weight of Mount Sinai on one's shoulders than the displeasure of the most insignificant of colonial administrators.

Wangrin was able to conquer calmly all the dangers sown along his path by circumstance and to accept setbacks philosophically when his otherwise good fortune took a turn for the worse. Always facetious, he nevertheless kept his word and all his promises religiously. In his bantering way he went so far as to warn his companions of the adversary tricks he intended playing on them. This was the sort of caustic refinement he would often indulge in.

As for me, I am most happy—through this work—to keep a promise made to a man who always kept his, so much so that it was said of him: "Wangrin's words are gold, and his promises are as durable as bronze."

Amadou Hampaté Bâ
6 November 1971

THE FORTUNES OF WANGRIN

Overture

Where did Wangrin come from?

Wangrin was born in a country both ancient and mysterious, a country where rain and wind, in the service of the gods, gnashed the mountainside with their invisible and useless teeth, creating in the process a flat and monotonous surface. A few ledges of granite or laterite managed to survive. Now they jut out at well-spaced intervals over the plain.

At the foot of one of the eminences that had rebelled against erosion was founded the foredoomed village of Nubigu which would later give its name to the country that surrounds it. Was it by mere chance that this name was given to the village, and later to that whole area? Fodan Seni, praise-singer of the god Komo, *Dan*[1] musician, and ritual dancer, strongly denies it. Without being a member of his retinue, at the beginning of the twentieth century Fodan Seni lived nevertheless at the court of king Metiogo Dani. Let us now listen to the Bambara thaumaturge as he tells the strange story of the birth of this country.

The plain stretching along the lower reaches of the Nubigu hills was one of the many centers where tutelary gods and spirits were wont to meet and discuss as well as determine the fate of the country.

Sanu, God king of gold, built on this plain a small hut called "Nubigu," and it was here that the great witch Nganiba came once a year to meet Ninkinanka, the immense Mande python who was seven hundred and thirty cubits long and weighed no less than fifteen well-fed donkeys. Unlike the boa constrictors and pythons we know, Ninkinanka did not use the three hundred and sixty-five rings that made up his impressive skeleton to suffocate his prey, but rather to plough in miraculous fashion the river beds now known to us as the waterways that originate in Guinea and the Ivory Coast. The care of Sanu's small hut, invisible among overgrown vegetation, had been entrusted to Tenin-Turuma, a sparrow plump as a pigeon. This bird had a tuft of feathers on his head and in his stomach a small white pebble symbolizing longevity and prosperity. He nested in the branches of an old gnarled *toro* whose invisible flowers had golden corollae.

Yuyayo, partner god of Nganiba, was patron of that stretch of land south of the country which consists of a succession of mountain chains, hills, and slopes, all the way to the Guinea Apennines. Led by Yuyayo, the guardian spirits of the southern Malian Massif traveled every year to the plain where Sanu had built his hut, there to hold their occult conferences.

According to the myth, this is the way Nubigu came into being. Now Nubigu is the capital of the region bearing the same name and it is there that the hero of our tale was born.

1 The Birth

It was the hottest time of the year; on that particular Sunday it was even hotter than on previous days. When the sun reached the middle of its parabola, all shadows withdrew underneath whatever object had been projecting them. Having attained its highest temperature, the sun shone implacably, blinding man and beast alike and making the gaseous surface that envelops the earth boil as if it were soup in a cauldron.

Men drank in deep gulps, sweat poured from their bodies in large drops. Chickens, their wings slightly askew, breathed fast and loud. Dogs, with flopping tongues and palpitating sides, unable to find a comfortable spot, panted and shuttled to and fro between the underside of the millet granaries and the narrow awnings that had been set up in front of the huts. Close to these unhappy creatures, a woman in labor thrashed about, pacing incessantly between the pallet that had been placed in one of the corners of the hut and a cluster of earthenware pots, where water was kept, in another corner of the hut. This woman was Wangrin's mother, overwhelmed by thirst, heat, and atrocious pains. She was attended by a toothless matron, heavy with age, who watched the mother-to-be arch her body like a spanworm, yet did not provide any solace except for a soft psalmody of the matrimonial chant handed down for generations by Nyakuruba, goddess of maternity:

Wooy wooy kyakuruba:[1] *a tinti!*
den wolo manndi Nyakuruba
den cee den wolo manndi Nyakuruba
a tinti!
Waay waay[2] *Nyakuruba, a tinti!*
den wolo manndi Nyakuruba

den muso den wolo manndi Nyakuruba
a tinti!
Eeh Eeh Nyakuruba
on den fla den wolo manndi Nyakuruba
a tinti!
tin bee tinti Nyakuruba a tin tin
nta tin tinti Nyakuruba a tintin.

Wuy way o! Nyakuruba, push hard!
Childbirth is laborious, Nyakuruba.
Giving birth to a boy is laborious,
Nyakuruba.
Push hard!
Waay waay o! Nyakuruba, push hard!
Childbirth is laborious, Nyakuruba.
Giving birth to a girl is laborious,
Nyakuruba.
Push hard!
Eeh, eeh, Nyakuruba! push hard!
Childbirth is laborious, Nyakuruba.
Giving birth to twins is laborious,
Nyakuruba.
Push hard!
Push hard all possible childbirths on earth, Nyakuruba,
Push hard!
Push hard this very childbirth,
Nyakuruba, push it hard.

The chanting of the old woman helped the future mother to bear the blows the baby was dealing to her belly with head, hands, and feet, trying to break free from the cocoon that prevented it from being its own master, an independent being who could live and move without any help from others.

Did Nyakuruba, goddess with great white eyes resembling huge rinsed cowries, hear the soft entreaties of the white-haired old woman? Whether she did or not, the delivery began. Maa Ngala, god of creation, parted the pelvic bones of the parturient mother and the head of the baby, soft as a wizard's egg,[3] peeped out, followed by the rest of the body. Little Wangrin let out the cry that announces the arrival of all babies in this baffling world where everyone must endure a thousand and one discomforts and which no one ever leaves alive.

The baby was draped all the way to the shoulders in a soft white tissue of flesh, supple and transparent. Even his head was swathed, as if he were sporting a bonnet. The "little brothers"[4] followed soon after. The old woman found it very hard to cut the umbilical cord that kept the child tied to his "little brothers": in the end she was obliged to go off in search of Wangrin's father who, seated in the shade of a great silk-cotton tree, was awaiting news of the birth, which could be: "very good and double," "good and double," or the opposite.

Traditionally, a woman in labor is compared to a soldier on the front line. When she has delivered, she is considered victorious, but if she dies in labor, it is said of her that she died honorably on the battlefield. The delivery of a boy is announced as being "very good and double news," that of a girl, "good news." The death of a woman and of her baby boy is termed a "double and very bad" announcement, while the death of a woman and of her baby girl is related as "double and bad."

When Wangrin's father saw the toothless matron running toward him so fast that her toes hit and scattered about every little object that stood in her way, he tore out of his mouth his earthenware pipe, took it in his left hand, and looked at the old woman intently, with staring eyes, his beard pointing upwards and his lips slightly parted. Before she had time to utter a word he stretched the open palm of his right hand toward the messenger[5] and said: "What news do you bring me, old woman?"

"Very good and double," she answered, "but you must come at once; my knife is too blunt to cut through the vessel that joins your baby to his 'little brothers.'"

Wangrin's father ran into his man's hut.[6] He brought out the fetish he kept in a black catskin, pulled out of his bag his sacrificial knife and a sachet full of active vegetable powder, and then followed the old woman to the spot where his helpless wife lay on her childbed, poignantly fearful for the life of her baby. Wangrin had been born, but not delivered. No one knew yet what his "little brothers" meant to do to him.

The father went into the maternity hut, nodded quickly at his spouse, and picked up a new calabash which he filled with water. He sprinkled into it his vegetable powder and began to invoke Nyakuruba and all the gods who protect marriages and maternity. As he recited these ritual litanies, he spat lightly into the water. This done, he threw his sacrificial knife into the calabash. A few moments later he pulled it out streaming with water, and with an accurate and sharp blow cut the umbilical cord that joined Wangrin to his "little brothers." The aged woman grabbed the "little brothers" and placed them in the folds of a wrapper made of cotton strips sewn together. Then she added seven millet pancakes, seven cowries,[7] seven balls of cotton fluff, seven kola nuts, seven small white pebbles, a tuft of hair cut from the head of the newly born baby, and finally a small strip of cotton stained with the baby's first urine and excrement. All this she buried in a place known only to herself and to the mother of the child.

After dinner the god Komo[8] came out of the sacred forest to Wangrin's father's compound. It was his way of welcoming a child into the community.

Komo announced to the father that his son would distinguish himself and lead an exciting life; his grave, however, could not be discerned among those of his ancestors. This prediction suggested that Wangrin would die abroad, far from the country of his birth.

Wangrin was brought up like a good son of the Bambara people. He walked about naked, wearing a bandoleer from which hung a small sack made of strips of cotton. Around his neck he wore a flute carved from a piece of sculpted wood. During his wanderings, he learned to ride horses, to hunt with a bow and arrow, and to set traps for birds and other small animals. He helped his father to till the fields and fetched water from the well for his mother. He never came back from the bush empty-handed. He always carried something home to his mother. The least he ever had to offer was a bundle of wood or a load of millet stalks for the kitchen.

There was no intimacy between the child and his father. Wangrin was deeply afraid of his father and before him lost all presence of mind to the point of not recognizing the objects that were placed in front of him. Yet he believed that his father was the strongest man in the world and thought with pride that some day he would be just as strong.

At first Wangrin was inducted into the association of uncircumcised boys, devotees of the lesser gods Thieblenin and Ntomo, and when he became a stripling, to Ntomo-Ntori. During the year of his second initiation, he was summoned to an establishment called "The School for Hostages."[9]

His country was the sad arena where conquering Yorsam, who sought to carve an empire for himself by fighting against Nubigu, engaged in lengthy conflicts, waging war at the same time against the French so as to protect the domains he had already conquered. The senseless atrocities inflicted by Yorsam encouraged the people of Nubigu to welcome the French conqueror with open arms. Many young people joined the ranks of the military which had been organized for the indigenes, to become later the Senegalese Infantry.

Although the population had sworn to capture Yorsam and deliver him to the Whites, this was only achieved after fifteen years of fighting.

At the same time, the French feared that chiefs and leading citizens might offer their loyalty to Yorsam in case he should manage to establish the least military advantage over the French troops. As guarantee against this contingency, they founded the School for Hostages in Kayes and enrolled all the children of pre-eminent families either amicably or by coercion. Wangrin—then almost seventeen—and many other young boys from all the lands conquered by, or allied to, the French who controlled the "Upper Senegal to Niger" area, which in those days included the territory between Kidira and Zinder, were sent to this school.

Young Wangrin learned to read and write very quickly, and also to do sums and speak French fluently. Every two years he would return to his native village, Ninkoro-Sira, for the holidays. His father took advantage of this break to have him circumcised and initiated into the society of Komo the god, thus conferring on him the status of a man. After that, it became possible for his father to discuss secret or intimate matters in his presence, and to speak openly before him of sexuality, of the symbolism attached to masks, etc.

Wangrin was proud of being a "Kamalen-Koro," a boy who had been circumcised, but he was equally proud of being a pupil in the School for Hostages. He took just as much pride in wearing school clothes, especially shoes made by a French cobbler, as in his round, red chechia adorned by a pompon of blue silk. Each holiday represented a memorable event, one that was awaited impatiently. Everybody in Ninkoro-Sira longed for his arrival, but all the beautiful young girls even more.

He completed his studies in the shortest possible time and was given the certificate for indigenes as proof that he had finished primary school. In those days no African was permitted to obtain higher diplomas. That bit of parchment—one of its corners crossed by the French stripes—was a miraculous key, an "open sesame." The Africans who owned this document were admitted into the lower cadres of Civil Administration and could be employed as instructors in indigenous primary schools, as office clerks—that is, secretaries entrusted with copying and dispatching correspondence—as telegraphists, nurses, etc.

Wangrin, having obtained the highest marks in his final examination, became an instructor, an employment that was reserved for the most deserving pupils. For two years he carried out his duties to the greatest satisfaction of his superiors, especially of the Inspector of Schools. As a reward, he was directed to found and head a school in Diagaramba, capital of Namaci, an area which the French had taken back from the indigenous chiefs in 1893. It was in this handsome and large city that his adventures were to begin.

At that time Wangrin had already adopted one of the most significant of his pseudonyms, Gongoloma-Sooke, a legendary deity in Bambara mythology. This god could neither be soaked by rain nor dried by the sun. Salt could not salt him, and soap could not clean him. Although he was as soft as a mollusk, no metal, however sharp, could cut through him. The elements did not affect him in the least; he never felt hot or cold. When he slept, he closed only one eye; because of this, he was feared by night and mistrusted by day. Simultaneously, he married dawn and twilight and had his union blessed by the scorpion Ngoson, one of the oldest patriarchs in the whole world. Before the sun, Gongoloma-Sooke was lunar and before the moon he was solar. He took advantage of this confusion to create dissent between the two heavenly bodies symbolized by "Kalomina," the eclipse, but blamed this mishap on the cat.[10] Moreover, he exploited the darkness caused by an eclipse to sow terror in the hearts of the *hadama denw*, or sons of Adam. Gongoloma-Sooke was also shepherd of the stars and took them to graze in the endless, uncharted plains of the cosmos. The Milky Way represented the bulk of his flock. Both kindly and ill-disposed, chaste and libertine, Gongoloma-Sooke, a weird divinity, used his nostrils to absorb drink and his anus to ingest solid food. His penis was planted right in the middle of his forehead. His mouth was tongueless and furnished with toothless maws—sharper, however, than a brand-new razor. These he used for sawing, cutting, sculpting, and digging, according to his needs. Each time that the news of a birth or a wedding was broken to him, Gongoloma-Sooke wept and wept until his tears eventually dried up; but when he heard of a demise, divorce, or any kind of calamity he laughed till he split his sides. He always walked backwards toward his destination, and rested with his head on the ground and his feet stuck in the air at right angles with his body. He hurled vulgar abuse at those who had been kind to him but warmly thanked and sang the praises of those who detested him and had caused him the worst kind of trouble. After the first crowing of the rooster at dawn and the last braying of the donkey at dusk, Gongoloma-Sooke climbed the vast mahogany in the sacred forest and shouted for all who wished to hear: "It is true that I am Gongoloma-Sooke, a weird divinity, but I also represent the confluence of all opposites. . . . Come to me and your wishes shall be granted!"

At what stage had Wangrin heard that call? When he was still mere smoke, between heaven and earth, or a particle of liquid in his father's loins? Be it as it may, he chose Gongoloma-Sooke as one of his "patron-gods." Let us listen to him as he tells the story of his covenant:

"Having decided to place myself under the protection of Gongoloma-Sooke, I procured a chicken with black and white feathers. Then I called the spirit of the god and invoked his patronage. I had already learned the appropriate sacramental formula; now I was to recite it; I slit the chicken's throat and let its blood drip on a stone that would symbolize the dwelling place of my chosen god. At this point I was to drop the chicken so that it should not die in my hands. Having accomplished this ritual, I let go of the bird, who leaped in the air, fighting against death. My heart was beating fast and large beads of sweat ran down my body; I feared that the god might reject me. But the chicken fell on its back for the last time, wings outspread and legs stretched in the air.

"I was positively overjoyed! This meant that Gongoloma-Sooke had adopted me and ritually undertaken to protect me."

Wangrin did not try to conceal the fact that he counted on Gongoloma-Sooke's inspiration and assistance for the day when he was ready to trigger off what he called the "stupendous enterprises that would place him in a good many awkward situations."

Thus accepted by Gongoloma-Sooke, Wangrin adopted the name of that god as a pseudonym. Many more were to follow.

After circumcision, and when Wangrin had been initiated into the society of Komo, his Sema,[11] Numu-Sama, who had drawn up the horoscope of each newly circumcised boy, had warned him: "You, my boy, will have a successful life if you can persuade Gongoloma-Sooke to accept you, and your luck will hold so long as you have in your safe-keeping the pebble that represents your alliance with the god. I do not know how you will die, but I can see that your star will begin to set the day Ntubanin-kan-fin, the dove with a black ring circling half her neck, comes to rest on the dead branch of a kapok tree in full bloom, cooing seven times distinctly, then leaves that branch and alights on the left-hand side of your path. From that moment on you will become vulnerable. You will be at the mercy of your enemies and ill luck will dog your steps relentlessly. Guard against that moment; this is my advice to you."

The narrative which is about to begin will show just how exact that prediction turned out to be.

2 Diagaramba

A well-established custom prevailed in Diagaramba, capital of the Namaci empire: every morning after breakfast a large number of men would gather in the shade cast by the walls of houses that surrounded the main square, named Eldika, or "pebble." Nearby was the market reserved for the sale of kola nuts. Everyone came in elegant attire, as if to attend a ceremony, and bought one *gondio* or *siga* kola nut, according to his taste or means and, above all, his social status.

The *gondio* kola, which originates from the Gold Coast, now Ghana, is red, wrinkled, and very hard. It is thought to have virile properties and is sold to warriors, while the softer and almost sweet *siga* kola, which comes from Gutugu in the Ivory Coast, is sold to more sensitive souls, such as marabouts or women.

Every customer, having bought the quantity of nuts necessary to himself and his family, would send home the ones he was not going to consume on the spot. He was now ready to join his chosen group. There were seven of these altogether, and they assembled according to criteria of age and class differences.

Each person would begin to chew his kola nut, and talk to his companions. This morning ritual would last an hour, sometimes even two, depending on the season and what people did for a living. The spot had become so well known that it was sung by poets, and a number of strangers were prepared to come to Diagaramba from faraway lands so that on their return they might boast: "I have chewed kola nuts in Diagaramba's 'Eldika.'"

Eldika was the twin of Telerke, a much larger square, where boys and girls forgathered when the moon was full and amused themselves, singing, dancing, and conversing. But it was also an area for wrestlers, and the setting for the performance of famous storytellers and eminent lute players always surrounded by crowds of admirers.

Kullel, the great narrator, sang thus:

Come to Diagaramba.
come in the morning and chew kola at Eldika,
and join the evening celebrations at Telerke,
then return to your country and die. You may
be certain that the angels in heaven will say to
the Lord: Show clemency and compassion towards
that man. For he has "done" Eldika and Telerke.
He has been purified.

It was at Eldika that news would spread, that present and past events would be discussed. In the corner reserved for the marabouts, conversation centered on theological issues and juridical debates, while in the corner occupied by the old *Sofas* (warriors who had been defeated by the troops led by Colonel Archinard and reduced to a state of depressing idleness) one heard nothing but bitter recriminations against the French and against the regime of King Buagui who had been coerced by circumstance into an alliance with France, and had later become king of Diagaramba.

On one of the mornings of the year 1906, while everyone was busy talking and chewing kola, a convoy suddenly wound its way into the square. It consisted of five porters, who carried luggage tied in the European manner. A horseman followed. He wore a khaki jacket over baggy trousers, elegant boots, and a conical hat of the kind then known as "colonial helmet."

Comical as it was, that headgear elicited no laughter. On the contrary, it inspired great fear, for it had unmistakable official connotations. It was the regulation headgear of the Whites, those sons of Satan from beyond the vast salty lake who, armed with their guns that snapped in half and were loaded through the arse, in a few years had annihilated the local armies, enslaving kings and subjects alike. As a result, whenever anyone appeared wearing a real colonial helmet, even a misshapen old thing, one thought alone sprang to mind: chickens, eggs, butter, and milk must be fetched at once, and offered to the "helmeted gentleman" as an exorcism against the misfortunes that his presence was likely to cause.

In fact, once the conquest was over, only the Tubabublen, or "White-Whites" born in France, and the Tubabu-fin, or "White-Blacks"—Africans who were employed as close adjutants or domestic staff by the former—were allowed to wear such a helmet, an emblem of nobility that automatically empowered the wearer to claim shelter, food, bribes, and, should he be that way inclined, finely limbed young damsels for his nocturnal pleasure. Indeed, the "helmeted gentlemen" did in fact love warming themselves with that feminine flame which tends to invigorate rather than consume.

In Diagaramba itself, helmets were highly regarded, even respected, but as the forbidding shadow cast by King Buagui continued to hover above that area, the wearers were not able to indulge in the sort of excesses that elsewhere had become a matter of course.

Who, then, was this helmeted horseman who had appeared in their midst? He was the new instructor whose appointment in Diagaramba had been announced to the Commandant by "means of the wire"[1] a month earlier. It was known that he was a Bambara, born in Ninkoro-Sira, a large village in the Nubigu region, who had done his schooling in Kayes and according to rumors had learned to speak French so well that when he used that red-tailed-quelea-idiom[2] even the real Whites, born of real white French women, hearkened to the sound. It is said that ten years at least are needed to learn the mannerisms that adorn French utterances, the most typical being as follows: stretching one's neck forward from time to time, as well as staring, shrugging, and frowning; now and again folding one's arms at right angles to the torso with the palm of the hand turned upward; crossing one's arms and looking intently at one's interlocutor while pouting one's lips in many different ways, having little spasms of cough, pinching one's nose, or holding one's chin, etc., etc. . . . Not to know, however, how these gestures should be timed to emphasize the words that tumble out of the mouth of the speaker is to be the object of pitiless ridicule.

But this was certainly not the case where Wangrin, the first teaching instructor in the town of Diagaramba, was concerned; when his convoy reached Eldika, everyone, marabouts and common folk alike, rose prompted by a mixture of respect and curiosity, and greeted the morning traveler in a loud voice, welcoming him and wishing him a pleasant stay. Could it be that Wangrin had suddenly become aware of his importance, or had the "white" ways to which he had been inured got the better of him? Be it as it may, instead of answering in the African manner, he simply raised his right hand—a thong of hippopotamus skin dangled from his wrist—then dropped it abruptly. He repeated the gesture several times, accompanying it with a haughty nod. If the truth must be told, Wangrin was just as comfortable responding in the European manner as any real "white-White" nurtured on the lukewarm milk of a well-bred French-born mother.

It was in this manner, then, that Wangrin crossed the town of Diagaramba for the first time. He made straight for Hintsi, a district situated behind the river Maaye, whose unusual feature was a large pocket of water called Iwaldo, or "the rumbler," later renamed "the marsh of the sacred caimans." The river Maaye, affectionately nicknamed "Maayel" by the Fulbe singers, was as popular as Eldika and Telerke in the land commonly known as the "loop of the Niger."

Hintsi had been the abode of Diko-Lomi, a skillful warrior in the days of Al Haji Omar, and also later, during the reign of his successor. At that time an immense protective wall called "Tata" had been built round Diagaramba. Diko-Lomi refused to remain within that enclosure. "Never again," he had said to his sovereign, "will I allow myself to be besieged as we were within the walls of Hamdu." And he had crossed the river Maaye and founded on its left bank the district called Hintsi. When Diagaramba was conquered in 1893, King Buagui installed himself in the palace within the Tata enclosure, while the French troops occupied the Hintsi district which was later to become the French "Residence."

Having reached Hintsi, Wangrin presented himself at the Residence, where he was received without delay by the Commandant. Since the staff of the Civil Administration lived in Diagaramba proper, a large compound was placed at Wangrin's disposal. Owing to the diligent work of Maabo Sammyalla, the King's agent in charge of lodging and supplies, everything had been made ready for his arrival.

King Buagui was a shrewd politician, who treated all new arrivals handsomely and saw to it that their stay was agreeable, provided they did not interfere with his affairs. He was the first person, then, to send Wangrin the sheep and kola nuts that are offered traditionally to a distinguished guest. The gift was delivered by a young griot of the royal family, Kuntena by name.

The second person who greeted Wangrin on his arrival was Lakim Fal, eldest son of King Buagui. Lakim Fal, formerly a king himself, but later dethroned by the French, had been confined to his father's kingdom in Diagaramba. Thanks to his intelligence and versatility (he built a number of roads which have remained in good condition to this very day), he had managed to carve a place for himself in his father's kingdom. This was contrary to the wishes of the French Resident who had been instructed by the authorities to see to it that Lakim Fal kept a low profile and had no say in the running of the country. An astute way, this, to distract the Prince from any thought of taking over from his father at some time or other.

Lakim Fal, again through Kuntena's agency, also sent Wangrin a large sheep to signify his welcome. From then on, Wangrin decided to adopt Kuntena, for he realized how useful that young griot who had access to all the best families in the country could be to him.

Having settled in and rested two whole days, Wangrin presented himself once again at the Commandant's office, where he was to be given instructions before embarking on his teaching activities. Wangrin had expected to be led into the office at once, but he was soon undeceived. A man dressed in white, his left hand smothered in huge silver rings, came to stand before Wangrin, and regaling him with a broad smile, said:

"Good morning Sukul Massa, you don con wel?"

Who could this man be, dressed like a king, who addressed visitors so casually before leading them to a seat where they would have to wait until the Commandant was ready to receive them? He was the *Dalamina*, the Commandant's mouthpiece, or, more explicitly, the interpreter. Unlike Wangrin, he had not had any schooling and spoke *forofifon naspa*, or pidgin French. In *forofifon naspa*, verbs had neither moods nor tenses and nouns, adjectives and pronouns, neither number nor gender. The interpreter shook Wangrin vigorously by the hand, pointed to a bench, and said: "Sukul Massa, mek you si don hia. Mek you wet for wen Oga Commanda I wan si yu. I no de press o, tek yu taim. Na so I dey wit den big man."

Dismayed by hearing the beautiful tongue he had learned at school so ill used, Wangrin sat down with a singular lack of enthusiasm. An hour later, a shout of "Orderly!" was heard. A sentry, wearing a navy blue tunic, white denim trousers, blue puttees, laced-up sandals, and a large, tasseled, scarlet chechia leaped to his feet as if propelled by an invisible spring and started off at the double although the Commandant's door was only a few steps away. He straightened the heavy yellow belt round his waist, stood to attention, and saluting in impeccable fashion shouted: "Presensa, Oga Commanda!"

Wangrin heard the Commandant ask: "Is everyone here?" Without worrying his head about what sort of people might be waiting, the orderly answered automatically: "Efri body I dey, efen di new Sukul Massa sef."

"Interpreter!" shouted the Commandant.

Displaying the same agility as the orderly, the interpreter sprang in the direction of the office and came to a halt near the orderly who remained transfixed in his "salute the flag" position. After an obeisance so low that one could have easily balanced a pot on his back, the interpreter shouted: "Ah de, Oga Commanda."

"Let the people in one by one," replied the all-powerful.

The interpreter drew himself up and called: "Sukul Massa!"

But the Commandant interrupted him: "No, I will see him last."

Wangrin felt a shiver in his spine. He couldn't make out why he, who was the most educated African around, should be received last when everything pointed to the fact that he should be let in first. He consoled himself by calling to mind the words of a bearded priest he used to know in the Catholic mission at Kayes. The young pupils who attended the School for Hostages and the orphanage for half-castes went to mass every Sunday, he remembered, the former in order to get the sweets and appetizing titbits that were handed round from time to time by the priests to their catechumens and the latter because they couldn't avoid doing so. In fact, Catholicism was supposed to be the religion of their fathers, whose civil status, however, was deemed to be unknown by the authorities.

One day, that same bearded priest had told them: "Rejoice, my children, for Jesus Christ our God, Lord and Savior said unto us: 'The first shall be last, and the last shall be first.'" The promise made by Jesus was now fulfilled, at least as far as Wangrin was concerned. Upon reflection, he wondered whether in future it wouldn't be proper for him to revise his prejudices against Christianity.

Like all other pupils in the School for Hostages, Wangrin, whenever going to church, had been in the habit of crossing himself and murmuring a somewhat sacrilegious set formula. In Bambara, the correct translation of the sacramental formula:

> In the name of the Father
> and of the Son
> and of the Holy Ghost
> Amen.

should have been:

> *Faa*
> *ni den*
> *ni hakili-senu*
> *I togo la amen.*

But the pupils, who were all sons of animists or Muslims, had maliciously made up the following phrase, which they would murmur while making the sign of the cross:

> *Naa Keera min ye*
> *nne*
> *nin*
> *taa-la*

which means:

> Whatever may be,
> as for me
> there I won't be.

While Wangrin was immersed in his thoughts, the accusers and the defendants were being sucked systematically into the Commandant's room, in through one door and out through another on the opposite side. The Commandant settled some of the questions on the spot and referred others to the Native Customary Courts. The complainants came to him for a host of reasons: disputes over wives, quarrels over pasture land or wells, complaints lodged against them by the warrant chief, or by them against him, damage to their fields, debts, etc. What irritated the Commandant most was the lack of submission to discipline and the spreading of news that might harm French authority and prestige. Whenever the Commandant was heard shouting at someone, the interpreter would thump the poor wretch brutally as he came out of the office, and the orderly struck him a blow for good measure before kicking him out of the premises or throwing him in jail without ceremony.

The morning went by. Finally, nearing noon, the interpreter bellowed: "Eh! Sukul Massa, Oga Commanda sey mek yu enta for insaid ofis."

Wangrin rose and knocked on the door, as he had seen the French do, and waited to be invited in. The Commandant was busy writing. Without looking up, he answered: "Come in, my dear chap."

This "my dear chap" had a wonderfully soothing effect on Wangrin, who forgot at once the long, wasted hours of waiting inflicted on him. He walked into the office wearing a smile that exposed most of his teeth. This was followed by a deep bow after the manner of the great courtiers and knights of France and Navarre. The interpreter had accompanied Wangrin in. Generally speaking, the Commandant had no secrets from him—his private witness and his assistant in all things. Now for the first time the Commandant asked to be left alone with his visitor. Bewildered and anxious, the interpreter went out, in so worried a state that he decided to remain as close as possible to the door, in order to overhear a few scraps of conversation. As for the Commandant, he had at last found a fitting companion with whom to converse in the French tongue as it had emerged from its original matrix. The interpreter stretched both neck and ears, but although he heard distinctly and perfectly well what the interlocutors were saying, he couldn't make head or tail of it, so that when Wangrin left the office where he had spent at least an hour he couldn't resist saying: "Ah si, Sukul Massa, yu don talk boku boku wit Oga Commanda. But yu, yu de talk 'forofifon naspa,' yu yu de talk beta beta faranse laik den wain wey jus commot from Bordo!" From that Wangrin understood that he had been eavesdropping.

But let us listen to him as he himself relates his interview with the Commandant:

"When the interpreter left us, the Commandant slid back a little more comfortably into his seat and said: 'Take a chair and sit down.' I was overwhelmed, for all 'French subjects,' unless they are kings like Buagui and the Moro-Naba, or chiefs like Amadu Kasso, Bokari Surgu, and Seku Hassaye, must always remain standing before a Commandant, however long the audience. (Old men, however, were allowed to sit on the floor as a concession to the frailty peculiar to their age.) The Commandant took a long, careful look at me and went on to say: 'Young man, you are not like other natives. You have attended a French school and received a sound moral and intellectual education. You have been a good pupil and to crown it all you ended up top of your class in your final exam. Your certificate, I see, testifies to the fact that you have completed your primary school studies for indigenes with "distinction." This diploma gives access to the noblest of tasks: the education of children, that is, the molding of future men. You have been called upon to set up a school in a town full of fanaticism, in a country that is but marginally loyal to France. I am not unaware that in your work you will find more thorns than roses. But if you remain faithful to your promise to serve France wholeheartedly—body and soul—you will be able to rely on the solicitous support of your Commandant. On the other hand, as the representative of France in this country, I will tolerate no lapse or subterfuge. You must pay the debt you owe France by ensuring that she is loved and that her language and civilization are spread far and wide. In the whole history of mankind, these are the two most beautiful gifts ever bestowed on African Blacks. Yes, it is our mission to bring happiness to the Black peoples, if need be against their own wishes.

'I will inspect your school once a month, but you will report to me every Thursday morning; do not let this prevent you, however, from calling on me at the office or at home, during the day or at night, whenever you feel like it.

'I must warn you. Be extremely careful of the Tukulors. They are intelligent, shrewd, and violent. They have no affection for France, for she has ruined their hegemony. This I can sympathize with. Still French interests count above everything. The Tukulors see you Blacks as nothing more than captives to be auctioned like cattle. You will have to keep both eyes and ears wide open so as to be able to appraise, record, and then inform your Commandant accurately. This is an absolute must for a man as well educated as you are.

'That old idiot of an interpreter was thrust on me. He was orderly to some officer or other at the time of the conquest. He is very condescending toward his brothers and obsequious with Whites—an attitude I don't much admire. Besides, I don't altogether trust the two lance-corporals who serve as guards. Although they appear to be sincerely devoted to

France, since I know that one of them is the son of a *Sofa*[3] and the other of a noble Tukulor warrior, I very much doubt that the blood of their ancestors has undergone any great change in their veins. I am under the impression that either by instinct or deliberately they keep from me, or falsify, a number of interesting details, preventing me in this way from catching the subtler flavor of the local mood. I treat them kindly, while keeping an eye on them, but you must help me by watching them too. Old King Buagui is nearing the end of his days. I have been ordered to set him against his people, and them against him. His son, Lakim Fal, is a very open-minded man. He has chosen to overlook his princely status and is a very hard worker indeed. As such, he has succeeded in forcing his cooperation on me. He is a railroad and bridge builder manqué and is busy laying roads more or less all over the country. He speaks excellent French, which he taught himself. He is an extremely likeable man, but won't let anybody tread on his toes. I like him a lot.

'I would also draw your attention to my old court assistants. Although they are eminent people, well-educated in Arabic and greatly revered, they can be very dangerous. Happily for our policy, they are at daggers drawn among themselves and on the other hand they discreetly oppose King Buagui. Only one of them, Bubacar Holiwa, from time to time dares to tell Buagui what he really thinks of him. I will be very much surprised not to see his head fall if he chooses to continue to live in Diagaramba.[4]

'I have drawn you a brief sketch of the political situation in our district, but keep all this to yourself and take care that none of our conversation leaks out of here.'

"To show that our interview had come to an end, the Commandant extended his hand and let fall into mine three five-franc coins, the equivalent of the monthly pay of a *tirailleur* and half the amount of my own salary.

"I exclaimed: 'Oh, Sir!' The Commandant smiled with the princely condescension of the great man who has just bestowed favor on the needy. 'It is a mere nothing for someone who serves France as well as you do,' he replied. 'Just a small contribution to help you settle down in this wretched country where fetishists are known to practice human sacrifices to this very day!'

"I will never be able to tell which occult force made me shout, as I was leaving: 'Thank you, Sir! Hurray for France!' The old interpreter, who was waiting for me close to the office door, side by side with the petrified orderly, shouted in his turn—no one knows why—together with his companion: 'Thank you, Sir! Hurray for France!' The funniest thing of all is that my cry, by some irresistible communicative quirk, rebounded, and bounced, and ricocheted all the way to the great square, an arena of interminable discussions, not far from the Commandant's quarters. Everyone present, including some prisoners who were making up a water party and a few donkey drivers who were passing by, not far from that spot, shouted in chorus: 'Thank you, Sir! Hurray for France.'"

So Wangrin left the Commandant with the added weight of three lovely coins which the Fulbe had christened *taton taartiibe*, which means "the three naked ones." The five-franc coins current at the time did in fact bear on one of their faces the effigy of a man, a woman, and a child, all of them naked. The Fulbe, believing those coins to have been minted by magic, were convinced that whoever touched them ran the risk of falling under their spell and appearing naked and vulnerable, without perhaps even being aware of it, before the white-Whites born of white women on the shores that stretched way beyond the great salty lake. In Fulbe symbolism "to appear naked" does in fact mean to divest oneself of one's personality and of all human dignity, and to sell one's soul to evil powers.

As he returned to his quarters, Wangrin was deep in thought. He had every reason to be pleased with what he had heard. As for the sum that had fallen into his hands it was but a slight intimation of future bounty. Whether the Commandant had acted knowingly or not, the fact remained that he had placed Wangrin on wheels and now the least little push would send him rolling fast and free.

The Wenndu district, which was to be Wangrin's residence, celebrated the arrival of "Sukul Massa." In order to prove how happy and grateful he was, Wangrin asked to be admitted into the *Waalde* (an age-group society) which had organized his reception.

The *Waalde* was the biggest in Diagaramba: it counted one hundred and fifteen young members of both sexes and it controlled and gave protection to five other younger *Waalde* as well as laying down the law in the whole town. Its members organized ambushes against the *tirailleurs* and the district guards as well as anyone employed by the establishment who might attempt to abuse his powers against the indigenes. They were called *Yomptotoobe*, or "the avengers."

Wangrin knew what he was doing. As a member of that *Waalde* he would be protected and at the same time he would be able to probe into the secrets of the society. Should the occasion arise, he might even inform the Commandant. But he was quickly dissuaded from these naive delusions. On the very day he was accepted as member, the head of the society addressed these words to him: "As you are to be received into our *Waalde* of Wenndu, we bestow on you the same rights as to any townsman whose umbilical cord and placenta are buried in the soil of

Diagaramba. As a consequence, you owe the same loyalty in the pursuance of the welfare and peace of our town as any local inhabitant. Normally, we would mistrust you, since you are a civil servant who is paid monthly in *taton taartiibe* coins. But we prefer to give everyone the benefit of the doubt. Let me tell you, however, that we have multifarious ways of keeping check on everybody, including the Commandant. If the slightest scrap of our conversations were to reach his ears, placing anyone of us in jeopardy, we would seek out the informer, we would discover him and subject him ruthlessly to the treatment he deserves. If necessary, we would see to it that he is swallowed by the night."[5]

These were no empty threats, and Wangrin knew it well. The Wenndu *Waalde* was the "red terror" among police, district guards, and *tirailleurs*, and it was best for Wangrin to hold to the promise of keeping silent and lending help to the other members of the *Waalde* in any circumstances that were likely to arise. He paid his *waliluma*, or membership, which consisted of two sheep to be roasted and eaten by the society at large on a Sunday afternoon.

After having feasted in such fraternal communion, each new member was expected to choose a name for himself, and it was on this occasion that Wangrin decided to adopt the pseudonym Gongoloma-Sooke, the name of the god he had elected as his protector.

The young women who belonged to the Wenndu *Waalde* went off together to collect the rich black earth that lined the bottom of the Beelel Mabaalasi, or "the small Mabaalasi pond." With the mud scraped from the bed of this tiny lake, women decorated the interior of their houses with a pebbledash finish, accompanying their work with songs, both ancient and improvised. The custom meant that the man for whom this work had been done was not isolated like a lonely blade of grass that has been left unknown, but rather the member of a group which would be ready to answer his call at any time. Wangrin, then, found himself in the bosom of a family. There only remained for him to learn to speak the Fulbe language, Fulfulde. As he had a remarkable gift for learning languages, he mastered it to perfection within a year.

Wangrin opened a school in Diagaramba and enrolled a sufficient number of pupils to constitute one large class. After one year's stay, during which he led a quietly agreeable existence, Wangrin examined his situation and made a reckoning of all the political and financial advantages that would accrue to him if he were more closely connected with the Commandant. True, he was reasonably popular in Diagaramba and in all the environs of the town. Yet, in spite of being a *Jom-Kaanibol* (a reed owner),[6] as a civil servant he was still on the fringe of activities. The Commandant took an interest in him and even used his services from time to time, but he was neither needed, sought after, nor feared by the town's folk, the warrant chief, or village headmen, the merchants who handled large businesses, or by other eminent citizens. Besides, although his pay kept him at least from going hungry, certainly it did not enable him to lead the kind of life he had envisaged in his dreams. Not to mention the fact that the interpreter, Racutie, old *tirailleur*, whose fingers were vulgarly laden with cornelian and silver rings and who was as illiterate in French as he was inane in Arabic, came second in importance to the Commandant throughout the whole district. There were even times when the latter actually depended on him. Racutie organized or disrupted all sorts of machinations according to his whim. Anyone who didn't make up to him was sure to meet with some unpleasantness. For Racutie this was a time of hoarding. Tips rained on him; his evenings were cheered by songsters and lute players. He kept a good table for himself as well as his guests and his wives were running out of room in which to keep their amber, coral, gold, and silver jewelry. His two horses fed on delicate couscous and drank nothing but milk. He kept a pet sheep which was said to be his fetish.[7] Fat as a pig, this animal wore large gold earrings and a necklace of red agate beads.

Wangrin lived opposite the interpreter and couldn't help seeing all his activities and overhearing all that was being said in his compound.

To begin with, Racutie had lived in fear and trembling of Wangrin, who was able to communicate with the Commandant with the utmost sophistication instead of conversing with him in *forofifon naspa*. Now, however, he had taken heart. As far as he could see, Wangrin was no more than a captain in charge of a bunch of kids—his mind and his behavior testified to it. From the day Racutie had witnessed an "active" language lesson Wangrin was giving his pupils, he had stopped taking him seriously. Wangrin, he thought, was no more than a "childish adult," or a "bearded toddler." To heap ridicule on him, he would walk about town saying: "What can one possibly think of an adult who spends his days running, jumping, dancing, and singing with a crowd of brats, except that he, too, is either a tiny tot or a simple-minded fellow?"

Sadly mortified by this slander, Wangrin opened his heart to his griot Kuntena, who counseled as follows: "O my dear good friend, if a man who is physically and morally unclean kicks you under cover of darkness, you must repay him in kind, but theatrically, in full daylight; otherwise he will go about saying that you have come into this world without the limbs that are needed for retaliation. Show Racutie that you are far from being handicapped. Prove to him that God has given you very fine limbs indeed and that the ramifications of your torso are garnished with claws far more dangerous than those of a lion or a mighty leopard."

"What shall I do then?" asked Wangrin.

"Let us go and consult the old Jaawanndo, Abugui Mansu."

Abugui Mansu was the "godfather" of Diagaramba, where he wheeled and dealed according to his fancy. Both the warrant chief and the Commandant were powerless before him, and everyone else submitted passively to his authority. Kuntena and Wangrin went to visit the old Jaawanndo[8] and found him sitting in the shade of a wall in the great courtyard of his compound. Kuntena greeted him thus:

"Peace unto you, O Baba Abugui Mansu! My friend Wangrin, Sukul Massa, and I have come to wish you a good morning. My friend Sukul Massa asks me to offer you this small parcel. It is the least tribute of politeness a son owes his chosen father."

In the parcel were a large bubu,[9] a pair of baggy trousers, a turti,[10] and a piece of cloth measuring a little over two square yards, all of them in fine white percale. Fifteen francs[11] and a bottle of Hausa perfume[12] had found their way into the pocket of the ample bubu.

Abugui Mansu opened the parcel, donned the turti, then the bubu. As he put his hand in the pocket, he felt the fifteen francs and the bottle of perfume. At this point he called to his wives and children: "Oho, come here, all of you! Come and see what a blessed son offers his father!"

The whole family ran out and congratulated him. They thanked "Sukul Massa" with these words: "Wallay, by Allah, you *do* know how to honor your elders!" Taking advantage of the prevailing excitement, Kuntena interjected: "O my good mothers, aunts, brothers, and sisters, all of you who represent the family of Abugui Mansu, I seek your permission to announce that Sukul Massa has chosen you as his kin. He wishes to be one of you."

"He is one of us!" exclaimed Abugui Mansu's senior wife.

Then Kuntena turned to the old man: "Wangrin asks you the way,[13] and your blessing also."

The old Jaawanndo replied: "Let us go into my man's apartment[14] where we can talk in private."

Once they were all together in his room, Abugui Mansu began by saying: "Whatever the value of a gift, there is but one word that acknowledges liberality, and that word is—thank you. After having said thank you, and yet again thank you, I want Sukul Massa to know that I do really wish to adopt him into my family. From now on, he can count on my support; both day and night this house, and especially this room, bid him welcome. If a young man leaves his country and does not find either father or mother in an alien land, it means that he has not been a dutiful son. And now I would like you to tell me what I can do for Wangrin."

Kuntena gave Wangrin's hand a little pinch to let him know that he must keep quiet, and went on to speak in his stead. In Africa, this procedure is not unseemly. Custom demands that a nobleman speak little and that his griot speak for him, except in matters that entail a serious and irrevocable decision. In fact, if a griot goes back on his word, no one thinks it an unacceptable or surprising event; but if a nobleman behaves in this way, the whole affair is viewed in a totally different light.

Kuntena, then, turned to the old Jaawanndo and said: "O Abugui Mansu! Today Wangrin has nothing particular to say, except that he would like to entrust his head to you, hoping that you will place it between your flesh and blood;[15] he also asks that you may be present in his stead whenever he is absent and that you may shield him from the evil eye and slanderous tongues. What he is asking you, is merely to guide his steps."

Abugui Mansu stretched his hands towards Wangrin and said: "Place your hands on mine." Wangrin complied most humbly. Abugui Mansu recited the first chapter (or *surat*) of the Koran, called *fatiha*, "the opener." In this way he sealed their pact of mutual assistance, also witnessed by Kuntena.

This intimate ceremony over, Abugui Mansu said to Wangrin: "Tomorrow you will go and pay homage to the great marabout, Tierno Siddi. The day may come when you find yourself in need of his prayers. They are effective. According to the proverb, one must not wait to train a hunting-dog until the actual day of the shoot."

On the following day, Wangrin, accompanied by Kuntena, went to visit Tierno Siddi. To him he offered the same presents, plus a ream of "marabout" paper,[16] which Kuntena delivered after having recited the same litany as he had done in Abugui Mansu's house. Tierno Siddi also adopted and blessed Wangrin.

Later, Kuntena took Wangrin on one side and said: "Now that you are protected by Abugui Mansu and by the carapace that are Tierno Siddi's prayers, you are as a stone in a basketful of eggs. If the stone knocks against the egg, the egg breaks, and if an egg rattles against a stone, the same thing happens. Henceforth you are an indomitable stallion. You need no longer fear Racutie. Next time he attempts to ridicule you in public, as he is obviously fond of doing, begin by replying wittily; but if the need arises, show him, like the true Bambara from Nubigu that you are, how well you have learned to fight hand to hand, how well you can grab your opponent round the waist, lean forward against him, throw him off balance, and kick his legs out from under him. Show him that when you fight you are as swift as a catfish in water, with the difference that if the fins of a catfish flap gently in the waves, your *kurfinny* (fists) thump hard and heavy in the open air. In this way you will prove to

Racutie that in the 'white' school you learned, among other things, the new foreign way of wrestling which is so noxious to teeth, eyes, and jaws."

Suitably doped by the words of his griot and guide Kuntena, Wangrin had been transformed into a veritable booby-trap, ready to explode at the approach of poor Racutie.

3   First Confrontation

From the time the town had been conquered by the French, Sundays, which among Whites are days of rest, were celebrated like a lesser *Katran-zuliye.*[1]

On that particular Sunday, after the morning festivities, both the black civil servants and the young people of the town gathered at Telerke to have a good gossip while listening to the most skillful lute players. These were seven in number and were usually referred to as "the seven conjugated melodies." Whenever these seven lute players began to strum together, the mere buzzing of flies—even the gentlest breeze—became an intolerable intrusion. Unhappily, as it is human to be noisy, now and again a sigh of abandon or irrepressible contentment would escape from the crowd, and cut through that delectable harmony. Sometimes it might be a griot recalling the deeds of a warrior or declaiming a stanza in honor of a great king or marabout; at others, a young man full of his own importance bragging and, through indirect reference, aiming arrows at his rivals. Racutie belonged to the latter category.

When Yero Inna intoned the so-called "Baylel Tune," extolling men favored by fortune and kings who lavish gifts on griots, Racutie burst out laughing, took off one of his Turkish slippers (made in Djenne) and lifted it high above his head. Then, letting out a scream as if he were a warrior armed with a spear, he struck the ground with it. He rose and hitting his chest and brow with the palm of his hand, began: "I am Racutie, former *Fantirimori*[2] sergeant, Class of 1885, Regimental Roll 6666. Now I am the Commandant's interpreter—his eyes, his ears, and his mouth. Every day, I am the first and the last person to see him. I can slip into his office whenever I like and I speak to him without the help of intermediaries.

"Here, take a hundred thousand cowries, all of you—griots, cobblers, smiths, and household slaves. You may share them among yourselves and sing my praise until I see fit to stop you, and to tell you who to insult so as to fill my heart with joy.

"I am Racutie, who sits on a beautiful mahogany bench outside the door of the white Commandant. Is there anyone among you who doesn't know that both life and death depend on his word? Let me tell those who don't know that at the present time my mouth—praise be to God—is the one that is closest to his ear. The favor that I, Racutie, enjoy with the Great White Chief kindles mortal jealousy in the breast of someone I refuse to name, since in doing so, I would honor him beyond his deserts. Yet I swear by the milk I sucked from my mother's nipples that my enemy shall find out this much: the breast of the woman to whom I owe my life did not secrete the kind of liquid that gives life to idiots or ne'er-do-wells. Before many sunrises have done alternating with as many sunsets, I will see to it that he tastes my bitter cup. He will feet through his very skin what I think of ill-taught grown-ups who insist on remaining urchins when they are old enough to stroke a beard whose existence is a sign of imbecility rather than moral and intellectual wisdom."

This totally unexpected outburst astounded some listeners and roused indignation in others. But a few guffawed foolishly. The lute players, not knowing what accompaniment to provide for such ill-chosen remarks, stopped plucking at their instruments. The melody that had waded through the air was suddenly drowned in the uproar that followed Racutie's uncouth words.

Everything was suspended, as in the instant that precedes a tornado. There was a catching of breath. The more cautious began to withdraw, that they might decamp or at least get out of the way if the whirlwind that threatened were actually to swoop down on them.

Wangrin rose, and like a cartridge case elected from its housing, stood up before Racutie. A deathly silence ensued, enabling everyone to hear distinctly each word uttered by Wangrin with quiet strength, a sly smile playing on his lips.

It is impossible to say which was the more offensive, Wangrin's mocking and malicious air, or the patent look of disdain in his eyes and in the curve of his lips as he addressed Racutie. "Ah, you poor man," he began, "who boast of having been branded with the number 6666, just like a cow, let me tell you something: although a man may be forgiven for not recognizing his plateful of food when a number of plates are being handed round, he may not be pardoned his utter idiocy if he falls to grasp an allusion made to himself. If a man insults his enemies without naming them, it means that he is sheltering behind anonymity to avoid confrontation with an unwavering opponent. Things, however, take a different turn if a man states uncompromisingly: 'This is the very enemy with whom I had a hand-to-hand fight last night!' Well, that is exactly the sort of outspoken enemy I am.

"I don't happen to possess a hundred thousand cowries, and if I did, I would take good care not to use them to buy myself accomplices. You intend to prove to me before long that the milk of your mother's breasts was invigorating. I suggest you prove it now. If you don't, tomorrow you may wake to find that a great catastrophe has overtaken you."

Racutie, much taken aback by Wangrin's riposte, slapped him on the right cheek. Still possessed of a serenity that was proof of his strength, Wangrin burst out laughing: "Out of consideration for the audience, I shall overlook this slap in my face," he said.

Instead of taking advantage of this opportunity to change tactics and make amends, Racutie slapped Wangrin once again, this time on the left cheek.

Wangrin exclaimed: "Pity I haven't got a third cheek for you to slap, for the palm of your hand seems to be positively bursting with slaps!"

When he saw that Wangrin could not be provoked, Racutie lost his head. Bursting with rage, he lifted his hand. Just as he was about to dispense a third blow, Wangrin, with the rapidity of a bird of prey pouncing on a chick, grabbed Racutie's hand and, before the latter could recover himself, twisted it behind his back. Then, taking advantage of his enemy's uncomfortable posture, he flipped him over and having swung him round, pressed him to the ground with the whole weight of his body. Breathless beneath his opponent, Racutie was now kicking frantically in a vain attempt to prize himself loose, but Wangrin held his neck in a tight grip with his left arm, while with his right hand, with the skill of a professional boxer, he began to rain blows on Racutie's face. Racutie's jaws were dislocated and his blood, far deeper in hue than a mere blush, spurted from his mouth and nostrils, flooding his whole face.

Letting go abruptly, Wangrin got up and stepped back. Racutie rose unsteadily, and half blinded by his own blood, tried to charge. But Wangrin, who was watching him closely, side-stepped him and with a mighty kick to the belly sent him sprawling. Racutie fell like a mud wall giving way under heavy rain.

At that very moment the *alkati*[3] arrived on the scene, bearing his great sword. He blew his whistle, dispersed the crowd, separated the wrestlers and said to them: "Both of you are officials and for that reason I cannot think of clapping you in jail before tomorrow, as I should. I am letting you go, then, but I command you to show up punctually at eight in the morning at Government House."

Everybody went home. Kuntena and Wangrin left together, while Racutie made off in the opposite direction.

Throughout the night, in every house, lively tales of the brawl were told with an abundance of detail. Everywhere, both a description of the quarrel and a colorful illustration of the way the blows had been dealt dominated the conversation. Some extolled Wangrin's fists as an indisputable mark of superiority over his opponent, others expressed admiration for the way Racutie had been flung to the ground, while the remainder lavished never-ending praise on the skill shown by Wangrin in avoiding the charge of his enemy and in sending him sprawling on the ground with a powerful and unexpected kick.

In other words, every one of Wangrin's moves elicited a chorus of praise. His left arm was compared to the devil's cloven foot, and his right hand to a club of metal forged by David, who was Jehovah's messenger, Lord of Iron, and Father of Solomon.

Just as Racutie's bragging was mocked, so the restraint shown by Wangrin as prelude to the display of manly strength and courage which had undone his opponent was paraded around for everyone to admire.

Abugui Mansu began at once a campaign against Racutie. His task was the simplest, for in everybody's eyes and to everybody's knowledge Racutie was in the wrong. Not only had he provoked Wangrin with his words, but he had also been the first to strike him—twice—with no retaliation from Wangrin.

On the following morning, before eight, the *alkati* gave the Commandant an account of the quarrel. He leveled grave accusations against Racutie, not only because the latter had "lent his back,"[4] but because he had been visited by Abugui Mansu during the night and had been told by him that all the dignitaries of Diagaramba, led by the marabouts, were on Wangrin's side and would not hesitate to march in protest if the scales of justice were tipped in favor of Racutie.

Abugui Mansu had added: "As for you, don't forget that Wangrin is a member of the Wenndu *Waalde*, which is the most turbulent in the country. To defend its members, this *Waalde* is capable of stirring up the sort of trouble which might well result in your losing your impressive sword and the gorgeous silken tassel on your great big scarlet chechia!"

The *alkati* knew only too well that in that area people feared Satan and his horde of devils infinitely less than Abugui Mansu's tongue. . . . It must be said at this point that his tongue was indeed more murderous than a halberd, more pointed than a needle, and sharper than a razor. The worst that could happen to anyone living in Diagaramba was to incur Abugui Mansu's displeasure.

When the Commandant heard the *alkati*'s report, he could hardly believe his ears. He thought it over and decided to carry out a few inquiries of his own before coming to a final decision.

At that time, the degree of moral uprightness of an individual was judged, on the one hand, on the basis of how much he had contributed toward French penetration and, on the other, by the geographical position of his country of origin. Accordingly, Europeans were the most moral of men, followed by the people of Martinique and Guadeloupe, the black Senegalese from the four communes of Saint-Louis, Goree, Rufisque, and Dakar, the black veterans, and finally, at the very end of the line, the rest of the population. Consequently, the Commandant began by questioning Mamadu N'Diaye, master carpenter of the district and originally a citizen of the Saint-Louis commune. Having heard his evidence, the Commandant was convinced beyond any doubt that that idiot of an interpreter of his had gone too far. If this business were to be heard in court, not only would Racutie be beaten hollow, but he would also risk being heavily fined or imprisoned, both of which went against the local administrative policy. An interpreter who loses face is totally useless. In order to avoid such distress, the Commandant decided to appease Wangrin by giving him to understand that from then on he would be keeping an eye on Racutie; and that in fact Wangrin could be of great assistance to him in this contingency. As a result, the whole affair was settled amicably and then forgotten.

Yet, although the administration had taken care to suppress the business for its own ends, popular opinion had no intention of letting the gossip die down. Wangrin remained the hero upon whom all must shower fulsome praise, while Racutie, from Commandant's-splendid-interpreter had become poor-devil-with-a-dislocated-jaw-who-can't-win-a-fight.

When Racutie went about his business, instead of being greeted respectfully by the town urchins as in former times he would hear their cries of "Broken jaw!" or "Bleeding nostrils. . . . " The gibes that followed Racutie wherever he went poisoned his life to such a degree that in the end he decided to ask the Commandant for a transfer to another station.

The Commandant passed his request on to a higher authority, enclosing a confidential letter in which he asked permission to employ Wangrin, the local primary school teacher, as interpreter during the school holidays, until the arrival of the man officially appointed to replace Racutie. So it happened that Wangrin became an interpreter, which in those days was equivalent to slipping one's foot into a gold stirrup.

4 The Beginning of a Career

Wangrin not only acted as interpreter in official business, but also became secretary to the Commandant, distributed the post, prepared files for every case, and took painstaking care of the archives.

At the end of the long summer holiday, the Commandant went to Bamako in person to apply to the Governor and the Inspector of Schools, who was head of a division in the Department of Education, for permission to change Wangrin's status officially from that of teacher to that of interpreter. In this way Wangrin was transferred to the cadre of interpreters for Upper Senegal and Niger, and kept his posting in Diagaramba.

When a hyena falls into a well, may God and Death rejoice![1]

As a result of Wangrin's elevation, Abugui Mansu and Kuntena, his confidants and friends, also enjoyed greater prestige. Although their new situation was not entirely free of risks, it promised to be yet another "open sesame."

Kuntena, fine griot (*Kuate*) that he was, had never mastered the art of lute playing, a skill which would have multiplied his worth a hundredfold, while also swelling the ranks of his audience. In fact, a griot who can't play the lute, or plays it discordantly, is held in the same contempt as a horse with bandy legs.

Now the most frightful sound likely to reach one's ear in those days was poor Kuntena's strumming. Yet, obstinate as a mule, he would persist in playing. As soon as he began, people would go into convulsions of laughter and jokers would shout: "Hey, Kuntena, your donkey of a lute is tired of braying. Take it back to the stable before it kicks the bucket."

Kuntena was a good-natured fellow who never got angry. He would acquiesce and put away his instrument with the words: "Lean over there, my poor lute. I'd rather my friends laughed at me than that they should weep over my corpse."

On the other hand, the melody which the strings of his lute refused to release poured forth abundantly from his tongue and vocal cords. He was a truly gifted storyteller and praise-singer as well as an excellent mimic. So far as that went, he was second only to Kullel, the greatest of the great storytellers of the Niger loop.

Our three friends, Abugui Mansu, Kuntena, and Wangrin, hastened to establish a double intelligence network. The first culled news from the interior and brought it to Wangrin, while the second spread information around the area which had been both sifted and seasoned according to the wishes and interests of our trio.

Meanwhile Wangrin made use of the laborers which the administration had placed at his disposal to have his premises enlarged. In those days in West Africa every "French subject," that is, every native of each colony, was expected to do a fortnight of forced labor, and the district of Diagaramba had as many as two thousand unpaid workers permanently available.

Wangrin divided his house into three living quarters. One gained access to the first through a spacious rectangular hall which opened onto a vast courtyard, where Wangrin offered lavish lunches, or dinners, to the accompaniment of music and songs.

The watchman in charge of checking the influx of visitors sat in that hall. He was assisted by two servants, who kept an eye on every movement and listened discreetly to all that was being said.

The watchman's room was next to the hall and, with the aid of a small opening, served admirably as an eavesdropping cabinet. The watchman and his helpers were able to overhear a number of secrets exchanged among visitors who thought themselves alone and safe from indiscreet ears.

The second courtyard led to Wangrin's *thie-so*, his man's apartment. Although it was less imposing in size than the first, it did nevertheless boast an open shelter with a thatched roof where Wangrin could sit in the open air during the hottest time of day. It was there, too, that he had breakfast. Kuntena was always with him, and sometimes other guests as well. Often these dropped in casually, but whoever called on Wangrin at meal times never went hungry.

Wangrin's *thie-so* consisted of a number of rooms: a large reception hall, a study, a secret room,[2] a bedroom with a bath and lavatory, a boxroom, and finally two guest rooms, also very well-equipped with conveniences.

The second courtyard was connected to the third by means of a hall called "the women's hall." The latter was just as spacious as the first and it was surrounded by the living quarters, equipped with kitchens and lavatories for Wangrin's wives, children, and other close relatives. There were also posts to which Wangrin's two horses were kept tethered.

No male who was not a member of the family was allowed in this building. Wangrin's apartment communicated with the women's quarters through an extension built onto Wangrin's study as well as through the women's hall, so that he was able to visit his family whenever he felt like it without having to cross the large hall.

His house became an object of envy even to chiefs. Before long, it turned into the meeting place for civil servants, the espionage center for that area, and the hall for secret consultation between warrant chiefs.[3]

It would have been unthinkable for any traditional chief to turn up at Wangrin's house empty-handed. Visitors would unfailingly arrive with either a bribe or an interesting piece of information. On the other hand, no griot, woman of loose morals, old procuress, marabout, beggar, or man of any sort who came to ask for help, would ever leave Wangrin's house empty-handed either. It is true that Wangrin knew how to ask for, and even exact, gifts from those whom fortune had furnished with abundant means, but it must also be said to his credit that he gave generously to the poor and helped the wretched without ever asking for anything in return. Naturally they were all devoted to him and he was able to recruit his ablest informers among the blind beggars who walked from door to door and posted themselves along various roads or in the market square. He also had more than one informant among the children who frequented the Koranic schools in town.

Although he was obviously no fool, Wangrin had not established this extraordinary network, which stretched like a cobweb over the whole region, altogether single-handedly. His adopted father Abugui Mansu, his shady mentor, had spun all the necessary threads.

Just then, the Commandant, who was suffering agonies of loneliness, asked Wangrin to look out for a comely and shapely maiden.

Madame Commandant had refused to come out to the colony, for she hated flies and had a morbid fear of mosquitos. The mere mention of them would bring on a temperature, while the thought of a cockroach was enough to make her feel sick.

Sergeant Mandagout of the Colonial Army was heavily responsible for this state of affairs. On leave after a period of strenuous service, Mandagout had visited Madame Commandant in France and had given a vivid description of the situation that awaited her in the colony. He had dwelt especially on the subject of hairy scorpions and rattlesnakes which, according to him, were in the habit of insinuating themselves between bed sheets, and of spotted hyenas with extravagant manes which, driven by hunger, would pursue people into their very huts.

To ask his wife to come to Africa was therefore absolutely out of the question for the Commandant. On the other hand, no longer able to control the ever-more-pressing exigencies of the flesh, the Commandant, who in any case had never dreamt of taking a vow of chastity, decided to resort to the most obvious means of calming his nerves. If he had so wished, he could easily have commandeered any number of women every night of the year and in this way he might have cooled his ardors. This procedure, however, was likely to affect adversely his moral prestige and his authority as a high official, for Africans, while accepting polygamy, frown on adultery.

In the event, the Commandant decided to opt for what used to be called at the time a "colonial marriage" with a local woman. The bride, who was often compelled to agree to this step, was not referred to as "Madame," an appellation reserved for white women only; instead, she was called *musso*.[4]

French law, which as a rule takes such a serious view of bigamy, turned a blind eye on these colonial marriages. The real victims were the children born of these unions. They were officially registered as children of "unknown fathers" and forgotten when the civil servants responsible for their birth left the country.

It was Wangrin's considered opinion that a Commandant had every right to a really fine specimen. Doesn't the Fulbe proverb say: "If you are obliged to feed on a carcass, make sure that it is at least fleshy," which means: "If you are obliged to do something which is beneath you, at least see that it is worth your while."

Wangrin chose a very beautiful girl. Her family was poor but honest. According to custom, he assumed the role of father towards the girl, becoming ritually his Commandant's father-in-law.

It is easy to guess that Wangrin was determined to kill two birds with one stone. On the one hand, having acted as intermediary in the marriage, he had put himself squarely in the Commandant's good graces; on the other, he had every intention of using "his adopted daughter" to keep an eye on her husband's behavior.

The meals for the Commandant's little *musso* were prepared at Wangrin's house.

One could say that Wangrin's sun of glory and good fortune had risen radiant in a cloudless sky. His life in the good town of Diagaramba was bound to be extremely happy. Everyone agreed that Diagaramba was a pleasant spot, where one could live even better than in Kayes or

Bamako, one the former and the other the new capital of the colony. The fact that all the people from the neighboring areas had settled down there at the end of their term of service was positive proof of this fact.

The griots sang the following poem in praise of the town:

O, Diagaramba!
O, immense town!
Built in the shade
of the great cotton trees
which belong to Madom's father
and to Waguirma.

Your air
is pure and delicious,
your girls are comely and coquettish,
your stallions are fine, ebullient, and frisky.
The water of your springs
and of your rivers
flows clear and abundant.
It has the perfume of many flowers
and of scented roots like the vetiver
whose aroma keeps repugnant insects at bay.
Your splendid hills are a rich orchard
hung by God above vast greening plains
where thousands of milk cows
and fattening bullocks graze.

Everyone is always welcome
for you are the best of hostesses.
No men can leave you,
either by choice or necessity
without unbearable pain.
Yes, Diagaramba!
The white man leaves his heart
with you in his colonial helmet;
the old *tirailleur* in his large chechia,
the cook in his old pot.
Here, grooms forget their hooks;
shepherds their crook,
and great chiefs are fond
of leaving behind their aspirations
that they may return to look for them.

Wangrin's days slipped by happily—he was everyone's close friend. All good things seemed to flow in his direction, easily, abundantly, and delightfully. Why should he forgo the pleasures that fate was sowing so lavishly in his path? His ears were charmed by the sound of delectable music while his palate was refreshed by cool drinks mixed with delicious honey.

In this world of ours, however, bright days are followed by somber nights. And so it happened that great sorrow spread throughout the land. All the same, a particular event does sometimes bear different consequences for different people. Let us not forget that the selfish man's prayer runs as follows: "Dear God, may you hurry on its way the great disaster that will bring me happiness!"

Under Abugui Mansu's influence, Wangrin was becoming more and more selfish, and there was a good chance that with the passing of time his heart would grow harder still. At this point, his conscience seemed to have grown silent; if it spoke, he heard it merely as a distant echo.

5 Where the Calamities of Some...

As usual, Wangrin arrived at the office a quarter of an hour before the official time, but he found the Commandant already in his office, staring at a telegram on his desk.

"Good morning, Sir," said Wangrin.

Without looking up, the Commandant muttered a cold reply.

Aware that something serious must have happened, Wangrin made bold to ask: "Is the Commandant feeling well this morning?"

"Yes, Wangrin, I am all right," he replied, "but I fear my well-being may be of short duration. I have just received a most alarming telegram. Germany has violated Belgian neutrality and France is about to declare war."

On hearing this, Wangrin exclaimed: "Oh Sir, if only Europeans weren't such skeptics, I would advise you to consult the marabouts. They could easily forestall disaster through their prayers, either by halting Germany in her tracks or by letting her know what defeat tastes like!"

The Commandant smiled condescendingly: "I will ask the marabouts to pray for a French victory, but in the meantime find me all the census records so that we can get ready for the general mobilization decreed by our government."

At eleven that morning Wangrin left his office and directed his steps toward the residence of his adopted father Abugui Mansu. He wanted to tell him in confidence that France was likely to declare war on Germany.

Having devoted some thought to the matter, Abugui Mansu pronounced: "Things being what they are, our best plan is to go to Tierno Siddi, who will consult the oracle and tell us whether our future happiness lies in war or in peace."

They went to the marabout's house and found him dozing in his hall after breakfast.

"*As-salaamu-aleykum!* Peace be unto you!" was the greeting Abugui Mansu threw out to him.

"*Wa aleykum salaam!* Peace be unto you!" replied Siddi, somewhat startled.

"Has master Siddi's morning been a happy one? Has he breakfasted well?" asked Abugui Mansu by way of introducing the subject he had come to discuss.

The marabout drew himself up and replied: "By the grace of Allah, I have had a good morning and sated my hunger with a plateful of good *bintou-bala*[1] rice. Do come in, Abugui Mansu. Oh, good morning, Wangrin, come in peace. . . .

"Whatever has happened that you are both prepared to brave the scorching rays of the midday sun? It is in a spirit of peace you have come to me, I hope. . . . "

It was Abugui Mansu who replied:

"The Commandant has just told Wangrin in great secrecy that there is danger of war in France. We have come to ask you to consult the oracle and tell us whether there will in fact be a war and whether our personal well-being and that of our town are likely to be jeopardized. It is important for us to know."

The marabout rose and said: "Come with me to my *worwordu*[2] where we will be protected from all indiscretions."

Abugui Mansu and Wangrin followed the marabout into a rectangular and fairly spacious room, which was both light and well aired. It served at once as study, bedroom, library, and as a retreat where the holy man could pray and hold secret meetings. First of all Siddi made his guests comfortable, then he extracted from a pile of books a heavy manuscript, opened it, and perused at length several pages. He took a small board covered in red copper and traced on it a few cabalistic signs. He leaned over them and fell into deep meditation, abstracting himself from the rest of the world for a full half hour. As he was doing this, he oozed sweat like an earthenware pot full of water. Finally he looked up and noisily let out a deep breath, much like a diver when he returns to the surface.

"France," he said, "is a great, Christian-oriented country. The numbers which correspond to the era of Seydina Issa ben Maryam (our Lord Jesus, son of Mary) make up one of the numerological keys which enable us to penetrate the mystery in which is shrouded the destiny of the Christian world, and especially of France. Indeed, ever since the 'Spirit of God'[3] was born in this world, a different celestial spirit has been placed in charge of the Christian universe at regular intervals of eleven years. Hamshayael was the first. He watched over the first eleven years of Jesus Christ's life, which were spent in retirement. It was only in his twelfth year that Seydina Issa (our Lord Jesus) appeared in public and spoke to the wise men in the Temple. The hundred and seventy-fourth spirit operating at present is named Ba'azshayael. If war breaks out between France and Germany— as it will, inevitably—France will win, for the Spirit in charge of the Christian universe will come to her assistance. But Allah knows best. He can alter our vision and even that of the saints; he can act according to his unfathomable will. Whatever happens, this war will cause many deaths on land and sea; there will be many widows and orphans, many men will be maimed.

"You, Wangrin, won't be called up, and you will live to see the end of the hostilities. Also, war will put a great deal of money in your way.

"Many young people from our town will be sent to the shores beyond the salty lake and will fight valiantly, but all their glory will be acknowledged with recognition rather than with material rewards."[4]

Wangrin offered the marabout a horse, a hundred francs, a suit of clothes, and ten loads of cereals, two of them of white rice from Djenne.

A few days later a sound of trumpets and drums, as well as large posters displayed on many walls (which only ten people or so were able to read), proclaimed that war had been declared and general mobilization would follow. All the French territories overseas must contribute actively to the war effort of the mother-country in order to overcome the enemy.

The Commandant convened a meeting of chiefs and dignitaries from the whole area and made the following announcement:

"Germany has set light to all the gunpowder in Europe. Her emperor, William the Second, wants to rule the world, but first he will have to face our *Eternal France*, champion of freedom and of the rights of man. France demands that all her territories contribute men, raw materials, and prayers.

"The government has issued a decree whereby millet, rice, fats, and animals fit for slaughter shall be requisitioned. The prices of the various supplies will be fixed by a commission which is to meet shortly in Kuluba. Anyone who interferes by word or deed with these requisitions will be tracked down and punished as a traitor to France."

The news spread like wildfire.

Wangrin was given the job of keeping records of the requisitions and preparing forms for supplies. Abugui Mansu came to him at once and said: "I am now fully convinced of the validity of Tierno Siddi's prophecy. For you, this will be an abundant spring of profit. If you only wish it, you can become the richest man in the whole mountain area. . . . "

"By doing what?" asked Wangrin.

"By increasing the number of cows in every supply. I undertake to send to Kumasi in the Gold Coast any surplus that you can possibly manage. It will be worth its weight in gold. By the end of the war we shall have amassed an immense fortune." Wangrin caught on to the idea in no time at all. Abugui Mansu continued:

"If you want the embezzlement to go on for a long time without incurring any risk, we shall have to involve either the Commandant, through the services of his *musso*, or his adjutant, or even, possibly, the treasurer. . . . Leave it to me to buy the silence of the warrant and village chiefs. They will not betray us."

Just at that time the Commandant had been assigned a young adjutant from the cadre of clerks in charge of native affairs, as it used to be called. His name was Jean-Jacques de Villermoz. He was a count, but as he himself was fond of saying, a count without a bank account.

"My real fixation," he would readily admit, "is to mount, that is, to rise in all things. That bitch of a French revolution, mother of a Republic just as shameless as herself, has frustrated my ambitions. Nevertheless I have undertaken to serve her in the hope of *mounting* in rank; that will enable me to satisfy my passion, which is to *mount* beautiful girls, as well as fine stallions, to the hilt."

Villermoz was never to be seen in any footwear other than his riding boots decorated with glided spurs. He took them off only to go to bed. And sometimes not even then. How many times had his steward Antugumo found him napping in the afternoon complete with riding boots! Inevitably, he was nicknamed "The spur-booted Junior Commandant." It must be said to his credit, however, that he never booted any black behinds. On the contrary he was always most affable with the indigenous population.

Always the fine gentleman, Villermoz wore a monocle. His steward let it be known that this eyeglass was reserved for the scions of princely families from France and Navarre, and that all Villermoz had to do was simply to appear with his *insignia* before any French Treasury or Bank of Commerce; any amount of money he might wish to draw was then paid out to him.

Villermoz was as reluctant to exercise his limbs as he was shy of working. It was convenient for him, then, to leave everything to Wangrin, who seemed to be both an experienced civil servant and a model of dedication.

Part of the business of the district, such as minor palavers and matters touching on requisitions, were transferred to the sector which came under the Junior Commandant, while Wangrin remained in sole charge of the administrative and legal registers of the district as well as interpreter to the top men.

Villermoz hated to be woken up before nine in the morning, or before three in the afternoon. As if that weren't leisure enough, he spent most of his office hours horse riding. He owned the three finest stallions in Diagaramba: a splendid golden chestnut, a thoroughbred palomino from the Sahel, and one which was jet black all over except for a blaze and socks. He rode them all in turn and wherever he happened to be, one of these handsome specimens, already saddled, awaited him at the door.

To save Wangrin the trouble of running after him to get his signature, he signed about ten blank forms for requisitions, summons, and other business in advance. There only remained for Wangrin to fill in the forms and apply the district seal to the documents.

Wangrin was quick to realize the enormous advantage that would accrue to him from such abundant trust. Since fate had placed at his disposal an unhoped-for victim, there was no longer any need to involve other Europeans.

Abugui Mansu was introduced to Villermoz as the most important cattle breeder and merchant in the whole area, as well as exporter of sizeable quantities of cows to the Gold Coast.

As a preliminary test, Wangrin increased by five the monthly contingent exacted by the authority from the Diagaramba district. The supplement was diverted discreetly in the direction of Abugui Mansu's compound. From there it was sent swiftly on to Kumasi where it was sold against gold sterling, a currency which at the time was highly quoted and sought for.

Owing to the exchange rate, a cow costing a hundred francs in Diagaramba brought a net profit of around eight to nine hundred francs.

Wangrin insisted that Abugui Mansu should bring back two fine English harnesses and a few items of toiletry, household goods, and clothing from the Gold Coast, which could then be offered to the two Commandants as a good-will gesture. This absorbed the profit made from three out of the five cows, but it was a good investment.

Seeing that the business was turning out to be so profitable, Wangrin went to Villermoz and suggested that an extra ten per cent might be added to the existing contingent. This increase seemed perfectly reasonable, for it would enable the veterinary orderly to sort out cattle much more efficiently. But instead of returning to the owners the cows which had been found physically unfit, Wangrin sent them on to Abugui Mansu who sold them in the Gold Coast.

In this way, because of Villermoz's complicity, or at least culpable negligence, the business flourished and money began positively to pour into Wangrin's pockets. Every night he gave dinners, enlivened by delectable music, displaying his great wealth and causing his praises to be sung far and wide. In spite of being the worst lute player in the whole area, Kutena became the most comfortably housed and elegantly dressed griot to be found anywhere for miles.

6   The Storm Breaks

If the tiniest of tiny red ants chances to climb into an elephant's trunk, it can stir—alas—trouble enough to cause the death of the largest wild animal in existence. Thus, a few words uttered during one of those memorable dinners caused the most unfortunate cracks to appear in the seemingly solid existing structure, provoking a scandal that was to becloud the political atmosphere of the district for a whole year and scatter to the four corners of Niger and Upper Senegal those civil servants who had not had sense enough to keep out of the way.

One fine morning, Wangrin's messengers returned from Kumasi laden with goods: gold, tea, sugar loaves, iridescent fabrics, and bales of richly textured bombazine and fine percale. No less than eighty donkeys and twenty oxen had been commandeered for the transportation of so opulent a load.

On that occasion, Wangrin gave a sumptuous dinner to which he invited all the native civil servants. A fine couscous served with lamb, and several roasted sheep were followed by tea interspersed with delicious aromatic *jinjiber*[1] which pretty girls handed round until everyone had had his fill.

Kuntena, roused like a young boy who has had his first taste of alcohol, lost his habitual sense of proportion. All of a sudden he rose, and like one who has been stung by an evil insect, he began:

"Now that we're all replete with the kind of delectable fare we can never afford to eat in our own homes, I ask everyone to be quiet and hear me out. Once upon a time a snake bought a horse and then proceeded to flop across his back, that being the only comfortable posture he could possibly adopt. A monkey happened to come by, and seeing the snake lying in that position, burst out laughing: 'Hey! You death-inflicting slitherer,' he said, 'that is no way to ride a horse!'

'How then?' asked the snake, who was more amused than irritated.

"Jumping astride the horse, the monkey slipped his feet into the stirrups, grasped the reins, and spurred his mount, making him prance in an experienced and elegant manner. Then, turning towards the serpent with an air of mockery, he said: 'This is the way to ride, my dear slitherer!'

'Indeed, my dear Waadu,[2] you do ride extremely well. But now please get off my horse.'

"The monkey, who had no reason to refuse, dismounted. Upon which the snake climbed back onto the horse just as he had done earlier.

'A property owner,' he said to the monkey, 'does exactly as he pleases on his own land. If I choose to lie this way on the back of my horse, don't let it upset your fine horseman's sensibilities, my dear *imitation of man*.'"

The griot went on: "I have asked you to listen to this parable to show you that I, Kuntena, am entirely at home in Wangrin's house even though my fingers can only draw horribly discordant notes from my lute, sounds likely to shatter your eardrums.[3] Like the snake in the story, I behave in this house exactly as I please, and not the way some others would have me behave. Dayemaatien[4] used to say that words abhor the following three things: to be spoken before the proper time, not to be spoken at the right moment, or to be spoken too late. There are, then, suitable moments, places, and ways, when it comes to speaking. And today I, Kuntena, must speak in honor of the man who, having found me in a 'village full of garbage,'[5] embraced me, purified me, and installed me in a palace. I shall do it, however, without accompanying myself with the sound of my lute—for that, I grant you, would be a certain way of distracting your attention."

Then Kuntena turned toward Wangrin and decorating his words with elaborate gesticulations intoned:

"O Wangrin! O Wangrin! You are the phoenix, offspring of the Amibile. Between Fie and Sankarani and in the whole of Baya's Canton the mere mention of your name yields shelter and fare for travelers in distress. Between Wassulu-Bale and Sankarani your name provides means for those who have none. O Wangrin, you are the noble Lord of Sokolombani, the Banifing, and the Bague. Griots have sung with good reason that to most men Baya is a country of difficult access, but they have erred in omitting that you are the exception. You weren't yet circumcised, when Sambu was already intoning chants of praise in your honor in the alluvial plains. The echo that rolled off the terraced cliffs overhanging those valleys amplified and diffused his song.

"O Wangrin, it is not merely because you have learned to write from left to right that you are what you are. It is because of your birth. It is because of the milk you have sucked at your mother's breast, and because of your father's vermilion blood. You *are* today because yesterday you *were*. You are no copy or imitation, but a truly original model.

"Your belly has never known hunger, nor has your body ever stunk. True, you are not tall and therefore you look like an unfinished wall, yet if anyone chose to leap over you he would learn to his dismay that you are like a tree trunk which is difficult to bestride. You are not a wall that was left unfinished for lack of materials; it was simply a fanciful wish of nature that you should be made as you are. It must be said, O Wangrin, that you have Samba Gueladio Yegui's daring, Silamaka Ardo's temerity, and Pullori's wild enthusiasm. You have the pluck of Tata, son of Ali, who is buried under the rubble at Woytala, warrior city of the Segu land, grave of the Tukulors.[6]

"The feast with which you are regaling us tonight, and the number and quality of your guests, are proof that Simballa, a Marka merchant famous in days gone by, was neither wealthier nor more generous than you. Garba Mama and Torokoro Mari would die of envy were they to behold the repast you are offering us in this hall hung with rich fabrics and dotted with lamps whose incandescence could rival the splendor of Allah's firmament.

"Standards of value are established through time and place. It is certain that in former days you would have been a king, or rather an emperor, as were Tunka and Mannga. Nevertheless, even though this is no happy season for Africans, you play a most prominent role in society. Are you not the Commandant's mouth and ears, and the custodian of his trust?

"Verily, to be trusted by a king is more ennobling than being his presumed son. Now, doesn't everyone know that our two Commandants will never settle any matter unless you have investigated it first? Is that not irrefutable proof of the trust he places in your judgment?

"Thus, let all envious and jealous cousins swallow their displeasure. If Wangrin orders a plateful of yams, the man who out of contrariness would order cassava can go and share it with the devil, or consume it in jail if necessary.

"Wangrin, Allah has endowed you with the cunning of a fox and the agility of the panther who dwells in leafless forests.

"One does only say 'Hey!' to unknown men.[7]

"Brothers[8] and fellow guests, eat and drink, and eat and drink yet again. If tomorrow you feel like recommencing, come back, and you shall be given more refreshments. Here one feels as if he were in Allah's paradise. One can ask for all things at all times, and no payment is ever exacted."

These words stung nearly all the civil servants present to the quick, but particularly so the new clerk, Usman Samba. By nature violent and irrepressible, he resented social etiquette above all things, as well as rights claimed by his neighbors. Strong as a hippopotamus, only two things could demolish him: hunger and sleepiness. Alone he had beaten up a platoon of twenty-five *tirailleurs*, imparting also a mighty kick to the behind of their leader, a European NCO who used to boast that he had been a boxing champion. This brawl, and all the others he got into almost daily all over the place, had caused him to be transferred a number of times.

Now Usman rose and addressed himself to Kuntena: "Even if custom prescribes that a griot sing the praises of his patron, who for all I know may be a lout, a bandit, or a thieving pimp, I am not aware that it entitles him to insult other noblemen. As far as I am concerned, if a griot insults me, even if his mouth reaches from ear to ear,[9] I'll see to it that he gets into his mother's womb the same way he left it at birth."

Accompanying his words with swift action, Usman got hold of Kuntena, wrapped him tightly into his own clothes, and then raising him high above his head as if he weighed no more than a feather, smashed him against one of the storm lights. Poor Kuntena was set alight and was almost burned to death. As for Usman, he stalked out before anyone dared utter a word. The evening ended very sadly indeed.

On the morrow, Wangrin felt oppressed by an impending threat. Abugui Mansu reprimanded Kuntena most severely. "Your mouth," he said to him, "has dug out a pit that will engulf a number of people, including your own benefactor."

But Wangrin calmed him down: "This is no time for blame," he said, "but rather for finding a suitable shelter from the storm that is gathering around us all. It may turn out to be a long-lasting storm, one that will squeeze piss out of the walls of our huts, and drench all of our belongings."

This remark had a prophetic quality. And so it happened that one month later, a telegram announced officially that Count de Villermoz had been transferred to Zadun, a subdivision three days' walk east of Diagaramba.

Another telegram followed, announcing that an Inspector of Administrative Affairs might be sent out on a mission without, however, specifying when or why. This raised a great hullabaloo throughout the district. Everyone, including the Commandant, was perturbed. Why an inspection? . . . Several supposedly embarrassing registers and files were seen to be transferred from the office to a half concealed box-room not far from the municipal jail.

During the following twenty days everyone was on the alert. The Commandant was bad tempered; Wangrin felt anxious; and the court assessors, the veterinary orderlies, the warrant chiefs—in other words all the officials, whatever their rank, who were guilty of misappropriation— were on tenterhooks. Everyone was convinced that it was on his account that the inspector was being sent.

On the other hand, this juncture turned out to be a real windfall for the occultists and marabouts, as well as for geomancers, wizards, and fortune tellers. Every single civil servant sought protection through prayers or conciliatory ceremonies. Payment always followed.

This state of affairs continued for a couple of weeks, without the slightest intimation of the approach of a European from the capital, let alone an inspector. Thus oblivion, the most powerful sedative ever placed by God at man's disposal, began to do its work. If man were not forgetful by nature, if he ignored the comfort given by sleep, where would he get the strength to survive the spiritual and physical trials that life places in his path? Thus it happened that the alarmed civil servants calmed down, and gradually forgetting that an inspection was impending, regained both sleep and peace of mind, convinced as they were that the prayers they had offered up were not unconnected with alterations in the plans originally made by that unwanted killjoy, "the Inspector."

If wild animals are disturbed while they are busy feasting on a carcass, they abandon their prey briefly and take cover. As soon as they feel safe from danger, they resume their feast.

That is exactly what happened to our embezzlers in Diagaramba. As soon as the inspector's visit ceased to be a matter for concern, they went back to their shamefully corrupt ways with renewed vigor. They had obviously forgotten the Fulbe proverb: "When justice is slow in coming it's because it's gone on a long trip to look for sturdy, but flexible branches with which to chastise the culprit all the better."

Some pushed their forgetfulness so far as to actually make a mockery of the situation, whispering among themselves: "Hey! Has the *official rummager* dissolved into thin air on his way to us, or could he be riding a chameleon?" To which the general reply was: "*Pink ear* must have heard that there are fetishists around here who are none too fond of nosey parkers, who would not even hesitate, if necessary, to do a European in who insisted at all costs on being meddlesome. They might not even balk at making a drum out of his skin and using his hands to carve themselves drumsticks."[10]

In the end, people grew tired of croaking about the aborted mission and of jeering at it. One fine morning, however, on the way to the Commandant's office, the employees were extremely startled to see that the official rest-house had been taken over *unexpectedly* at daybreak and a lance-sergeant placed at the entrance to stand sentry. This fellow's uniform was decorated by epaulets and also by a length of gold braid which traveled down the left side of his chest, passed under his left shoulder, and reappeared over his chest before cascading down his side in the form of thick lengths of golden strands terminating in two small cylinders of silvery metal. This order of dress proved that the lance-sergeant did not belong to the Diagaramba platoon, but rather to the mighty government guard in Kuluba.

So the famous inspector had been able to leap after all over the barrier erected by all those prayers and had actually arrived on the spot without the least bit of warning! There was reason to believe that he was a devil incarnate. If someone throws a pebble in a stagnant pond full of croaking, overfed frogs, they react with deathly silence and dive to the bottom trembling with fear in the hope that they won't be noticed. The inspector's unexpected arrival elicited the same reaction from the overconfident civil servants.

The inspector from Administrative Affairs was a former cavalry officer. Although he was the greatest imaginable daredevil, death—be it peaceful or violent—had refused to have anything to do with him. He was born of a Protestant family and was a duke's grandson. His name was Charles de Brière and his ideal was to serve mankind by establishing the concept that all men had equal social and moral rights which were absolutely inviolable. He had brought along a bodyguard, an interpreter, and a cook-steward. He settled them all in the official visitors' encampment, not being the kind of European who can't stand living side by side with Africans.

Having been told by the night-watchman that an inspector had arrived unexpectedly at dawn, the lance-sergeant in charge of the station at Diagaramba ran as fast as his legs would carry him to report the fact to the Commandant. Unfortunately, the latter had left on horseback in the early hours of the morning to oversee the construction of a bridge on the road to Yaguwahi. The sergeant saddled his horse and galloped toward the site.

Seeing him come at full tilt, the Commandant understood that something serious had happened. "What is it?" he shouted.

"This is what it is, Sir," replied the poor sergeant breathlessly, "a great white chief, accompanied by a sergeant higher in rank than myself, wearing the gold lanyard of the governor's palace guard, has arrived in Diagaramba and installed himself in the visitors' encampment unassisted by any of us."

"Damn!" swore the Commandant. "The old son of a bitch! He didn't even deign to let me know that he was coming. . . . "

Leaping on his horse, he went off at a gallop to introduce himself to the inspector.

"Good morning, Sir," he was greeted by the latter. "Allow me to introduce myself. I am Chief Administrative Officer, Charles de Brière, Inspector of Administrative Affairs. I have been sent here on a mission."

"How do you do, Inspector. Marc-Gabriel Galandier, Commandant of the Diagaramba District."

After this brief introduction, the Commandant left the inspector and went to his office, feeling somewhat morose and perturbed by the fact that the inspector had not volunteered any information on the real object of the mission. Wangrin, even more dismayed than his superior, was rummaging almost mechanically among the stubs of the requisition sheets, talking aloud to himself. Visibly agitated, his anxiety was reflected in his troubled condition, so strange in someone usually unruffled.

Taking him on one side, the Commandant said: "I don't understand why the inspector has come to Diagaramba. We must watch out and above all avoid letting him know that we are preoccupied by his presence. If he has simply come to make an overall inspection of services in our district, then it is the most natural thing in the world. It is normal procedure and it is necessary, for trust does not exclude control. If, on the other hand, he is on an extraordinary mission, that alters the complexion of the whole affair. If that is the case, we'll have to be on our guard or we may come out of the inspection a little the worse for wear. M. de Brière is someone to be reckoned with. He is a duke, one of those noblemen who have espoused, not out of snobbery but for the sake of true humanitarianism, the belief that all men are equal, to the point of having swopped the aristocratic particle de for a dé à coudre (a mere thimble)[11] and of having chosen to work for a living. The trouble is, such men are not prepared to trifle with morals or justice. The thing I still don't understand is why Count de Villermoz was transferred to Zadun. Contrary to normal administrative practice, the central office did not consult me or breathe a word to me about the reasons for this transfer. I can only conclude that there is some vague feeling of suspicion in the air. We must try and find out what it is all about, and not wait until we are told."

Wangrin, suspecting that the cattle affair might have been discovered, said to his chief: "How would it be, Sir, if by chance the inspector wanted to look into the requisitions . . . ?"

"What makes you think that he might show any special interest in that affair?"

"I have heard rumors that in Segu and Djenne he was particularly interested in checking the deliveries and supplies of cattle provided by the local population as a contribution towards the war effort."

"Gather together all the documents relating to that question, and we won't be caught unawares. It won't be hard for you to do this job, since you've been in charge of the requisition records all along."

M. de Brière had set up his office in the encampment. He carried out a general inspection, dealing systematically with each department: post, dispensary, jail, law courts, treasury, communications, chieftaincy, agriculture, commerce, etc. He checked all the records of every department, addressing himself to the Commandant only when he wished to use him for summoning people he wanted to question in his own office. He worked for twenty eight days, with the exclusive assistance of his own staff, so that nothing transpired of the real objective of his mission.

His inquiry was so widespread and thorough that it would have been impossible for anyone to guess that the cattle affair was the object of his inquiry. Most people assumed it to be a commonplace investigation, but not so Wangrin, Villermoz, Usman Samba, Abugui Mansu, Kuntena, and some of the Fulbe chiefs who were in charge of requisitioning. They were interrogated often and at length. Although the questions asked concerned a variety of subjects, they inevitably came back to the requisition of cattle.

Before returning to his post, which he had left at the inspector's request, Villermoz had an interview with Wangrin. Demba Lakila, a secret agent who had been asked by the inspector to shadow Villermoz, found them confabulating and reported the fact to his superior.

The inspector was now ready to leave Diagaramba. He told the Commandant that he would receive in due course a report of the inquiry through normal channels. Then he packed his trunks and returned to Kuluba, where he wrote the report and placed it in the proper hands. The report spoke of a number of minor offences: unjustified detentions, the upholding of certain judgments which had in fact been quashed by a higher court, etc. These irregularities, which were due to negligence rather than to any real abuse of power, would be the object of an official but nevertheless confidential reprimand.

On the other hand, the file christened by Brière the "cattle affair," which had been set in motion originally by an anonymous letter received in Kuluba, spoke of serious misappropriation. The political bureau handed the whole affair over to the Department of Justice.

Since Galandier and Villermoz, both Europeans, were more or less involved, an examining magistrate was appointed by the Attorney General to inquire further into the findings.

A copy of the report presented by the inspector was dispatched to Diagaramba. Galandier was so upset by it that he took to his bed. He drew the excerpt concerning the "cattle affair" out of the file and sent it on to Villermoz in Zadun. Having read the document, the latter realized the full extent of his stupidity in having released blank signed forms to Wangrin. All he had wanted was to save himself the small inconvenience of being disturbed during his sleep, and now his honor was in jeopardy and he himself was in the kind of difficulty that was likely to deprive him of both sleep and appetite for a goodly long while. He had wanted to rise in rank and earn enough money to adorn his bed with comely damsels and his stables with fine stallions. Instead, he had become entangled in a most unfortunate affair which threatened to ruin both his reputation and his career.

7 The Count's Messenger

Count de Villermoz hastened to send a messenger to Wangrin, to fetch from the files all the requisition papers concerning cattle which he himself had signed at the time. Wangrin, however, was well aware of the disparity between the numbers marked on the sheets and those marked on the stubs and had already removed all compromising papers from his files in case anyone thought of checking through for consistency.

When the count's messenger delivered the note requesting him to hand over the papers, Wangrin did actually tie them into a parcel and gave them to the carrier before a witness, but at the same time he was very careful to hold on to the count's letter.

The messenger began his return journey to Zadun jealously clutching the parcel which Wangrin had sealed in the special way all official dispatches must be sealed. Having covered a distance of about three miles, he noticed a youth sitting on a rock. When he got close enough to speak to him, the youth jumped up, raised his arms to Heaven and intoned:

"Praise be to Allah, who said to the prophet: 'If I did not fear that the family of a lone traveler who has lost his way might cry unto me: O God, what have you done with our son?' . . . I swear by my own likeness and strength that I would allow any man who travels alone to lose his way.

"The words of our Lord echoed in my mind, and I was afraid to pursue my journey alone. My family have asked me to go to Zadun to track down some cattle of theirs which is supposed to be on the move just now. I hope you will permit me to go along with you as the companion who has been placed on your path by Allah."

"You have spoken truly," replied the count's messenger.

"Since I am younger than you," rejoined the youth, "permit me to carry your load, as our tradition prescribes."[1]

Without bothering to wait for an answer, he grabbed the load, balanced it on his head, and began to walk ahead of his companion. Whenever they stopped to rest, he would fetch water, prepare food, and share everything with his friend. And so they went on for two whole days. . . . When they arrived at a village called Gongo, the count's messenger turned to his companion and said: "I have a message for the village chief; can you keep an eye on my sack? I'll be back very soon."

As soon as his fellow-traveler was out of sight, the youth opened the sack, extracted the sealed parcel addressed by Wangrin to Villermoz, and proceeded to vanish into thin air.

On his return, the messenger saw that his companion had disappeared, but noticed at the same time that his load was tied just as he had left it, and apparently intact. The owner of the house where they had chosen to stop returned it to him with a snuff-box full of tobacco and a small parcel containing kola nuts. "Here you are: a little gift from your younger brother, who hopes to meet you at the next stop. He was told that the herd he is looking for might be approaching our village, so he had no choice but to go on in search of it."

As a matter of fact, a herd was crossing the village just then. Unaware of the misfortune that had befallen him and harboring no suspicion whatsoever, the messenger picked up his sack and started towards Edi, the next village, where he was sure he would find his companion. In Edi, the young man was nowhere to be seen, but the messenger was not unduly worried, as he knew perfectly well that his friend was expected to track down a herd which had not been heard of for several months. Having no time to spare, the count's messenger continued on his way toward Zadun, where his master was waiting for him in an agony of suspense. On arriving, he went immediately to the Residence, but was told by the watchman that the count had already retired for the night. "Tell him that I arrived late in the night, but will go to his office first thing in the morning."

The following day, just as he was getting out of bed, Villermoz heard of the return of his messenger. At once he sent a guard to fetch him. When the guard stepped into his lodgings, however, he found the messenger in a state of delirium, thrashing about on the floor like a dying boa constrictor and letting out deep groans interspersed with the words: "Woe is me! What have I done to deserve this? I am done for! And my whole family as well! What will become of me?" As it so happened, he had opened his sack that very moment and discovered that the parcel sealed in the official manner was nowhere to be found.

The guard saw that he could not convince the messenger to get up and follow him, so he decided to take him by the scruff of the neck and drag him along without ceremony before the count. The count, seeing in his turn that the guard was pushing the messenger roughly before him, suspected at once that something serious had happened. "What is it?" he shouted nervously. "Why are you handling him so roughly?"

Stammering, the guard replied, "Because, s-s-sir, he's told me something I c-c-c-can't repeat. I don't want to have my mouth 'r-r-ripped up to the ears.'"[2]

"Sir," sobbed the messenger, "a thief has pulled the sealed envelope that you sent me to collect from Wangrin out of my sack!"

"O God, come to my rescue!" were the first words that came to Villermoz's lips. It had ever been his habit to mock those who invoked God's assistance in his presence, but nothing is more efficacious than adversity or ill luck in persuading a man to recognize the futility of human endeavor and to declare his faith in God.

Now he began pacing his verandah, with his head bowed and his arms folded on his chest, very deep in thought. In the end he exploded at his orderly:

"Take this bastard to the lance-sergeant. Tell him to throw him in jail and leave him there to rot in a narrow cell until death sets him free."

The orderly, who had been eagerly awaiting the orders of his superior, gave a violent shove to the unfortunate messenger and promptly dragged him to jail.

While the poor wretch is decomposing in a cell dark and malodorous as a grave, what has become of the thief? And, indeed, who might he have been . . . ?

With the help of one of his followers, Wangrin had arranged for the parcel to be stolen before reaching its destination. Wangrin was no fool. He knew perfectly well that if he let go of the requisition sheets signed by Villermoz he would never be able to prove that he had been a mere instrument in the cattle affair. He understood also that Villermoz was anxious to recover those documents so that he could destroy them and wipe out every trace of his participation in the affair, shifting the whole weight of responsibility on to Wangrin. If he could only manage that, Wangrin's fate would be sealed.

Besides, as Wangrin knew, any case that involved, rightly or wrongly, a European would be very hard to settle in a colony. No doubt it was preferable to ignore a crime—however serious—than to pass sentence on a European, all the more so if the latter was part of the establishment. The prestige of the colonizers was at stake, and when it came to that sort of thing policy saw to it that problems of conscience did not stand in the way. In view of that particular situation, Wangrin felt he could discard all his own scruples and behave just like his counterpart. To defend himself with every means at his disposal became his only object. Villermoz now represented a heavy and sturdy cloak which he thought it prudent to adopt as protective garb. Too bad if, in the process, morals and justice had to fall by the wayside.

The man who had stolen the parcel was a well-known house-breaker. Although young, he already had nine convictions for aggravated theft to his name. He was in the habit of saying: "I only allow them to take me when I feel like having a little rest in jail." Although his real name was Worde Addu, he had been nicknamed *dutal-bayre*, which means: the vulture who hangs out on the cliffs.

Wangrin had used his influence to mitigate Worde Addu's last sentence with a view to employing him for his own ends, should the occasion ever arise. He had not had long to wait, nor had Worde Addu disappointed him.

Meanwhile, yet another of Wangrin's agents had arrived from Zadun bearing the news that the count's messenger was languishing in jail, dying a slow death. If no one exerted himself on his behalf he had no more than three months to live. Wangrin realized that he was to blame for his detention and made up his mind to help. He consulted Abugui Mansu, hoping that the latter might find a way to inform Galandier that the count's messenger was being detained illegally.

"Europeans cling to one another like the stitches of a knitted fabric," he said to Abugui Mansu. "If we make a formal accusation stating that Villermoz has thrown a man in jail without trial and has arranged to have him maltreated to boot, Galandier will be angered and will make us pay for our daring. He already hates the guts of the informers who have set this whole thing in motion and considers them responsible for the unpleasant situation we have been in since the inspector's visit."

"Don't worry, we'll find a way," replied Abugui Mansu. On the same day he brought along a *dyula*,[3] by name Mory Diakite.

"I have brought you a man," he said to Wangrin, "who will lodge a complaint against the count's messenger Sammba Buri. All you have to do is to introduce him to the Commandant and translate his statement."

Needless to say, Mory Diakite had been bought by Abugui Mansu on behalf of Wangrin and had learned to recite by heart his presumed grievance. So that when he found himself face to face with Galandier, he was able to proclaim unblinkingly: "Some time ago I entrusted a few heads of cattle to one Sammba Buri, with the understanding that he was to give me some account of my livestock every six months or so. Having been left without news, I sent my brother to find out what had happened.

Now he is back with the news that Sammba Buri has not been seen these last two months, and that his family refuse to disclose his whereabouts. I have come to appeal to the authorities to help me recover my property."

Whenever the word *cattle* was mentioned, the Commandant opened his eyes very wide and pricked up his ears. He sent at once an official telegram ordering Count de Villermoz, Assistant to the Commandant of Zadun, to find, and then order to Diagaramba the above-mentioned Sammba Buri, supposedly a cattle-breeder in that town.

When he saw the telegram the count went more or less berserk. What sort of evil spirit was this that was haunting his every step? He hastened to release Sammba Buri and advised him to run away to the Gold Coast to avoid a life sentence. He also promised him to take care of his family and if the necessity arose to send them to join him in Kumasi.

Sammba Buri left town under cover of darkness, not without having spoken words of comfort to his family. He was sad to leave them, but they, on the other hand, were thankful that he had managed to get out of the veritable hell which had been a threat to his health and might eventually have cost him his life.

Count de Villermoz waited a few days. When he was absolutely certain that Sammba Buri was no longer in his territory, he sent a telegram to his superior, informing him that the man in question had gone off to the Gold Coast without leaving an address. However, his brother Sory Buri, who was his legal representative, would be sent to Diagaramba in his stead.

Accordingly, three days later Sory Buri arrived in Diagaramba and, as custom prescribed, reserved his first call for the Commandant's interpreter, who in the event was Wangrin. The latter exploited this opportunity to take Sory Buri into his secret, and explained what needed to be said to the Great White Chief. When he was admitted into his presence, then, Sory Buri was ready with his admission that, yes, a herd had actually been entrusted to his brother by Mory Diakite; but his brother was in fact not guilty, for before his departure he had been careful to make known the whereabouts of the herd. No more questions were asked and everything went back to normal. An admirable trick had been played behind Villermoz's back, and under the unsuspecting nose of the mighty Galandier.

8 The Trial

Two weeks later, however, a completely different picture emerged. Both Wangrin and Count de Villermoz found themselves in an extremely awkward situation; even the mighty Commandant did not escape totally unscathed.

Having been put in charge of the cattle affair, the public prosecutor's office in Bamako decided to send one of their own examining magistrates—a short, corpulent Martinican with a head of gray hair—to Diagaramba to round off the inquiry. Because of the voluble, nasal cataract of words that hurtled out of his mouth, this fellow gave the impression of being an irascible busybody, but on second thought it was hard to tell whether this was his natural way or simply a posture. He was quite capable of thumping his desk or threatening people with a trip to Cayenne over a matter of not the slightest consequence and he seemed to be driven by a consuming desire to scrunch up Whites. Paradoxically, he also hated Blacks. One would have thought that he held a grudge against the two races which, by mixing, had adulterated the breed from which he had sprung, filling him with an abundance of complexes.

It must be said to his credit that in spite of his singular behavior, his manner of judging was unquestionably upright. He wrote an impartial report, based on facts. These proved beyond doubt that Senior Commandant Galandier had been naive and careless rather than dishonest. The magistrate recommended that discipline be enforced merely through a sound rapping of the Commandant's knuckles; a rapping vigorous enough to break his joints, however, would be out of proportion with his offence. Galandier's brilliant military career, together with his fine humane record, enabled him to exit from that nasty business with no greater chastisement than an official six-month leave—to be spent in France—and at the end of it a transfer to another station. But for Wangrin and Villermoz, things did not go quite so smoothly. Both were destined to endure a great deal of suffering as a result of their involvement in the unfortunate affair.

Fifty witnesses came forward. Wangrin and Villermoz were indicted and their case was transferred to the French court in Bamako. The affair dragged on six whole months. Wangrin lost twenty pounds and Villermoz aged fifteen years.

That they were both guilty was beyond any doubt, but Wangrin took the attitude that small fry are compelled to carry out orders at all times rather than question them or even verify them.

Although the requisition sheets had disappeared from the files, the examining magistrate had been able to establish the number of cattle which had been requisitioned, and through a system of cross-checking, those actually delivered to the military and civilian authorities. The discrepancy amounted to two thousand six hundred animals. On the basis of the rate of exchange that obtained for English currency during the First World War between French West Africa and the Gold Coast, it represented a sum of roughly two and a half million francs.

Aware that Wangrin had not even once alluded to the requisition sheets, Count de Villermoz eventually convinced himself that the parcel had indeed been stolen by someone else. In the lower court he protested his innocence and asserted that he had been deceived by Wangrin, who, he claimed, had abused his trust and had tampered with the already completed requisition sheets.

The case could not be brought to a conclusion in Bamako. It was transferred to the Assize Court in Dakar, which sat twice a year. Wangrin, Villermoz, and their witnesses were summoned to appear before that court.

Before leaving Diagaramba for Dakar, Wangrin went to call on his protector Tierno Siddi, "the marabout," and said to him:

"My most revered marabout, the proverb says: 'What is the use of being close friends with a monkey if one doesn't use him to pry loose one's cane when it gets caught in the branches of a tree?' At the moment, my life is balanced as precariously as a cane on a tree top. My job and, worse still, my honor and my freedom are at stake. I have come to ask you for a blessing that will act as protection. I know that your prayers are not for sale—therefore I am not offering you money. But I do wish to appeal to your compassion. I find that I am engaged in battle with the son of an aristocratic French family. His people will back him up, they will do everything in their power to save him. The only way they can achieve their end is by destroying me. The trial will be a mere mockery. I know full well what I am in for."

"Are you, or are you not, guilty of the crimes of which you are being accused?" asked Tierno Siddi.

"I am no more guilty than Count de Villermoz. To begin with, he was not aware of my subterfuge, but that was not for long. All he did was to warn me to behave prudently. Now that the banquet has turned to rotten flesh, he'd like me to be the one who eats it. *Lassidan-Deeral,*[1] who is in charge of accounts, and the *Neguediuru-tigui*[2] have both received lavish gifts of gold and sterling as well as precious objects. I have proof, but have thought it best not to uncover my trumps for fear that someone might destroy them surreptitiously. I knew all along that the trial would be transferred from Bamako to the higher court in Dakar. I have been proved right."

Tierno Siddi had listened to Wangrin with an impenetrable countenance. Now he rejoined:

"I am against anyone who abuses his power and intelligence, or any other quality he may possess, for the purpose of deceiving and robbing his fellowmen, but I am equally opposed to powerful men who make less powerful ones pay for their own misdeeds. Although both situations apply to you, I feel pity for you because of the second one, and therefore I will pray that the amount of poise needed to submit the kind of evidence you say you possess may not forsake you. I would advise you, however, to use it only at the very last minute, that is, just before sentence is passed." Tierno Siddi continued:

"When the muezzin lets out his first call to afternoon prayers, you will go on foot to the banks of the Maaye. There, you will look for a quiet spot covered with fine sand, unsullied by the excrement of man, beast, or insect. You will wait there until sundown. At the first cock crow, before the sun actually sets, you will take seven handfuls of sand with your left hand. At the second cock crow, you will take another seven with your right hand. At the third you will mix the sand in a brand-new calabash, one that has never been used up to that moment. You will not budge until the sun has set and then you will bring the whole lot to me before the last evening prayer. During this whole operation you will fast."

Wangrin carried out Tierno Siddi's instruction punctiliously. As night fell, he carried the brand-new calabash and its contents of fourteen handfuls of uncontaminated sand back to him. The marabout stretched on the ground a piece of black linen called Guinea cloth. He poured the sand onto it, then smoothed it out as if he were about to mark out a geomantic design, but instead of the usual signs, he traced a rectangle within which he inscribed a very long word indeed in Arabic writing.

"While I am deep in prayer," he said to Wangrin, "you will stare unrelentingly, and blinking as little as possible, at that word. Your body will remain motionless. You will repeat voicelessly the word *Amen* without interruption until I myself utter the word *Amen.*"

Then he sank deeply in a long, silent prayer, which ended with the word *Amen*. Wangrin, whose limbs had become very stiff, was about to stretch, but Tierno Siddi stopped him:

"Remain in the same position and try to look at each separate letter of this word, which is one of the mighty names of Allah. "

After Wangrin had carried out his orders, the marabout traced a diagonal line, dividing the rectangle into two equal parts. In this way he obtained two equal triangles; he gathered the sand from each into a pile. Thus, the holy word was cut in half. Then the marabout wrapped each little heap of sand in a scrap of white linen and made two sachets which he handed to Wangrin, saying:

"You will place one of these in the calabash, which you will leave behind in your house, in a quiet corner, where it will be hidden from all glances, especially those of menstruating women. The second sachet you will take along wherever you go. By the grace and the might of Allah you will return safe and sound from your ordeal, for I warn you, it is nothing less than an ordeal you are about to embark upon! As soon as you return, however, and before you drink water you must empty the contents of the one that remained behind. You will then throw the whole lot back on the spot whence it came. Afterwards, you will sacrifice a bull and distribute the pieces among the poor, without forgetting to feed some to your family."

Came the day of departure. The count and his witnesses, Wangrin and his own, left Diagaramba, bound for Dakar.

Although at every stop Count de Villermoz was cheered by the warm welcome accorded to him by his fellow countrymen, his physical condition remained pitiful. As for Wangrin, wherever he went, he heard nothing but gloomy remarks reminiscent of the lugubrious call made by birds of ill omen. Yet, whenever he reached for the sachet full of blessed sand which he had slipped into the bandoleer that never left him, a feeling of secret reassurance pervaded his whole being, and the threats that pressed so heavily on his mind were lifted in the way that dreams are dispelled by sudden awakenings.

In Dakar, the authorities sent a young man to meet Count de Villermoz and his two witnesses, and to accompany them to the catering rest-house reserved for French civil servants only. Wangrin and his witnesses on the other hand were ignored, but happily for them, African hospitality did not fail. The head of the family living in the first house on whose door they chanced to knock was most happy to receive them all.

Wangrin, whose wits never deserted him, made inquiries in the town and learned that their case, which was listed last on the roll, would not be heard for three months at least. Since the trial was expected to last about two months, Wangrin reckoned that he would have to live in Dakar between five and six months. He decided to make for the port and find a job as a daily paid laborer in the warehouse where the coal shipped from France was weighed, later to be sent on by train to Niger and Upper Senegal. For this purpose he bought two overalls made of coarse cloth and from that day on he always went around looking as grubby as a miner who has just climbed up from underground.

Whenever he was summoned by the examining magistrate, Wangrin turned up covered in coal dust from head to foot and with a look of starvation about him. In this way he hoped to make the right impression and to convince everyone that he had not kept the money made from the illegal sale of cattle. No secret agent, however skillful, succeeded in un-masking him. Meanwhile, a campaign of intimidation had been under-taken. Wangrin's witnesses were given to understand that if they per-sisted in wanting to help him they would eventually be deported and abandoned on desert islands where carnivorous animals would inevita-bly feast on their flesh.

At last the case was given a solemn hearing. It lasted five whole days. With the exception of Abugui Mansu, Wangrin's witnesses were, or at least seemed, ill at ease. Whatever the reason, they made contradictory statements, rendering their own testimony rather suspect. Wangrin had advised Abugui Mansu to admit to having sold cattle, but to explain that he had done so at Wangrin's request, having been told by the latter that the proceeds would go to the treasury, which in war time collected funds exacted by the government from French nationals. This included citi-zens, subjects, and French-protected persons alike.

Came the day Abugui Mansu was interrogated for the last time:

"Have you, or have you not, been selling cattle which had been put in your way by Wangrin, the interpreter, who is here in this court to-day?"

"I have," he replied.

"To whom did you usually hand over the money?"

"To Wangrin, in the office and in the presence of the Junior Com-mandant, Count de Villermoz, who afterwards dismissed me. A couple of days later, Wangrin would come to my house with my commission."

"Did you not suspect the deal of being somewhat shady?"

"I did not, since the Junior Commandant and *Lassidan-Deeral*[3] knew all about it. *Lassidan-Deeral* himself would change into French silver coins part of the sum of gold pound sterling I used to bring back from the Gold Coast."

"How many heads of cattle have you sold all together?"

"About two thousand five or six hundred."

"Do you have anything special to add to your testimony?"

"Yes, I have. I was prompted by a feeling of devotion for a France that at present is impoverished by the war. If the Junior Commandant had not been involved, I might have hesitated; but I firmly believed that a white man could neither steal nor lie, since he represents strength and justice, and comes here to educate and civilize. Moreover, Count de Villermoz, our former Junior Commandant, is the scion of an aristocratic family. He always wears a single eyeglass[4] which, I have been told, is an emblem of breeding among Whites. He is also a kind-hearted man and loves horses. Our people consider it a sign of great nobility."

Turning towards Villermoz, the judge addressed him thus:

"Count de Villermoz, this court asks you for the very last time to acknowledge the truth of the accusations that have been leveled at you in this sad case in which a name as aristocratic as yours should never have been implicated. Your superior, engaged as he was in other duties, had chosen to place blind trust in your cooperation. See where that has led you. . . . Both in your own interest and for the sake of the reputation of the corps to which you belong, I am asking you now to prove your innocence or confess."

"My lord," replied the Count. "I am the victim of a heinous breach of trust and of a conspiracy organized by Wangrin, an individual who, beneath an honest and devoted exterior, hides his true nature of devious underling; here is a man who has used the education that France has freely given him to deceive his superiors and to steal from his fellow townsmen."

The judge interrupted Villermoz:

"No insults, please. The gifts offered by France are in no way connected with the justification I am asking you to submit to this court."

Villermoz held his peace. Without having been so instructed by the judge, he walked out of the witness-box and returned to his seat.

"You are in a great hurry to go back to your seat, Count de Villermoz," said the judge. "Be so kind as to get up, return to the box, and stay there until such time as I see fit to dismiss you. I advise you in your own interest to show respect for this court. Answer my question."

"I plead not guilty," replied Villermoz. "I admit that I have been negligent, but I deny the accusation leveled at me by Wangrin and by his witness who is patently his accomplice."

Then the judge heard the witnesses for the defense brought by Villermoz. Their statements and their replies left much to be desired.

The hearing was adjourned.

During that interval, Count de Villermoz's situation was greatly improved by the efforts of his companions-at-arms, his powerful family connections, as well as various factors of a political nature.

For the last time, the court, which had already made up its mind, heard the case of the "cattle affair." A mere formality, since everyone knew that Wangrin would be found guilty and get a sentence hard enough to dissuade him from ever trying to compromise a white man again, especially one born of the French aristocracy and a member of the state civil service.

During the hearing Villermoz was interrogated once more. He denied any knowledge of the facts and reiterated that Wangrin had betrayed his blind trust.

Then Wangrin was called to the box and addressed by the judge:

"It has been proved that your one remaining witness is indeed your agent and your accomplice. The court cannot accept his testimony, so that you are left with no witness at all. Can you produce any other witness in your defense?"

"Yes, my lord," replied Wangrin, standing in the box. This caused a great stir among the audience.

"I do have a last witness. I have forborne from using this piece of self-defense, believing to the last that Count de Villermoz as my superior would exert his influence on my behalf. But he has done nothing but shirk his responsibility and shift the blame on to me. He has asserted that I have abused his trust and have ordered, unbeknown to him, larger numbers of cattle than were prescribed by the law. My main witness, I am told, is unacceptable. I have no other way left, then, than to quote Count de Villermoz against himself. I trust the court will see where the truth really lies."

Accompanying his words with a flourish of the hand, Wangrin pulled out from under his gown a large parcel sheathed in leather, resembling an oversized amulet. He unstitched the outer binding and placed on the judge's bench an envelope containing a number of requisition sheets, all in perfect condition, and signed by Villermoz himself.

"This evidence, my lord," he said, "cannot be refuted by Count de Villermoz." The judge took one of the requisition sheets, perused it carefully, and checked it against all the others. Then he handed it to the public prosecutor who asked the count to look at it and to say whether the signature at the bottom of the page was actually his own. At the sight of this sheet of paper, Count de Villermoz lost all control and bellowed at Wangrin: "You dirty swine! It was you, then, who stole these . . . " Unable to go on, he burst into tears. His hands began to tremble like palm fronds fluttering in the breeze.

The judge intervened: "These papers will be examined and admitted as evidence." Then he adjourned the hearing.

All the Europeans present, members of the court and spectators alike, were filled with painful consternation. They cast indignant glances at Wangrin. Some whispered: "How unfortunate, how shameful! We must find some way of destroying this scoundrel who has dared to sully a Frenchman's reputation."

Fearing a lynching, Wangrin stayed on in the courtroom. He took advantage of a secluded exit, which an usher had left open by chance, to make a quick getaway.

Wangrin and his witnesses went underground for a whole week, and one could hardly blame them, for any kind of accident was likely to befall them; they might even have to deal with some vicarious provocation in the streets.

Finally the day came for the last hearing.

Visibly embarrassed, the judge rose and pronounced:

"The case concerning the so-called 'cattle affair' having been sufficiently tried:

"Whereas the government of Upper Senegal and Niger has referred the so-called 'cattle affair' to our jurisdiction before having made adequate inquiries so as to determine the political consequences that might accrue from the case;

"Whereas those circumstances represent a serious handicap for the colonial judicial power;

"Whereas any case having political connotations, whatever it may be, falls necessarily within the jurisdiction of the Bureau of Political Affairs;

"The summing up of the Public Prosecutor having been heard;

"The court hereby decides to remit the so-called 'cattle affair' to the administrative authorities so that further inquiries may be made as to the political consequences which this case may entail."

On hearing the verdict, Wangrin understood that the affair was going to be hushed up to protect the count from an ignominious sentence. He rose from his seat and declared:

"My lord, Count de Villermoz has insulted me publicly, accusing me of being devious and dishonest. Since it has now been proved that I was a mere agent in the whole business, a man who was bound by oath to obey and serve his superiors, I wish to institute an action against Count de Villermoz for having cast a slur on my name. I could never have brought myself to exhibit the sheets which prove beyond doubt his involvement if he hadn't attempted to discharge his responsibility on my shoulders, consigning my fate to the hands of justice."

The judge answered that Wangrin's verbal complaint would be dealt with by the appropriate court, and the hearing closed in an atmosphere of increased moroseness on the part of the Europeans, all of whom ex-

pressed displeasure with a court that had allowed Wangrin to ask repara-
tion for insults he had only too well deserved instead of cutting off his
tongue.

On the same afternoon, Wangrin was summoned before the Bureau
of Political Affairs, which was directly responsible to the highest authority. He was asked to withdraw his suit so as to avoid the continuation of
a scandal which might cost him his job, and perhaps even more. . . . As
an interpreter for the colonial administration, Wangrin was no novice in
matters of political proceedings within the colonial administration. At
once he asked: "What advantages will accrue to me if I withdraw my
complaint?"

"The cattle affair will be classified, you will go back to your station,
and will be paid all expenses you have incurred in connection with the
trial."

Wangrin accepted the bargain. He was given two thousand five hundred francs out of secret funds.

Shortly afterwards, Count de Villermoz arranged a meeting with
Wangrin. Approaching him, he said:

"You dirty nigger! You've won, but I'll make you pay for it one day.
Don't you ever forget that wherever I meet you—anywhere in the world—
I'll crush you like the cur you are. But it's much too fine a compliment to
compare you to a dog, an animal who never betrays his master or benefactor, while you—you bite the hand that has fed you. Filthy rascal!"

"Wherever you meet me, Count de Villermoz," answered Wangrin,
"I'll be on my guard and will protect myself with the same amount of
energy you intend to expend on my destruction!"

Wangrin spent a few days purchasing a number of items and then
went on his way to Diagaramba, which he reached safe and sound, just
as Tierno Siddi had predicted.

Meanwhile Diagaramba had been regaled with a new Commandant.
The latter, however, was most careful not to rely on Wangrin's services
exclusively. As a matter of fact, deep down he detested him, but never
allowed himself to show his real feelings.

In the end, he applied by confidential letter for Wangrin's transfer
because, he claimed, of the recent events and of the exaggerated popularity Wangrin had achieved among the natives by managing to return to
his former station totally unscathed.

9 The Donkey Who Drank Honey

And so it came to pass that one beautiful morning the Commandant found among the official papers a letter that ordered a promotion but also, alas for Wangrin, a transfer to Gudugaua, a town about three hundred miles from Diagaramba.

If Wangrin had had any choice in the matter, he would have preferred to be reduced to a lower rank and remain in Diagaramba, rather than be promoted and transferred. But orders are orders. Although Wangrin keenly felt the administrative blow that had been dealt to him, he also knew that complaining was out of the question, since it had come in the shape of a reward specially reserved for worthy civil servants.

That evening, as soon as he arrived home from work, Wangrin walked straight into his "man's apartment" instead of calling on his wives before changing, as he had been in the habit of doing daily.

His favorite wife, whose turn it was to prepare his meal on that particular day, filled a cup with water and carried it to her husband, wishing him at the same time a warm welcome home after a long day at work full of interminable palavers. Wangrin answered with a whisper so faint that it seemed to fall into the folds of his bubu. He took the cup from his young wife, who was kneeling in the respectful *sonsoron*[1] posture, but merely brushed the surface of the water with his lips. He gave her a strange look, then turned his back on her.

The poor woman was perturbed. She ran in search of the senior wife who, as tradition prescribes, always protects her young fellow spouses.

"*Bamuso*,"[2] she cried, "*Dutigui*[3] is angry. His eyes are darker than a stormy, windy night, and he refuses to drink. How have I sinned? What sort of gossip might he have heard about me?"

"About us, rather," rectified *Bamuso*.

"Go and see him at once. If it isn't with us that he is angry, he must have heard some disagreeable piece of news." The corners of her mouth, usually curled into a joyous smile, set into a pitiful grimace.

"True, it's the first time he's gone straight to his man's apartment without coming to greet us first," *Bamuso* assented. She went to Wangrin, and found him disfigured by an indescribable feeling of anxiety.

"What is the matter, *Dutigui?*"

"Well, as you know, it's impossible to be happy every day of the year. Just like day and night, joy and sorrow succeed one another in the heart of man, first affecting his mind and later becoming manifest. I can't tell you how upset I am. A letter has just come from the governor. I have obviously fallen from grace, even though my misfortune is being glossed over with a spurious sort of varnish. I am transferred to Gudugaua in Mossi country and we have no alternative but to leave within three days."

Bamuso was even more stricken by the news than her husband. Her eyes filled with abundant, warm tears, and it was for Wangrin now to come to the rescue. He comforted her, asking her to conceal her grief, that the rest of the family might not be unduly alarmed.

"Our enemies would rejoice if they knew that we consider this transfer a misfortune," he told her. "When one's enemies plot to harm one, one must continue to smile in the face of adversity. In this way one's enemies will miss the opportunity for rejoicing they had so much looked forward to. They will begin to doubt their success, and that will cause them to suffer the pain they had intended to inflict on others. The ability to conduct oneself in such a way as to disappoint one's enemy's expectations enables one to take revenge with dignity and without any outward show of emotion. I did expect trouble. As a matter of fact, when I returned from Dakar, I brought back a number of outfits and other items that I know marabouts tend to be rather fond of. I offered them to Tierno Siddi, but he refused them, since he had not prayed for me with a view to material gain, but rather out of compassion, in a spirit of obedience to the Prophet who allows every man at least once in a lifetime to violate the law prescribed by the Koran, provided he is truly prompted by pity. He knew perfectly well that I was guilty in connection with the cattle affair, nevertheless out of compassion he prayed for me. He said: 'You will encounter great obstacles in your path. I fear for you. Your destiny is engulfed in a darkness so deep that I can't see the end of your life.' Could this be the beginning of that fateful night? Whatever happens, you, *Bamuso*, keep up your strength and make sure that your sisters, my other wives, do not discover my true feelings."

Within a few hours, practically everyone in Diagaramba knew that Wangrin had been transferred. He put all the affairs still pending with Abugui Mansu in order, and entrusted his herd to him.

The *Waalde* (the young people's society which Wangrin had joined on his arrival) held counsel and decided to honor him with a great farewell banquet. One of the African paradoxes is that happiness and unhappiness, joy and sorrow, are all celebrated in like manner. The Diagaramba *Waalde*, feeling deeply the loss of a member who had been both active and bountiful, celebrated Wangrin's departure as it would have celebrated a funeral—with a lavish feast followed by music and song.

The next day, fifty horses accompanied Wangrin all the way to a village thirteen miles from Diagaramba. Then Wangrin's small caravan, which consisted of ten people—women, children, and servants—journeyed eight whole days before reaching Yaguwahi, residence of a great king. There, Wangrin and his family intended to rest for a few days before continuing their journey, on the fair assumption that it would prove a pleasant interlude, for Romo Sibedi, who acted as interpreter to Yaguwahi's Commandant, happened to be their fellow townsman.

Romo Sibedi, unlike Wangrin, was not a product of the School for Hostages. He had come from the *Fantirimori*,[4] exactly like Racutie, and like him, spoke *forofifon naspa*.

Romo Sibedi was by no means a nonentity. Very corpulent, he was over six feet tall, and weighed about two hundred and seventy pounds. He had belonged to a group of young people who had sworn to make Yorsam the conqueror pay for the nameless atrocities he had committed in the Nubigu region. Having managed to survive the upheaval, he and those who shared his allegiance had pledged that they would allow themselves neither rest nor respite so long as Yorsam continued to live and to be free. They had enrolled in the French army as one man, and until the days of independence no district in Mali had been able to boast more veterans than Nubigu.

Romo Sibedi, having served under several officers, such as Mangin, Marchand, Quipandon, etc. at the time of the conquest of Western Sudan, ended up serving under Captain Gouraud. Having attained the rank of sergeant,[5] he enrolled among the district guards.[6] He rapidly climbed all the intervening steps and was discharged with the rank of lance-sergeant. As a reward for his faithful service to France, he was then appointed administrative African interpreter.

It was with great pleasure that he now received his compatriot and colleague, Wangrin. He invited him to stay and allocated to him one of his own rooms, while his wives, children, and servants were installed in the family quarters.

Romo Sibedi was the second most important citizen in the district, second only to the Commandant. It was conceivable that the Junior Commandant might not be told certain secrets, but not so Romo Sibedi. Everything passed through his hands. With a finer house than a warrant chief, Romo lived in the kind of opulence that could not help but boggle Wangrin's imagination. He was held in such high esteem that no one except chiefs dared speak to him standing up, or raise their voices in his presence. The king depended on him more than he on the king.

To compare the Yaguwahi district with Diagaramba was rather like comparing a man who enjoyed full sight with a one-eyed man, or paradise with purgatory.

Wangrin sat many a long hour in a corner of the market, admiring the beauty and riches of that country, reminiscent of the tales in *A Thousand and One Nights*.

The young Fulbe women were as light as mulattoes, while the Mossi and Bambara were dark as ebony from the Sahel. All were so slender and graceful that to see them in the market square was like watching a beauty contest. Cattle abounded to such a degree that the griot Belko Ilo was able to sing: "There are more oxen in the Fulbe cattle pens than insects in any ant or termite nest."

The trade with the Namaci prospered so that on the route to Mapata, its commercial capital, one met hundreds of caravans, mainly donkeys and oxen, laden with rich merchandise.

Every evening for a whole week, Romo Sibedi honored his guest with splendid musical entertainments provided by ten lute players, female singers, and percussionists. The sessions continued into the early hours.

Millet, rice, aromatic butter made from cow milk, fresh milk, curds, quarters of sheep, juicy humps of young bullocks, fine Timbuctoo tobacco, European sweets, tea, sugar in lumps and in cones—in a word, everything that people who understood and coveted delicacies might have wished to eat could be had in that house. Indeed, one might have mistaken it for a provision store, but one that was stocked free of charge and supplied goods in great bounty.

Romo Sibedi lived in greater splendor than the king himself, yet without vainglory.

Wangrin's dismay at the sight of all this magnificence plunged him into a state of despondency which he found himself unable to conceal. The ostentatious luxury displayed by Romo in an effort to be kind to him served instead to exacerbate the selfishness and greed that were gnawing at his heart. At the sight of all those beautiful women and fine mounts, the spontaneity with which the chiefs heaped gifts, including all sorts of bribes, on Romo, Wangrin forgot all feelings of moral uprightness, decency, justice, and gratitude. Such notions as these served only to cloud his judgment and weaken his resolve.

For him, life had turned into a cruel struggle. It was either destroy or perish, play tricks on others or be their helpless victim. His conscience and concupiscence found themselves in desperate conflict, but in no time evil triumphed over good and the voice of what had once been his conscience was silenced; it became a distant echo, and finally even the echo died down. From the demise of his earlier conscience there emerged a unilateral force: in the future he would have no care except his own well-being, he would have no object other than the fulfilment of his desires.

On the evening that saw the completion of this inner revolution, he went to bed with the firm resolve that he would return to Yaguwahi. It would be just too bad if his resolution were to mean supplanting his benevolent townsman!

"A man can be impudent without becoming devious," thought Wangrin. "Tomorrow, I will let my host know that I mean to have him decamp so that I can take his place."

Accordingly, the next morning, after a breakfast as abundant as a sumptuous dinner, Wangrin turned to Romo Sibedi.

"Brother," he said, "I must be on my way. In a few hours I will leave Yaguwahi, bound for Gudugaua. I owe you much gratitude for your generous hospitality. I have never enjoyed myself quite so much in my whole life. It was extremely good of you to introduce me to this town. Up to now I regarded those who believe in earthly paradise as simple fools, but from this day on I won't mock them any more. Thanks to you, I have come to realize that there are a few privileged places on earth which can only be described as annexes to the Garden of Eden! You will not take it amiss, then, if I do my utmost to return here and take over your office."

Romo Sibedi assumed that his townsman was joking and replied in what he thought was the same spirit:

"Have you ever seen anyone step into paradise and then abandon it?"

"Yes," answered Wangrin. "If we are to believe tradition, our father Adam and his bride, our mother Eve, lived in paradise, but they left it after all. . . . "

"Gently, Wangrin! They didn't exactly choose to leave. It was an avenging angel, brandishing a fiery sword, who compelled them to go."

"My dear brother Romo, let me remind you that history constantly repeats itself. Periodically, events occur, fade out for a time and then come back full circle. Only the protagonists change. In the same way, in a few weeks' time the drama of the avenging angel banishing Adam from the Garden of Eden will be re-enacted in Yaguwahi."

"I find it difficult to follow you. Explain yourself a little more clearly, my good Wangrin."

"Yet I'm being very explicit. In my opinion, a former cattle driver, even if he did at some point become a sergeant of Senegalese *tirailleurs*, then lance-sergeant in the guards, and finally interpreter, will always remain a flunkey. It seems improper that a *goujat*[7] should disport himself in paradise, deafening everyone's ears with his atrocious *forofifon naspa*, while literate men on whom blessings and bounty ought to be raining down from heaven and from France are suffering tortures of want. For that reason I have decided to return here as interpreter. I realize that you won't be exactly filled with enthusiasm at the prospect of leaving. That is why I have compared you to Adam, and myself to the avenging angel. Don't worry—however—I won't use fire to chase you out of here. All I need are a few lines of writing on a 21 by 27 format sheet of paper. In case you are not in the know, I am referring to what is generally called an appointment."

Romo Sibedi was absolutely stunned by this unexpected declaration. Was this not the most consummate show of ingratitude with which to regale one's host?

Inwardly, Romo wondered whether Wangrin might not be drunk. Otherwise those cynical and outrageous words could be blamed only on a sudden attack of insanity.

But Wangrin had never been more lucid in his whole life, or less concerned with traditional properties (which in that particular moment he considered an encumbrance). It was easy, then, for him to guess the nature of Romo's inner monologue.

"O my brother," he exclaimed, "don't rummage any further in your poor brain. I am neither drunk nor insane. I am simply a rare phenomenon—an impudent, yet candid, individual, a badly brought up enemy who shows his intentions and weapons before engaging in battle. It's for you to try and avoid being swallowed up by the vulture that I have turned into."

"If you were armed with fire, Wangrin," shouted Romo, who at last was regaining his wits, "I could put it out. But you are no more than the natural offspring of a woman who let herself be screwed at random by any scoundrel who happened to come along, and for nothing into the bargain."

"Now, Romo! don't go sullying your mouth with insults. You'll be much better off trying to sharpen your claws against me—Wangrin—also known as Gongoloma-Sooke. You say I am a bastard, as though my father had not given me a proper name and surname at the chosen time. Never mind, my civil status has nothing to do with this affair. What will matter when we come to competing for the job of interpreter in Yaguwahi are my cunning, my poise, and my occult powers. In any case, you have only yourself to blame. It is you who, unwittingly no doubt, have prompted me to behave so ungratefully. Dear brother! could it be that you have forgotten the tale of the old *dyula's* donkey? In case you don't remember it, let me refresh your memory.

"There lived in Kong, a holy city and commercial capital of the African West, built a thousand years ago on the edge of the southern forests, an old *dyula*, Soriba by name. His only possession was a donkey, but a sturdy and courageous creature at that. Soriba made a little money by carrying goods on the back of his animal, and that was just enough to keep them both alive. Soriba fed his donkey reasonably well on dry grass, bran, and rock salt, which he let him lick for ten minutes in the evenings. The animal was perfectly satisfied.

"Now, one day, the donkey did such good work that Soriba earned more money than usual. This reminded him that his donkey deserved a little treat. Accordingly, he went to the fair and bought a large quantity of provisions as well as a number of seasonings, including several pots of honey. Then he invited his fellow townsmen to dinner. Everyone accepted, for they were curious to see what an old ragamuffin like Soriba, who lived more or less on charity, might have to offer.

"Soriba served such dishes and refreshment as the monarch of Kong himself might not have disdained. The dinner was followed by a musical performance; drum and string players, as well as players of monochord instruments and flutists lulled the assembled guests with the sound of a harmonious melody until the very end of the evening.

"When it was time for the guests to leave they all congratulated Soriba, who exclaimed: 'Wait! I want to give my donkey, the devoted and faithful companion of my lean times, some proof of my love and gratitude in front of you all.' And in so saying he offered his donkey a calabash of water mixed with honey—a drink fit for kings—which the donkey swallowed in large gulps.

"Everyone exclaimed: 'O Wallahi! Old Soriba, you have given us a dinner the equal of which was never seen, not even at the courts of kings; for this is the first time a donkey has been given honey to drink.'

"When he woke up the following morning, Soriba noticed that he had not even one cowry left in his pocket, so he proceeded to unfasten his donkey with the idea of going back to work. He offered the animal a calabash full of water, which the latter had been in the habit of drinking before setting off to work. But the donkey would have none of it, and consequently his work suffered. By mid-morning he was already worn out. The donkey, however, continued to refuse to drink and in the end died of thirst, since Soriba was no longer in a position to offer him honey.

"The moral of the story is that donkeys must never be encouraged to taste honey, for if they do, later they won't be able to live without it. If you, brother Romo, had not let me taste of the many pleasures and riches of this land, I wouldn't have felt the urge to rob you of your present job. Although you are my elder brother, I mean to teach you that those who hesitate to repay good deeds with ingratitude risk dying in bondage."

Romo Sibedi allowed his rage to explode at last:

"I refuse to countenance any of this nonsense until something actually happens. Then I will teach you to change your tune. You will know, then, who I really am."

After this stark and painful exchange, Wangrin and the members of his household set out again in the direction of Gudugaua. The rest of the journey was going to take another week; the stations that dotted the way were announced from time to time on unusual placards. Some read: "Danger—Lions," others: "Danger—mosquitos," and still others: "Danger—snakes." But the most threatening of all was the one in Zindinnguesse[8] which warned in large letters: "Danger—thieves, mosquitos, lions, and snakes."

When he saw it, Wangrin said to himself: "Well, well! This place is obviously the rendezvous for everything that is unpleasant in the whole area!" This thought had not quite crystallized in his mind when a large rattlesnake began to sound the vibrations of his deathly jingle. Wangrin barely managed to jump clear. With a swing of his mighty stick he sent the snake rolling by the wayside. Thus injured, the animal couldn't slither away fast enough to avoid the fatal blow which crushed his head.

Wangrin felt it to be a good omen. Intuitively, at that moment he became certain that he would be able to overcome his enemies as easily as he had killed the rattlesnake.

The placards proved to be fairly accurate. During the night a huge lion managed to penetrate into the station courtyard, killing a donkey and seriously wounding one of Wangrin's horses. Unable to carry away his prey, the lion spent several hours of the night prowling and roaring all around the station. Although none of the members of the small party had slept a wink, tormented as they had been by mosquitos and by the wretched lion, no one had noticed that a thief had slipped in and grabbed a loadful of household items belonging to Wangrin's wives.

The night spent at Zindinnguesse was to remain engraved forever in Wangrin's memory!

At last, seven days after his departure from Yaguwahi, Wangrin arrived in Gudugaua in pouring rain. Not knowing where to go, he asked to be led to the administrative quarters. In those days, the town of Gudugaua wasn't yet subdivided into blocks and districts demarcated by streets and paths; it was just a huge, flat piece of land dotted with a multitude of tiny villages and fields cultivated with crops. One could say that each family lived right in the middle of its own *lougan*.[9] The next day Wangrin, armed with credentials, showed up at the Personnel Office, which was run by Monsieur Quinomel. But let us once again listen to Wangrin's own account:

"The man was about five-foot-six tall and at a glance looked as if he might be only half his expected weight. His face was flushed and his skin blotched by an excessive intake of strong liquor. His voice was sepulchral and his conversation often interrupted by a series of hiccups which twisted his mouth into a semblance of ludicrous merriment. One needed quite a lot of self-control not to burst out laughing at the sight of this strange individual. The tip of his long nose was practically buried in a thick, bushy moustache shaped like a scorpion's tail over a curling, snarling upper lip. His back had been irretrievably bent by the full pack of the old infantry in which he had served for many years.

"Quinomel had been a bad soldier. In twenty-five years of service, he had copped three hundred and seventy-five punishments. On the other hand he was a daredevil. An irrepressible volunteer on the most perilous missions, he had fought like a hero during the four years of the World War, and later in the Near East. Having been demoted twice after attaining the rank of sergeant, he was able to regain his stripes both times and was discharged with the rank of Chief Warrant-Officer. The Legion of Honour, the Médaille Militaire, and the Croix de Guerre with three clasps figured among the ten decorations that bore testimony to Quinomel's fighting spirit. He still loved military life and had a weak spot for the former *tirailleurs* who had fought side by side with him in faraway lands.

"The Europeans of the colony didn't like Quinomel. They had nicknamed him 'Living demijohn,' and thereafter carefully avoided him. And Quinomel, who had braved death a thousand times, was anguished by the contempt shown him by his fellow countrymen and groveled under their disdain like a mean coward. Anxious to drown his sorrows, he had taken refuge in drink and allowed his valiant spirit to founder. He had become brooding and solitary."

Wangrin had gathered information on the governor, the secretary general and his under-secretary, the personnel manager, the Commandant, the police inspector, and the local king. He had asked for information on the four traditional ministers, each of whom fulfilled a very well-defined role. All attended the ruler's levee every morning and renewed vows of fidelity by swearing an oath on the country's tutelary fetish.

Wangrin knew that Quinomel was a little hard of hearing, and he also knew that whenever he wasn't dead drunk he would work himself into a boiling rage at the thought of a newcomer—unless he was a former soldier—and was likely to bare his teeth, blackened by alcohol and to-bacco. Even the governor's chief of cabinet wasn't spared this treatment. There was only one way, then, to be liked and accepted by Quinomel—it was to show up in the guise of a former soldier.

Under his peculiar exterior, however, Quinomel hid a basically senti-mental and generous nature. He shared his pay with the poor who sur-rounded him. He was fond of joking: "I much prefer my wretched black beggars, my sons-of-convict-princes, my tattered kings, and my aristo-cratic grooms to any of the European colonials!"

Such was the man Wangrin had come to meet.

As soon as he got into Quinomel's office, Wangrin came stiffly to attention, as if he were an old sweat of the Imperial Guard, and recited his surname, name, and qualifications. This introduction acted like magic on Quinomel. Instead of grunting as he always did, he smiled pleasantly, extended a hand and said:

"We are no longer in the army. Stand at ease, my good friend, sit down. Let me see, when did you get here?"

"Last night, Lieutenant, Sir! . . . "

"Of course, of course, I could have reached that rank, but my con-duct prevented me. . . . Twice sergeant, twice reduced to the ranks—by the time I mended my ways it was too late. Nevertheless, I was made Chief Warrant-Officer. Anyway, it is ancient history. . . . Let me see what sort of corner we can fit you in."

Quinomel called: "Tramen, Tramen! give me Monsieur Wangrin's personal file."

Tramen, the copy clerk in charge of files, brought Wangrin's file which had arrived in the post a few days earlier. Quinomel ran through it quickly and then, leaning back in his chair: "Good! Very good!" he said, "I see from your file that you are intelligent. You speak French fluently, and five African languages as well. What more can one ask of an interpreter? What is your religion?"

"I don't have any special religion," answered Wangrin. "As an inter-preter, it's my job to get on with everybody; I am as much at ease in a mosque as I am in the sacred groves of the animist villages."

"Where do you think your talents would be best exploited?"

"My own personal wish would be to serve in Gudugaua, as it is in the chief town that one has the best opportunity to learn. However, in Yaguwahi I would be of real use to the government, and I care more about that than about my own inclinations. I speak all the languages commonly used in that town, and I am well acquainted with that part of the country, for it borders on to the Diagaramba district, where I served for many years."

Quinomel asked to see the file concerning the interpreter at Yaguwahi. Tramen brought Romo's file. Quinomel leaned forward to scan it. When he saw who the man was, he exclaimed: "Oh! Oh! It's Romo Sibedi, who is an excellent civil servant, and has a lot of big shots pulling strings for him. I can't promise you anything, Wangrin, but I'll see what I can do to help you. Meanwhile, get settled. You have a whole week to do it in. For the time being, you are attached to Personnel Management."

Wangrin took advantage of his free time to establish new and useful relationships and to win over to his side the attractive young Fulbe woman who shared her life with Quinomel. He distributed gifts among Tramen's wives and children. He managed to make himself known to the staff of the governor's cabinet. He offered his friendship to Demba Dicko, who was head copy clerk and confidential secretary to the governor.

In addition, he visited the three greatest marabouts resident in that town—Abaldi, Madau, and Ulmaye—and asked them to work on his behalf. The first, who had a reputation for his learning in the occult sciences, was to tie Romo's tongue and that of the Commandant's into a magic knot so that they couldn't prevent Romo's transfer. The other two were to pray that the white chiefs on whom rested the decision to transfer Wangrin from there to Yaguwahi be kindly disposed toward him.

Having secured these secret and mysterious interventions, Wangrin knew he could also rely fully on support from Tramen and Demba Dicko.

Quinomel did suggest to the governor that Wangrin might be transferred to Yaguwahi to replace Romo who, in turn, would join the staff of the Gudugaua district. During the customary little administrative inquiry, Demba Dicko pleaded deftly for Wangrin in the governor's cabinet, invoking his ability and the exceptional quality of service he would be able to render in a place like Yaguwahi, situated as it was near the border of another important territory.

When the inquiry came to a close, Tramen drew up the papers concerning the appointment and submitted them for signature to the governor. No one got wind of this maneuver until the governor actually signed the document. An official telegram was despatched to Yaguwahi, announcing Wangrin's appointment and Romo's transfer.

The news exploded like a bomb. Never before had the town been quite so taken by surprise. Romo was considered a fixture no one could budge. It was said everywhere that the country was like a coach drawn by two stallions—one representing the king and the other, the Commandant—while Romo was the coachman who led that powerful conveyance to any destination and in any manner he chose.

Faced with the *fait accompli*, the Commandant had no alternative but to accept an appointment that proceeded from high places. After having made a glowing report on Romo, he invited him to hold himself ready for the official handing-over which was to take place before his departure.

It took Wangrin a week to get to Yaguwahi, but this time he was careful not to break his journey at Zindinnguesse, that ill-fated intersection.

Finally he reached the town in the very early hours of the morning and directed his steps to the official visitors' encampment, preferring not to go at once directly to Romo's residence, where the likelihood of some sort of scene was by no means to be excluded.

Jean Gordane, the local Commandant, had perused Wangrin's personal file and gathered from it that he would have an assistant more adept than his predecessor, but also more audacious and astute. As it turned out, from time to time he was indeed to regret the loss of his amiable old interpreter who had been as pliable as curried leather. Wangrin couldn't even be remotely compared with Romo, who had done nothing else all his life but serve Europeans and obey them like a robot. A robot which, however, did not miss a single chance of exploiting them without awakening the least suspicion. . . .

On that same morning, as soon as the offices opened, Wangrin called on the Commandant who put him in touch with Romo so that they could proceed with the official handing over of duties. Grim-faced, Romo acquainted Wangrin laconically with all pending files, then walked out of his office for the last time to go to a relative in whose house all his luggage had already been deposited so that Wangrin could move into his palatial official residence.

Before leaving town, he asked Wangrin for an interview, to which the latter agreed. As soon as they were alone, Romo gave full vent to his indignation:

"You evil son of a bitch! So you've been successful with your criminal scheming. You have actually dared to repay my generosity with the blackest ingratitude. I swear to you that I shan't have any peace until I arrest you with my own hands and clap you in jail. Your confinement will be painful, for I will see to it that while you're there, you eat your own shit and drink your own piss. I will watch with great enjoyment while your belly becomes bloated as a pot until it bursts like a balloon!"

"My, my! dear elder brother and countryman, I see that this is the real thing! that you want a fight, that you'll give me no quarter! But you are unwise, for I am always on the lookout. The day you set out to arrest me, that very same day, I will play a trick on you far more diabolical than the one that now compels you to leave this paradise. Nor will you ever be allowed the pleasure of leading me to jail. Meanwhile, you can bite your finger up to the second knuckle in anticipation of the helplessness you will feel. And since we have declared war on each other, let me give you one more bit of good advice. Don't leave behind your son Dumuma Romo, temporary overseer of road works. Just now there are only three of us in this room: God, you, and me. I know that God won't denounce me, therefore I can be frank. I am not keen to have your son here. I have come to embezzle and to become rich, just as you have been doing for years. I have no intention of having a spy like your son on my trail. If you don't take him along, you can be sure that I'll get him out of circulation and that I'll have him locked up, what's more, so that he doesn't stand in my way."

Romo Sibedi had thought that his insults would offend Wangrin, but the plan had misfired. In a spirit of bravado he replied:

"I refuse to take my son along. He shall stay and cause you relentless anxiety. He will watch your every move and will let me know every detail. Don't worry, one of these days, I'll have you arrested all right. That much I promise you!"

"In that case you will have been responsible for the misfortunes that will befall your son," replied Wangrin. "Now we have nothing left to say to each other, so I entreat you, my dear elder brother, to remove your elephantine bulk from my presence. Otherwise I shall have to accept the fact that your visit was paid in a spirit of provocation, that you violated my threshold with every intention of playing a dirty trick on me. It is a crime that entitles me to lodge a complaint against you. . . . Choose! . . ."

Romo Sibedi had learned at his own expense that Wangrin was capable of anything. Hurling insults at his father and mother and wishing him the worst imaginable hell, he at last made his exit.

Wangrin gathered in his hand the dust which bore the mark of Romo's footprints, and scattered it to the four winds, crying: "Hey, you elephant of a man, turn round and look at the ill wind that blows the dust stirred by your incurably gouty feet!"

Enraged, Romo mounted his horse and went to join his family, who were waiting for his return so that they could leave.

Wangrin was neither stupid nor did he lack perception. He knew very well that he had made a powerful enemy. So he said to himself: "Wallayi! My dear Wangrin, now that you've grabbed the tail of a large and ferocious beast you had better not let go of it. You'd be wise to watch out lest the animal turn round and make a clean sweep of you!"

Then he returned indoors, breakfasted, got himself up into natty clothes, and left for the station where the new job awaited him.

Commandant Jean Gordane always came to his office on time. He made greater demands on himself than on his employees. He was always the first to arrive and the last to leave. Wangrin was extremely surprised to find him already working away at his desk and quickly realized that if their relationship was to be easy it was best for him to set his watch according to his master's time.

He knocked on the Commandant's door and on being invited in recited the sacramental litany:

"Good morning, Sir. I trust you have slept well?"

"Good morning, Wangrin," replied the Commandant, without any outward show of warmth.

Somewhat taken aback, Wangrin went on: "I have come to take up my new duties and to ask my superior for instructions and for advice also, so that I may serve him according to his wishes."

Gordane looked up and let his glance rest on Wangrin. "I have examined your file," he said. "I see that up to now you have a first-class record. I hope you will continue to feel committed to your work and that I won't have cause to regret the loss of my good old Romo Sibedi."

"I give you my word I will, Sir."

"I see that you speak Fulfulde fluently, while Romo did not. It is the second most important language in this area."

"Yes, Sir, I do speak Fulfulde fluently, and I give you my word that I shall serve you devotedly."

Then Wangrin added: "Sir, may I tell you something in confidence? By way of letting you into a secret?"

"Why not? Go ahead!"

"Well, Sir, old Romo, before leaving town this morning, was impudent enough to force his way into my quarters and heap on my head a number of vulgar insults. Apparently he means to put all manner of obstacles in my way to make me feel sorry that I have supplanted him. The truth is, I had nothing whatever to do with my transfer. The decision to reshuffle all personnel that had served longer than five years in the same area was taken in high places, and Romo happens to be victim of an indiscriminate measure rather than the result of what he likes to call 'my machinations.'"

"Don't worry," replied Jean Gordane. "I won't allow anyone to come and sow seeds of dissent in my district. I don't give a damn about your rancor and grudges and in any case I can't believe that Romo would ever want to play a dirty trick on me. However, I'll be on my guard and keep my eyes open."

"It is as well to be watchful, Sir! According to the proverb: 'One's buttocks are threatened so long as there is a scorpion inside one's trousers, however baggy they may be!'[10] Romo is a Nubigu Fulbe, but still a Fulbe, and Fulbe people are quite capable of keeping their eyelids shut without, however, being asleep."[11]

By the time Wangrin left the Commandant, he felt certain in his heart that from now on his superior would mistrust Romo and his acolytes, especially the son he had left behind in Yaguwahi. He returned to the small office he had been allocated next to the one occupied by the Commandant. In addition, he had the use of a chair which stood under the verandah beside the door of the Commandant's office.

After one month, Gordane was already so delighted with Wangrin's work that he rewarded him with almost total trust. This did not prevent him, however, like almost all other Commandants, from occasionally receiving special informers at home in secret and late at night so that he could cross-check with them all available information. No interpreter could countenance this kind of behavior without attempting to frustrate it. There was no question of Wangrin having peace of mind until he discovered the identity of the Commandant's clandestine informers. To achieve this, he needed to ensure the loyalty of a member of the Commandant's household. . . .

His head steward and his *musso* were the obvious choices—the latter would be even more useful than the head steward.

Jean Gordane's *musso* was called Rammaye Bira. She was no beauty. Small and puny, she had a complex about her physical appearance. She hardly ever went out and frequented only her close relatives. Having never succeeded in finding an African admirer, she bore a grudge against all the male members of her own race. To some people she was just a little woman blown up with self-importance, who had become disdainful as the result of an unhoped-for association; to others, a creature who suffered from a complex because of her failure to get an African husband, and of her adoption instead by an *annassaara*[12] who considered her a mere sedative and would never dream of taking her back to his own country.

Wangrin wasn't the least bit affected by all these opinions. All that mattered to him was to find a means of making Rammaye Bira his pawn, so that he could use her to spy on the Commandant. Aware that no African child dare disobey its mother, however unreasonable she may be, Wangrin decided that it was necessary to ingratiate himself with Rammaye Bira's old mother Reenatu. But how to go about it!

Well-versed in matters traditional, Wangrin knew how to convert adages, proverbs, and parables to practice. Now, isn't there a Fulbe proverb that says: "As bees are drawn to flowers because they release an enticing scent, so will old people allow themselves to be charmed by the obliging ways of the young"?[13]

On a Sunday afternoon, Wangrin, dressed to the nines, just like an ear of corn,[14] leaped on his elegantly harnessed mount and pointed him in the direction of old Reenatu's house, taking along a few equally well-attired and elegantly mounted companions. As they approached Reenatu's entrance, Wangrin asked the griot in his retinue to begin his song of praise while he himself capered about on his handsome mount whose impeccable training had earned him the nickname "performing horse." The griot intoned:

"O men, women, and children of Yaguwahi, make haste, come out and behold a sight so beauteous and brilliant that it will stir your imagination, dazzle your eyes, and dispossess you of reason. How fine he does look, our Wangrin, mouthpiece to our Commandant[15] and earpiece to *Mousse Gofornere*[16] of all the territory, who was chosen among three hundred and thirty-three *Goforneres*, all *white-White*. Whites from France, from Bordeaux and Marseilles, which are home ports for 'smallboats'[17] and terminals for two narrow, parallel metal rails.[18] The latter resemble twins lying side by side, and stretch on the ground like inordinately long boa constrictors. On them 'terrestrial canoes'[19] glide as fast as the hawk diving on his prey! O come and see his performing horse! He is neither lop-eared nor docktailed. His neck is slender, unlike that of a bull. He is neither bandy-legged nor knock-kneed. His back does not resemble that of a mule. He is neither disobedient nor shy. He knows all the steps: rhythmical, quick, and high steps. He can skip and jump. Is there anything he cannot do? Not that I know of.

"I exhort you once again to come out! Come and behold the beauty of this stallion, who drinks milk and kneels before pretty girls. Come and see the 'performing horse,' who is as adept at racing as he is at warring or parading, and a full thoroughbred too!

"We have come here," the griot continued, "to pay our respects to our mother-in-law,[20] Reenatu, mother to our sister Rammaye Bira, who is like pure amber in a snuff-box made of gold. The exquisite scent that emanates from the hollow of Rammaye Bira's armpits has led us to the source of which she, perfumed with musk, is a visceral concretion."[21]

Never before had a delegation of young people come to pay homage to Rammaye Bira's family. It was an event that could not pass unnoticed. The chanting of the griot and the clip-clop of the horses' hooves set the whole neighborhood aflutter. Children poured in from all directions, pushing and shoving to get a better look, shouting, calling, even crying. Some of the grown-ups, who didn't think they needed to step outside to see what was happening, simply stood in their doorways or behind their enclosures; some climbed up and leaned on their balconies, observing the scene. They looked at Wangrin's little band the way they would have looked at wandering performers on a day of public rejoicing.

Reenatu couldn't grasp what was happening to her at all. It was the first time in her life that her house had been surrounded by well-wishers.

No one had ever come to pay homage to her out of a feeling of gallantry toward her daughter. The old lady was utterly confused. She began to walk aimlessly in and out of her house, mechanically removing mats which she put down instead of the skins used for prayer, and placing the latter where her cooking utensils ought to have been.

Wangrin and his friends made their way in under the open shed that had been erected in front of Reenatu's house. It provided ample shelter, and the white sand that covered the ground was spotlessly clean.

Although Wangrin was now standing before Reenatu, he allowed his griot to speak for him, according to the prescriptions of traditional demeanor. The griot intoned once again:

"To me this day is comparable to the one when the rich harvest produced by the seeds grown during the seven years of abundance in Egypt, under the vizierate of Joseph, Prophet of God, was garnered at last. To me this day resembles a sunrise of riches whose golden rays will dispel the darkness of my indigence. Never again will I fasten round my waist this ancient pair of trousers—my poor waist marked all round by calluses, for numberless lice have sucked my blood for so long that there is almost none left. Those lice are so numerous that every time I stretch my ragged old trousers out in the sun, they are dragged back by the lice into the shade, to my utter despair.

"Thanks be to Allah! My indigence has come to an end, as does the drought when the rainy season sets in!

"Wangrin! Wallayi! You are as rich as the rainy season, but more generous still. True, the rains yield water, but water that is accompanied by thunder, and by lightning that may strike men, animals, and crops. But you, Wangrin, rain lavish gifts on the poor, on the aged and on us, your insatiable griots, without rumblings or dangerous flashes.

"While aristocratic misers whose right hands are riveted to their necks and whose left hands are stuck to their backsides[22] chase us away with sinister and contemptuous looks, you, Wangrin, with an engaging smile, encourage us to come forward. You give us all things, always and tirelessly.

"I thank you, Wangrin, for all those who either patently or secretly owe you a great debt. *Thank you* is a modest little phrase indeed, but it is spoken only by lips that desire to express gratitude.

"One may be born a nobleman, yet lose that station through avarice and greed. True nobility is contingent on values. It resembles a building which has foundations, walls, and roofing. Foundations are inherited, while walls and roofing are built by one's own effort, else the building would remain a mere outline and would risk reverting to wasteland.

"There is no such danger where you are concerned, O Wangrin! You have inherited a solid aristocratic foundation[23] upon which you have skill-fully created sturdy walls and a roof so fine that birds stop in mid-flight to admire it and men cannot believe their eyes when they behold it."

Having praised Wangrin with such extravagant eloquence, the griot turned towards Reenatu:

"O mother of Rammaye Bira! Wangrin and his young friends whom your venerable eyes now behold are paying you a visit this Sunday—holy day of the *annassaaras*[24]—as a mark of respectful deference. Allah blesses a woman with a beautiful and virtuous daughter when he wishes her mother to be held in high regard by the young. Accordingly, Wangrin has come to ask you to consider him henceforward your son and your ser-vant, as he considers Rammaye Bira his sister and friend. She may well become his lover, or be his potential wife, for who but Allah knows what the future holds in store? Life is certainly longer than all distances be-tween all countries in the world put together!

"When speaking with old people, what great comfort it is to find that they capture the essence of what is being said even if it is merely suggested, or merely mimed.

"One does not visit one's mother-in-law empty-handed. Wangrin of-fers you a four-year-old milk cow and her five-month-old heifer. Also this suit of clothes, which includes white robes for your prayers. A hundred francs are added, to help you face the expenses involved in the obser-vance of Ramadan, which begins next week.

"As for me, griot to you all, I have been given by Wangrin two em-broidered bubus with matching underwear and two pairs of trousers that I may cast off my ancient pair, which is but a nest of lice and a doss-house for fleas and bugs of all sorts. Wangrin has placed ten francs in the pocket of each bubu and in my own hand the sum of thirty francs. On this day, then, so blessed for you, O Ma Reenatu, also blessed for your daughter Rammaye Bira, and finally twice blessed for me, I have received from our inexhaustible Wangrin the sum of fifty francs. I will buy myself one of the finest stallions in the country, will name him 'Thanks-be-to-Wangrin,' and will choose Bira as his *Yettoore*."[25]

Reenatu rushed indoors and stole a quick glance at herself in a large mirror which Gordane had offered to her daughter. She wanted to see her face so as to be sure that she had not been transformed into a beauti-ful Fulbe princess by one of calamitous Njeddo-Dewal's conjuring tricks. She knew that this legendary witch was fond of casting spells on the poor, helpless people she encountered on her way.

Unable to accept the fact that her appearance, such as it was, could elicit so much admiration, Reenatu retraced in her mind every step of her long life. The earliest recollection was of a little orphan dressed in her one and only wrapper, threadbare and stinking of indigo, with painfully bleeding chapped heels and little hands whose palms had hardened with calluses drawing water interminably from deep wells. After that, she could only call to mind the picture of an emaciated young woman with disheveled hair blown in all directions by the wind, like grass on the plains. She also saw a walking creature balancing on her head a large calabash full of milk in which lumps of butter were swimming. The poor wretch offered her provisions from village to village. She would stop at every door. At times she was given a polite brush-off by charitable souls, at others she was chased away by nasty dogs. Some days she was even robbed by dishonest men. And always, on her way back towards the station which bordered on a village, she had to face threatening youngsters, heat, cold, rain, or disquieting darkness.

Later still, she saw herself a poverty-stricken woman married to a seedy man who had nothing but his hands to hire out to others.

She saw the birth of her daughter Rammaye, at a time when she didn't own a single sheep to sacrifice, according to custom, on the occasion of the naming ceremony.

Yet all that had vanished like a bad dream. Rammaye had become a Commandant's *musso*. Now, even that unhoped-for ray of sunshine was made all the more dazzling. The interpreter, second in importance among all citizens in the area, had come to her, Reenatu, former inhabitant of the "village of filth."[26]

So she thanked Allah from the bottom of her heart, went out radiant as a goddess, and said to the griot:

"O my griot of good omen! I do welcome warmly my son Wangrin, all those who accompany him and you too, you who are here to speak on their behalf. There are moments when one's feelings of joy and happiness are so intense that they glue the tongue to the palate and make a lump in the throat, preventing words from flowing with adequate strength of expression. What I can do is to ask you to say to Wangrin: 'Thank you! I do accept you as my son, and my daughter shall be your sister. May Allah bless you all!'"

It was in this way that Wangrin succeeded in winning over Reenatu, who naively believed all the protestations which the griot, paid for the task, had ladled out with so much emphasis and volubility.

As Fulbe custom forbade a suitor from taking any nourishment whatever[27] under the roof of the parents of a girl or young woman who had aroused passionate feelings in his breast (parents and parents-in-law were equivalent by association), Wangrin now took his leave from the woman who had become his mother, mother-in-law, and unconscious accomplice. He arranged a great *mechoui*[28] for his friends. That was a memorable Sunday of revelry and drinking, enlivened by the harmony of lutes and by women's songs. The explosion of innumerable blank cartridges echoed in the night.

Wangrin had given the Commandant to understand that the party had been arranged to mark the inauguration of a society named "Friends of France." His superior sent on two cases of red wine and later put in a personal appearance, as his country's representative, with Rammaye Bira. He also handed over a large French flag to the society on behalf of the local governor who represented the governor general, head of all the Whites working in West Africa at that time. Thus, a nonexistent society came to be officially recognized by the government. It was pure Wangrin!

Rammaye Bira was deeply touched by the homage that had been paid to her mother. On a subsequent meeting with Wangrin, she said:

"I don't quite know how to show you the gratitude I feel for the way you have honoured my mother among all other mothers in this town."

"If in the near future my sister were to grant me a *tête-à-tête*, I could show her ways in which a well brought up and beautiful woman may demonstrate her gratitude to a brother who has tender feelings for her," replied Wangrin. "To attain its highest value, gold must be wrought by a goldsmith and displayed against the exquisite background of a female body. Like a gold ingot, I need you both as goldsmith and female body to set me off. Neither of us will have anything to regret."

"I am not quite sure what you are leading to, my brother, but I would like to be as honest with you as you have been respectful and lavish toward my mother. I am not particularly impressed by the presents you have given her. Thanks to my husband, I can give her as much, even a hundredfold. But for the manner of your giving, which is peerless, I feel deeply indebted to you. However, I don't see that I must give myself to you because of your kindness to my mother. I prefer to be your sister, rather than your lover. I have never deceived my husband, or known the embraces of any other man, and feel no desire whatsoever to embark on an extramarital relationship."

"O my sister Rammaye!" replied Wangrin. "Thank you for being so frank, so direct. A clear, well-defined path is always so easy to follow. If you had said to me: 'When I lose my husband, no one else shall ever have me,' I would have died of despair. This way I can go on, living in hope. . . . Our Commandant isn't African. One of these days he will go back to his country. As you know, marriage between Fulbe and Bambara is permissible, so you can guess what I have in mind? You see, Rammaye, I don't want you to become a *Tubabu-Musso-Koro*,[29] for that unfortunate label reduces the value of an African woman in the eyes of her compatriots by three quarters at least. A piece of silliness, I grant you, but tell me who hasn't suffered at some time or other because of this kind of nonsense? My arm will be always there to support you! I promise you—you will be able to lean on it whenever you choose and you may be sure that when you do, you won't fall into a contemptible situation with a painful crash. Thanks to my name, everyone will respect you, and your intelligence will help me to make better plans for a future which I hope you will share. You will give me fine children and I will leave it to you to choose their names, relinquishing to you the right, which all fathers cherish so dearly, to name their descendants."

Rammaye Bira lowered her eyes and said with a smile: "Permit me to leave you before my 'whiskers–no beard'[30] is made restless by my absence."

Wangrin, delighted at having elicited such a saucy little jest from Rammaye Bira, took her hand and made as if to caress her buttocks, but the young woman resisted him. "Be correct, brother," she said. "Don't try to take what isn't yours. If I am everything that is sweet and yielding and let you rub against me as you please, what will there be left for you to do when I become your wife?"

"O my sister Rammaye, since you wish it, I will try to control myself. But remember that love is like a river. Its waters flow on unchecked, and its wellspring can neither be made dry nor deviated. Go by all means to your lucky 'whiskers–no beard' and whenever he holds you in his arms, surrender your body to him. He has a right to it. But your thoughts, you must keep for me. It will help me to wait for the night when the thirst of my soul will be quenched at last."

Rammaye Bira eased her feet into her oriental slippers, pulled a veil of embroidered muslin over her head, and walked away saying: "I wish you a pleasant night with your wife!"

Wangrin realized at once that Rammaye, just like a catfish, had bitten into the bait.[31] It wouldn't be long before she swallowed the hook. He knew that when an African woman alludes verbally to the wife or lover of the man who is courting her she is letting him understand that his suit is accepted. This wheedling address is called the "fond kicks of the female animal before yielding to the male." And the male who submits willingly to this treatment will eventually be rewarded. As we all know, an old monkey doesn't need to be taught how to grimace, and our Wangrin didn't need any instruction in the art of seducing women or making a warrant chief—or even a Commandant—entirely dependent on his services. Poor Rammaye Bira was to learn as much at her own expense. . . .

But he answered: "Make sure that your 'whiskers' doesn't ever get it into his head that I might be in love with you."

"Don't worry," she replied. "My husband knows perfectly well that I don't allow myself to be used as a trough[32] by passersby."

On this note the potential lovers parted. One was convinced that she had found herself an African husband, an authentic husband, traditionally speaking, for later on, and the other an unwitting, yet promising acolyte.

10 Romo's Son and Beautiful Pugubila

Time was passing.

While life in the district ran its course in the most agreeable manner, Wangrin's quarters turned into a veritable club. Every Saturday, the cream of society was invited to spend the evening there. The guests' only preoccupation was to gorge themselves on succulent and varied meals enhanced by tea prepared according to the Moorish custom, to drink alcohol in vast quantities, to listen with languorous abandon to the melodies provided by ten or more lute players, and to . . . how shall I put it? well—because of the respect I owe you, dear reader . . . I'll limit myself to saying that this weekly gastronomic and musical debauch resolved itself in heavy sleep for some, and for others in the embraces of some beauties who had been brought in for the purpose of dispensing favors to the highest bidders.

Through his hospitality Wangrin managed to set up such a powerful intelligence network that literally nothing could happen in that district without his getting to know about it at once—down to the least detail. And Rammaye Bira, without realizing the role she was playing, fed him information about everything that went on in the Commandant's house. This is how Wangrin succeeded at last in identifying the private agents who had been acting as informers behind his back. They were about a dozen. One by one, they were caught in Wangrin's web. Some ended up in jail; others discovered that the Commandant no longer trusted them. The most important head to fall was that of the overseer of public works, Dumuma, Romo's son. Wangrin, you will recall, had threatened to have him jailed when his father, on leaving, refused to take him along. This is how it all happened.

A few days after Romo's departure, Wangrin had summoned Dumuma Romo to his house and spoken to him as follows:

"My dear boy, I am as much your father as Romo.[1] But he will insist on bearing me a grudge for having stepped into his shoes. I imagine that he thinks of me as his enemy; perhaps he has even warned you to be on your guard. In that respect, he's entirely misguided. Even if I were fighting Romo openly, I would never be small-minded enough to persecute his son, whom I consider my own child. If it were true that I dislike you and actually did try to harass you, our relatives in Nubigu would never forgive me: I would lose face, as you are neither my rival nor my equal. I am your father and I want you to think of me as such. My house is yours. Come here whenever you wish and behave exactly as you would in your father's house, but don't listen to or keep company with my enemies, lest in disposing ruthlessly of them, I unwittingly drag you down as well. Ask me for anything you desire—money, gold, cattle, horses, millet, rice, and even women, if you feel so inclined—and you shall have them."

Wangrin had opened wide the doors of his house as well as the flaps of his wallet to Dumuma, and the latter took advantage of his offer with an astonishing lack of restraint.

Meanwhile Wangrin had bribed the postman, who brought him all the administrative correspondence, both European and African, and left it to Wangrin to arrange the delivery. Wangrin took advantage of this irregularity to open and read any letters addressed to agents who seemed dislikable or untrustworthy. It was his good luck to stumble on a letter in which Romo congratulated his son on the amount of information he had been able to gather and forward to him about the personnel of that district. Romo went on to say:

"Above all, I want to know what Wangrin is up to. That scoundrel has played a filthy trick on me and one of these days he is going to pay dearly for it."

Already suspicious, Wangrin redoubled his vigilance. Thanks to Rammaye Bira's indiscretions, he found out that Dumuma, accompanied by a number of shady-looking individuals, paid a good many visits to Gordane in the dead of night.

As overseer of public works, Dumuma was responsible for choosing and assigning to the various sites the thousand or so young men and women to be employed there as forced laborers.

Unfortunately for him, Dumuma had "no control over his trousers"[2] and this weakness was well known to Wangrin. He was also very fond of money, and this was equally known to Wangrin.

One day, Wangrin invited him home for a confidential chat: "I have just heard a few rumors, my boy," he said, "which fill me with consternation. I'd hate to be put in the position of having to sacrifice a fine red-eyed black bull.[3] I hope you will be able to convince me that the gossip I've heard is untrue."

But Dumuma Romo, besides being amorous and immoderately fond of money, was also a smug little ass. Just because Gordane, unbeknown to Wangrin, saw him secretly both at his house and at the sites, he firmly believed that his hour had come. Instead of acting cautiously, one day he allowed himself to be heard bragging in a tavern: "I am Dumuma, Romo Sibedi's son. People think that I am no more than a tiny red ant. But if an elephant were to let me sneak into his trunk, he would be infinitely the worse for it, for I'd make him die an undignified death. I owe that much to my father. I must prove that I am worthy of being his son. Don't the Fulbe say: 'Be patient with your father's assassin. Wait till you have a fine dagger and the murderer is within easy reach. Then, strike at his heart with both hands, and with both eyes tightly shut!'"[4]

This remark was faithfully reported to Wangrin, who received the news with peals of laughter: "Romo's offspring mistakes the tooth of a young warthog for the tusk of an old elephant. He tries to peep a little too often out of his cocoon. His crowing is beginning to disturb my sleep. I can see that there is nothing for it but to wrap him in a bundle of rags and drop him in the murk-and-heat."[5]

And so he finally made up his mind to investigate Dumuma's affairs thoroughly. For Dumuma, that spelled the beginning of the end. . . .

Wangrin opened an inquiry to find out what treatment Dumuma Romo meted out to the laborers he engaged within the area under his jurisdiction and discovered at once that Dumuma allotted labor to a number of people in exchange for payment. Other laborers who were better off redeemed themselves by bribing him with a suitable amount of cash, while women and girls paid him in kind. For our libidinous overseer they represented an inexhaustible harem.

Wangrin secured the help of a former *tirailleur*, by name Tennga, and had him appointed adjutant to Dumuma. He was to watch the latter, but above all to encourage him to get entangled in some thoroughly unsavory business. Tennga was very good at flattering Dumuma, calling him always *mon captenne*[6] and springing to attention whenever he spoke to him. Thanks to information received both from Tennga and other sources, Wangrin gathered enough evidence against Dumuma to justify a formal denunciation which he meant to make through some other person. At that point an even better opportunity offered itself, facilitating his task. Dumuma had gone to the Togo district to recruit one hundred and fifty laborers of which twenty-five were girls. One of them, named Pugubila, was unusually handsome. Dumuma, who was always careful to keep a few good-lookers around for his own personal pleasure, refused the sum that the young woman's parents and fiancé had offered him to prevent her conscription, and sent the girl to work on a new road that was being built thirty kilometers away from her village. Pugubila, too far from her parents to commute, was compelled to remain on the spot for the duration of her conscription—that is, twenty days.

Dumuma took her aside and said: "Your job will be to take care of my food and lodgings. You will come to rub my feet, my arms, and my back whenever I feel like it. You are far too beautiful and shapely to be sent off digging and carrying bucketfuls of soil. When your conscription is over, I'll give you money and fine clothes. I don't want you to get tired. I find you very attractive, and as I am an important *captenne*, I can do whatever I please. The Commandant, the interpreter, the 'pen bearer,'[7] and even Rammaye Bira, all of them depend on my services. If you are nice to me, your parents needn't go on working as laborers. On the other hand if you resist me you will have only yourself to blame if your family has to mend potholes and carry heavy loads every day of the year. . . . "

Pugubila listened quietly because she was frightened, but certainly not for want of a pert rejoinder! In any case she was obliged to remain at the station and to prepare Dumuma's meals, but she persisted in resisting his frequent advances.

Dumuma couldn't bear to be turned down by a mere little village wench. Didn't he have all the means at his disposal to coerce her and even make her beg for mercy? But as he didn't seem to succeed in getting what he wanted, he went about making life impossible for her. He fabricated a thousand excuses so as to find fault with her and make her do the same thing two or three times over. He slapped her viciously for no reason at all. Still no results.

Dumuma was unable to subdue his desire for this girl, which by now had turned to obsession. He felt sick with it, to the point of losing his appetite. Possess her he must, and he decided that the time had come to shed all restraint.

One afternoon, a tiny little old man covered in talismans, with a goatskin bag hanging from his bandoleer, was seen to make his way into the camp. After a long confabulation with Dumuma, the latter handed him the sum of ten francs as payment for a sachet full of vegetable powder. Taking advantage of a moment when Pugubila was out of the way, Dumuma mixed the powder with the food the girl had set aside for her evening meal. Later, when Pugubila had finished eating, Dumuma ordered her to come and rub him down as she had done so often in the last few days. When the girl appeared before him he was so gentle with her that she couldn't help wondering at his unexpected amiability. But she obeyed the command of her master and tormentor and proceeded to massage his limbs.

After a quarter of an hour she felt an immense tiredness spread throughout her body. Little by little, she lost control of her willpower. In spite of her efforts not to yawn, her mouth began to open and close convulsively. She tried to fight the torpor which was benumbing her senses, preventing her from rubbing Dumuma's limbs with the necessary vigor. She was afraid that he might slap her; ordinarily every yawn earned her a backhanded blow across the cheek. As she was sinking into unconsciousness, she was astonished to see Dumuma smiling, even trying gently to keep her head from falling on her chest. Then she sank into a cataleptic sleep.

At last Dumuma Romo had this long-coveted prey in his power! Pugubila's sensitivity was totally suspended—he could do with her just as he wished. He would find no resistance or obstacle. There she was—a corpse in the hands of the undertaker. The narcotic bought by Dumuma from the little old man dripping with amulets would keep the girl profoundly asleep for ten hours at least.

Dumuma undressed his victim and, laying her out full-length on his pallet, contemplated the youthful nakedness of that creature whom God had spared no effort in sculpting. Pugubila was perfectly proportioned and as lovely as a statue. Her bronze skin was smooth as down, her teeth beautifully set and white as ivory. It was impossible for any man to behold her without being seized by a frenzy of desire. Dumuma began to caress her body.

Suddenly, he felt a pang of guilt. His hands stopped stroking. "What risks am I running by taking a girl this way?" he wondered. "Isn't this abduction, breach of trust? Couldn't her parents and her fiancé prosecute me?"

But soon desire got the better of the prudent thoughts that had momentarily flooded his consciousness. Passion beclouds reason. Even the wisest of men is enslaved by his basest instincts. Dumuma threw himself on the defenseless girl. She was a virgin. He violated her.

Having perpetrated the deed, he felt the full weight of his misconduct, and the realization dawned on him of the serious consequences it might entail. He wiped away carefully every trace of virginal blood, took the unconscious girl in his arms, carried her to her shelter, which was fairly close to his own and Tennga's, and there laid her down on her pallet.[8]

Since he was paid by Wangrin to spy on Dumuma, Tennga had got into the habit of waiting up until his master went to sleep. Ever since the day of Pugubila's arrival, he had been perfectly well aware of the chief overseer's intentions and had carefully noted down Dumuma's behavior toward the girl, so that he might report to Wangrin. Having secured a promise that he could have Dumuma's job as soon as extortion or malpractice were proved, Tennga didn't miss a trick. He knew that rape was dealt with by the indigenous magistrate courts within the criminal offences' section. Yet, to justify a lawsuit, an official complaint must be lodged first. . . .

Pugubila woke up late in the morning. It didn't take her long to realize that she had been deflowered. She buried her face in her hands and began to weep softly, abundant tears streaming down her cheeks. Tennga, who knew exactly what had happened, and had been watching her all along to record her reactions, came up to her and said: "What's the matter, my poor girl? Dumuma must have been maltreating you again, isn't that so?"

"No," she replied, "but I feel homesick, especially for my mother. I feel ill. I'd like to go back to my family, but I have one more week's duty."

Tennga wanted to hear Pugubila herself give an account of what had happened. He began to question her:

"Did anything special happen between Dumuma and yourself last night?"

"Nothing. He asked me to rub him down as usual. As I was massaging him, my head began to weigh terribly on my shoulders. I started yawning, teetering from left to right, and lurching forward. When I began to yawn, Dumuma didn't hit me as he usually does. Then I sank into a deep sleep, I lost consciousness altogether, and didn't wake up until this morning."

"Since you fainted away in Dumuma's hut, how did you manage to get back to your shelter?"

"That's what I've been asking myself. I have no idea."

"Only one of the 'devil's bearers' could have brought you here on his shoulders. . . . "

Pugubila remained silent.

As it so happened, during his night-watch Tennga had seen Dumuma in the act of concealing his blood-stained bedcover in a bundle of straw. As soon as Dumuma had returned to his hut and fallen asleep, Tennga had got hold of that irrefutable piece of evidence.

Early in the morning, before sunrise, Dumuma went to his hiding place to retrieve and destroy the compromising blanket. Finding it gone, he didn't quite know what to think. Could it be that a wild cat or a stray dog had made off with the thing because it smelt of blood? He wondered. It wasn't a very likely explanation, but a mind that fears reality accepts any construct of the imagination, provided it soothes besetting anxieties.

Tennga went to Dumuma and said:

"You know, I'm afraid something serious may have happened to Pugubila during the night. I saw her with her face hidden in her hands, weeping a positive torrent of tears. She told me that she misses her mother, but I couldn't help noticing that there was something odd in the way she walked. It looks to me as if she has a wound in some secret part of her body, but doesn't want to own up to it. Since you are the boss, I would advise you to send that girl back to her mother. There is no time to lose. If her condition requires special care, then her parents can see to it that she is treated at once."

Although Dumuma had been in the habit of sending Tennga to the devil whenever the latter made any kind of suggestion, this time he listened to him without interrupting. Then he said:

"How can we fiddle it? Pugubila owes us one more week of labor."

"Sickness is a case of force majeure," replied Tennga. "You can always use it to justify her leave."

Adjusting himself to that line of reasoning, Dumuma returned Pugubila to her parents.

The girl's mother was by no means fooled. Very soon she discovered that her daughter had lost her virginity, and in unusual circumstances at that. But in order to prosecute she needed to be able to prove the fact, and Pugubila couldn't remember a thing. True, she had been assiduously pursued by Dumuma, but she couldn't state categorically that it was he who had raped her.

Pugubila's parents weren't ruling out the possibility that a libertine demon, yielding to his dissipated and unruly impulses, might have slipped into Pugubila's shelter and perpetrated his crime while she was asleep.

To get to the bottom of the affair, however, they decided to consult the great geomancer, Bila Kuttu. Bila knew how to interrogate the invisible and elicit answers from devils, spirits, and genii. He composed an elaborate design and examined the data produced within the sixteen geomantic squares. Then he said:

"Well, well! It's always demons who get the blame! It's true that your daughter's secret abode has been violated, but certainly not by a demon. The culprit is a son of Adam, young, vigorous, and dark-skinned. But he is by no means a man of no consequence. I see his counterpart sitting in the shade of a large tree, and that means he's protected by powerful people. In this particular case, a tree represents a chieftaincy. If you want justice to be done, you must sacrifice two chickens to our ancestors. You will distribute their flesh to the brats you will find playing around the market, but not without having thrown the entrails to a dog with a sandy pelt."

Pugubila's parents sacrificed to the ancestors in the required manner, and waited.

That same day Tennga went to see Wangrin and gave him a detailed account of what had happened, not forgetting to mention the little old man covered in amulets, whom Wangrin was able to track down and grill so skillfully that he managed to extract, at a price, Dumuma's secret. Then the little man was told:

"Now there only remains for you to come to the Commandant's office tomorrow morning and admit in front of him that Dumuma Romo compelled you to sell him a powerful sleeping potion to be used you knew not how, and to say that you want to decline all responsibility for any accident the medicine may have caused." Then Wangrin added: "If you don't do it and the scandal explodes—and it is going to explode any moment now—you will be accused of complicity and you'll risk a heavy jail sentence."

On the following morning Wangrin awaited serenely the arrival of the little old wizard. He introduced him to the Commandant, who heard his statement as translated by Wangrin.

At first the Commandant did not perceive that the sale of a sleeping potion might have serious consequences. "Perhaps," he thought, "Dumuma Romo needed some powerful concoction to make him sleep in order to regain his strength, undermined by so many long days in the sun?"

But Wangrin told him: "In our country, a sleeping potion is always administered with criminal intent and only evil malefactors ever think of buying one. Now I have been informed that Dumuma Romo wanted to sleep with a young laborer very badly indeed and had tried every possible means to that end without success—cajoling, gifts, and the whip. I wouldn't be a bit surprised if he had resorted to a powerful sleeping potion in order to get what he wanted."

"Sort this out for me," said the Commandant, "and if necessary set up a file."

"I would be happier if you entrusted this inquiry to your deputy, the Junior Commandant," retorted Wangrin. "If it were to turn out that an offence has been committed, I wouldn't like to give Romo the chance to be able to say that I got rid of the son because I hate the father."

Accordingly, the Commandant's adjutant was put in charge of the affair. He opened an inquiry on Dumuma Romo's activities.

Through an intermediary, Wangrin supplied all the information he had gathered day in and day out on Dumuma's behavior. Within a week, one of the most damaging files that could ever be got together against a civil servant had been drawn up: embezzlement, illegal employment of forced labor, mental and physical cruelty, sexual relations with women recruits, etc. Yet all these offences were dealt with in the magistrate's court, and the worst that could happen to Dumuma was a relatively heavy prison sentence. That didn't suit Wangrin at all. For the son of his rival he needed to rig up an ignominious sentence which would entail banishment as well as a heavy prison sentence. Rape of a virgin would be the crime best suited to Wangrin's purpose, but unfortunately the only instance of Dumuma's misdemeanor had not emerged during the inquiry.

Wangrin sent a messenger to Pugubila's parents requesting them to come to him at the so-called hour of "rats, beggars, and thieves."[9]

When the girl's father and mother arrived at his house, he spoke to them as follows:

"I suggest that tomorrow you go to the Junior Commandant and say to him: 'Our daughter has been raped by Dumuma Romo. We have kept quiet until now because we were afraid. Dumuma had told us that all women and girls who are placed at his disposal for the tarring of houses and roads belong to him, body and soul, during the whole extent of their period of employment. That if they refused to obey him, they would be sent to jail and their parents seriously harassed. The Nassaarasablaga[10] are great chiefs, and we believed they had every right over the Ninsablaga.[11] Thank God we have been undeceived. It has never been true, it turns out, that Dumuma had a right to fornicate to his heart's content with the women and girls he recruited for his tarring.'

"Then you will add: 'We have heard that the Junior Commandant has ordered all those who have a grievance against Dumuma to come forward.' Then you will make your statement."

Pugubila's parents were overjoyed. So their sacrifice to the ancestors had been fruitful after all! Their daughter would be avenged, and their honor rehabilitated. Besides, they could count on being supported by Wangrin, the Commandant's "mouth and tongue."

On the day that followed that nocturnal meeting, Pugubila's parents showed up at the Junior Commandant's office and testified against Dumuma Romo who, they claimed, had raped their daughter who was still a minor.

The Junior Commandant heard out their complaint, then he sent for Pugubila, asking at the same time the medical officer in charge of the dispensary to examine her. The result was positive; the girl had indeed been deflowered very recently.

When interrogated, Dumuma denied everything hotly, trembling all over as he was speaking—one couldn't tell whether it was out of indignation or fear.

On her side, Pugubila related the facts up to the moment when she had lost consciousness. The Junior Commandant asked her how she had felt when she woke up, and the girl confessed that she had realized at the time that she had lost her virginity. Then she added that Tennga was the first person she had spoken to after coming out of her long sleep.

Tennga was questioned. He confirmed that Dumuma had deflowered the girl after having administered a powerful sleeping potion. Dumuma protested violently, accusing Tennga of trying to incriminate him so that he could step into his shoes.

At this point Tennga went to fetch the bloodstained blanket which Dumuma had hidden on that fateful night. He produced it for all to see.

Faced with that crushing piece of evidence, Dumuma burst into tears, crying: "I am undone! Do have mercy on me, sit!" Then he submitted a full confession.

He was transferred to the Native Law and Custom Tribunal, where he was sentenced to eight years in jail and ten years' banishment from Yaguwahi. He was also relieved of his post as overseer of public works.

When Romo heard the sad news his rage against Wangrin redoubled. In his fury he even thought of going to Yaguwahi purely and simply to kill Wangrin. But his wife Binta Sangare dissuaded him. "Be patient," she said. "Don't expose your flank to the enemy. There is no question that Wangrin is powerful. Wait for a more propitious moment. Days succeed one another, and no single day resembles the next. . . . "

Romo managed to hold his choler in abeyance. Since he had to wait for a more favorable opportunity, he decided for the time being to recruit a large number of marabouts whom he set in motion against Wangrin so as to compel fate to place his enemy at his mercy.

Meanwhile Dumuma was transferred from the jail in Yaguwahi to the Gudugaua central jail. At last, Wangrin had a free hand! Romo had no one left in town to inform him except Moy Fala, a marabout of small renown.

As for Tennga, with Wangrin's assistance he was appointed overseer of public works in place of Dumuma Romo.

Hardly had the Dumuma Romo business been settled and the convict been duly transferred to Gudugaua when an incident occurred which enabled Wangrin to exploit to the full his talent for intrigue and moneymaking.

11   The Death of a Great
Chief and What Came of It

One day, as Wangrin was sitting outside the Commandant's door, wondering by what sort of machinations he could amass even more money than he had during his stay in Diagaramba, he suddenly heard:

"Salaamu aleykum! Peace be unto you!"[1] He looked up, and saw a young Fulbe dressed in white and riding boots planted right in front of him. No doubt the haggard look on his face meant that he had come to deliver some very disturbing piece of news. His discomposed features proved it.

"Aleykum salaam! Peace be unto you too!"[2] answered Wangrin. Then, scenting the possibility of some profitable business, he asked:

"Who are you? Where do you come from?"

"I've been sent here by Loli, son of the chief of the Witu and Guban provinces, and the news I bear you is by no means happy. I have come to announce to the Senior Commandant that the province chief Brildji Maduma Thiala died last night in his own house around eleven and in accordance with his last wishes was washed and buried before daybreak."

"I have been asked to break the news to you, Wangrin, so that you may bring it to the ear, first of your great Chief, then of King Bana Griti, then of the imam, and lastly to all the eminent citizens of Yaguwahi."

Wangrin led Loli's messenger to Gordane's office and announced the demise of Brildji Maduma Thiala. The Commandant was deeply moved. He had always held the late chief, who had administered his province in the most felicitous way, in high esteem. In his lifetime, Brildji Maduma Thiala had not merely been a chief who was second in importance only to King Bana Griti, but also a highly cultured marabout and the owner of the largest fortune in that area. He was so generous that the griots used to compare him to the rainy season, which lavishes its bounty far and wide.

Gordane asked Wangrin what a Commandant was expected to do, traditionally, in such contingencies.

"If Brildji had not already been buried," replied Wangrin, "it would have behooved you to be present at his funeral; but since he has chosen to be buried without pomp, it will be quite sufficient to send me to condole on your behalf with his widows, orphans, and relatives. If besides you were to offer an animal whose slaughter would help nourish the many visitors who will be pouring in from all over the land to show their grief at the loss of a man as respected as Brildji, it would be good policy and everybody would appreciate your gesture."

The Commandant handed to Wangrin nine hundred francs, a sum that would comfortably purchase three large bulls.

After a few hasty preparations, Wangrin leapt on his horse and started for Witu, accompanied by Loli's messenger. In order to get there, one had to pass through Guban. Karibu Sawali, who was both Brildji's younger half brother and the legitimate pretender to the succession of the chieftaincy in Witu, lived in the town by that name.

Wangrin stopped his mount at the entrance of Guban and turned towards Loli's messenger: "Go to Witu ahead of me," he said, "and announce my arrival for tomorrow morning: I'll be there by the time the cow-milking is over.[3] I am going to spend the night here. I want to speak to Karibu Sawali. I hope tomorrow he will come with me to Witu. There, I intend to lodge at the government rest-house. See to it that the place is properly cleaned and well stocked with water."

When his companion had left, Wangrin rode into town and went to call on Karibu Sawali. He found him in his courtyard surrounded by a crowd of potential courtiers and men who wished to ensure the future *Lamido's*[4] benevolence, goodwill, or favor in advance.

Without dismounting, Wangrin waved his hand in greeting after the manner of the Whites. Everyone rose. The whole place echoed with the words:

"*Wangrin wari! Wangrin wari! Simmilla ma Wangrin, foo-fo-ma!*" (Wangrin has arrived! Wangrin has arrived! Make yourself at home, Wangrin. Good day to you!)

A servant helped Wangrin to dismount. Karibu took Wangrin's hand between both of his and sent for a wooden chair which he had specially purchased so that any white-White or black-White who called on him might sit in the manner to which he was accustomed.

Wangrin had his wits about him and so refused with the words: "I am not in a government office here: I am in the house of a worthy brother, a man of impressive lineage. I'd much rather sit on a mat, just like everybody else."

Without wasting too much precious time, Wangrin began to explain the reason for his visit. "The Senior Commandant sends me to you," he said to Karibu Sawali, "to convey to all members of the family the deep sorrow felt by France at the loss of so illustrious and devoted a servant as was your brother Brildji Thiala. I have chosen to stop here before going on to Witu, to offer the official condolence of France, of the governor of this territory, and of Commandant Jean Gordane in addition to my own as your African brother. I will spend the night in your house, and tomorrow morning you will accompany me to Witu where I intend to call on the widows and the orphans of your late brother and pay homage at his grave. On behalf of France and of the governor who represents her, the Commandant has given me the sum of nine hundred francs to be used for the purchase of three large bulls as a contribution to Brildji's funeral."

Upon which Wangrin remitted publicly the sum to Karibu Sawali, who was moved to tears. Everyone expressed gratitude to France, to the governor, to the Commandant, and to Wangrin, the great district interpreter!

Wangrin was lodged in one of Karibu Sawali's apartments. This would enable him to talk freely to his host in the late hours.

After a substantial meal, punctuated by frequent and loud belches— a traditional way to show satisfaction and satiety throughout the African Savannah country—Wangrin took Karibu Sawali on one side and said: "When every light has gone out and the noise of steps has subsided in your courtyard, come and see me. I want to talk to you. Your happiness and your honor are at stake. The night will be all the more discreet as it is lit only by stars—an adornment to the celestial vault rather than a means to illumine space."

At the proper time Karibu Sawali, draped in an ample and somber wrapper, scratched at Wangrin's door. Having been let in he took a few steps and sat down. Wangrin lit his lamp, but took good care to shield the light so that it could not be seen from outside. Then he began to speak:

"It has come to the knowledge of the Senior Commandant," he said to Karibu, "that you didn't conduct your brother's remains to the grave. Is this true?"

"Yes," answered Karibu. "My brother died in the middle of the night. His sons and domestic slaves[5] attended to his corpse and saw to the burial in the small hours unbeknown to everybody else. It was only later, on the following day, that they sent someone to bring me the news. I went immediately to Witu, where I was told that they had simply obeyed my brother's last wishes. Although I felt indignant, and my pride was wounded, I didn't think that was quite the right moment to show my anger."

"So you didn't say anything?" asked Wangrin.

"What could I say, or do, against the will of a dead man? I felt bitterness at the affront I had been made to suffer by my brother. But they faced me with a *fait accompli....*"

"Karibu Sawali!" Wangrin upbraided him. "I'd never have believed that a Fulbe of birth and quality could so light-heartedly allow a bunch of children and domestic slaves to ridicule his honor and hereditary interests. Who had greater right than you, destined to be Brildji's successor, to dispose of his remains? Brildji's eldest son, Loli, is your son also.[6] There is no doubt, then, that he is second to you. He has no right to speak, and even less to act, without your permission. If you allow things to happen to you without reacting, your authority will suffer. How on earth can you claim that you are the successor of a chief who has been buried under your very nose while you were asleep? No, my dear Karibu Sawali. You must react as firmly as possible, and prove that the authority of a man, powerful as he may have been in his lifetime, ceases the moment he breathes his last. You are the head of the Thiala royal family and you must prove it by striking a mighty blow."

"What sort of blow can I strike, now that I have lost face in front of the whole population?"

"That depends on you. I am your friend, and I have enough mischief in my mind to uproot a whole chain of mountains. If you are prepared to pay, my guile will be placed at your service. And since we are friends, I owe it to you to let you know the real truth about myself. I haven't come to Yaguwahi to indulge in religious practices with a view to gaining access to paradise. I have come to make money, and I am prepared to serve well any man who will pay me handsomely, but discreetly."

"And what sort of blow would you arrange for me to strike if I were to reward you adequately?"

"I will have your brother exhumed, so that everyone will know that you are the true head of the family. You will conduct his second burial and you will lead his remains to a place chosen by yourself."

"How much do you want me to give you?"

"A hundred ten-year-old bulls."

Karibu Sawali was prepared to pay the price.

"Where do you want the animals delivered?" he asked.

Wangrin smiled. "I have mentioned a quantity of bulls," he replied cynically, "only to establish a basic estimate for the sum I want from you in cash. How do you think I could smuggle a hundred bulls out of here, raising and clashing their two hundred huge horns and bellowing their ear-splitting moos for all they are worth? Taking cattle as payment is out of the question. You will settle your bill in gold, that most royal of metals. Hard, yellow, and silent, it acts efficaciously where many a vigorous arm might fail. A hundred bulls at three hundred francs each makes thirty thousand francs. Gold is sold at three francs per gram; that sum, then, will buy ten kilos of pure gold mined in Bure."[7]

The bargain was struck. Karibu Sawali and Wangrin shook hands on the agreement.

Karibu Sawali was not quite as rich as his brother Brildji, who had owned the largest fortune in that area, but he was a man of property nevertheless. His cattle numbered over twenty-five thousand, and he owned double that quantity of goats and sheep. He had over five hundred domestic slaves in his service. As for his riches in gold, silver, and collections of jewelry, such as amber, agate, and carnelian, it was impossible to assess their worth.

Very bucked up at the thought that soon he would be able to avenge himself for the calculated affront inflicted on him by his elder brother, Karibu Sawali parted from Wangrin and went off to enjoy the sweetest of slumbers.

Early next morning, Karibu Sawali's domestic slaves began to play the royal music of Witu and Guban on their flutes, as it used to be played every morning outside the late Brildji's room to announce to his people that he had awakened. The sound of the flute was accompanied by the beating of drums. A few courtiers sang: "Praise be to Gueno[8] whose will it is to encircle the head of Sawali's valiant younger son, our Lord Karibu, with the turban of Witu and Guban."[9]

Indeed, the Guban principality, which was the residence of the heir apparent, had in a way represented a small state within a larger one. The inhabitants of Witu were by no means at daggers drawn with those of Guban, yet a strong sense of rivalry did exist between them. During his long reign, Brildji had resented this state of affairs and had always blamed it on his half-brother Karibu Sawali. Rumor had it that this was the reason why he had willed that his contentious brother should not behold his remains. It appears that he had said to Diofo, the head of his domestic slaves, confidant, and trusted retainer: "Don't give my brother the satisfaction of seeing me prostrate, inert, impotent, and noisome."

Accordingly, he had been buried at night, and Karibu Sawali had not been informed.

A band of horsemen consisting of Wangrin, Karibu Sawali, and about ten courtiers, griots, singers, and lute players left Guban for Witu, ten kilometers away. Regardless of the sad cause of their journey, flutists and drummers began to improvise a hymn which the griots and singers modulated according to the *Eerel-Maana* melody.[10]

When they reached the outskirts of Witu, Karibu Sawali ordered his ten horsemen to perform a "fantasia," and accordingly they galloped off at great speed, riding with utter abandon. By the time they reached the quarters that had been prepared for Wangrin's reception, their equestrian parade was a remarkable display, but how wounding for the dead man's family!

Brildji's eldest son Loli, surrounded by about fifty dignitaries, was awaiting Wangrin, interpreter and special envoy of the Senior Commandant. What he didn't know was that his guest was carrying in his wooden traveling trunk ten kilos of gold from Bure—a gift offered by Karibu Sawali—who was most anxious for revenge and wished to save his honor as well as consolidate a reputation without which he could never hope to wear the turban of Witu and Guban comfortably.

The head of the domestic slaves and Loli looked at each other. In their own separate ways they understood the significance of the display made by Karibu Sawali's people.

Diofo walked towards Wangrin, but first he said to his young master Loli: "Water changes its natural state only through the addition of a foreign body. Your uncle's demeanor hides something equivocal."

"Suspect, even," expanded Loli. "But the sun of truth will rise presently, and we shall know what it is that 'puffs up' my uncle to the point of making him desecrate the memory of his elder brother and overlord Brildji."

After this brief exchange, bitter but private, Diofo and Loli greeted Wangrin according to custom. Loli helped Wangrin to dismount and Diofo did likewise with Karibu Sawali.

Diofo, who was so faithful a domestic slave that for him no god existed except his master Brildji, and no saints except his master's children, showed plainly in his face the weight of sorrow that oppressed his heart. He managed however to control himself and to say to Karibu Sawali:

"My Lord! Similla—similla! Welcome! My deep dejection and the devastation of my features are caused only by the death of my master, your illustrious brother. Death alone could subdue him. Death is unconquerable. Death has vanquished kings, saints, heroes, and wise men and will prevail upon everyone's life, except that of our One and Only Eternal God. My Lord! Similla—similla."

Karibu Sawali understood that his behavior had wounded Brildji's family deeply. As he had striven to achieve that very end, he couldn't help experiencing a certain feeling of triumph. However, he was careful to hide it. He leaned on Diofo's shoulder and dismounted. Everyone gathered under a large shelter where beautiful mats and billowing cushions had been tastefully arranged to welcome Wangrin and his retinue.

A few minutes later a rain of kola nuts[11] and a cataract of calabashes full of milk descended on the guests. To signify his welcome, Loli sacrificed five large bulls and ten household sheep.[12]

Wangrin took a mouthful of milk, and then a kola nut, which he split in half and began to chew lustily.

"Similla—similla, Wangrin!" said Loli. "You have left your house to come to us, but here you are equally at home. Make yourself comfortable and feel free to do anything you please. We are indebted to you, and consequently are your servants. Command, and you shall be obeyed. Express a wish, and it shall be granted. Similla Wangrin! Similla—similla!"

It was Wangrin's turn to reply. He said: "O my mother's son,[13] how I would have preferred to come to visit you on a more cheerful occasion than the one that brings us together today! But our Lord Allah must do as he pleases. I have come to you on behalf of the Senior Commandant, who represents the *goforner*, who represents his senior brother the *goforner zenderal*, who represents *Franci*,[14] to be present at Brildji Thiala's funeral. The Senior Commandant wished to come in person, but he was summoned to Gudugaua to a meeting of Commandants. Before long, however, he will come to pay his respects in person at the grave of one of the most illustrious men who ever served France in this area."

Hearing the words "to be present at the funeral . . . " all those present looked at each other, their eyes and mouths wide open with astonishment. It was easy to see that all the inhabitants of Witu felt profoundly anxious. A deathly silence descended on the gathering.

Diofo, his eyes brimming with tears, cried in a strangled voice:

"Wangrin, Brildji has already been buried. It was his wish that the site of his grave should remain secret; all I have done is to obey my master's last wishes. In God's name, and bearing in mind the respect we owe to the dead and to Brildji's sorrowing widows, orphans, and relatives, I entreat you to settle this business. We will be eternally grateful to you and will prove worthy of your benevolence."

"Settle what?" replied Wangrin, his face brightening with a look that boded no good for the dead man's relatives. . . .

"You claim that Brildji requested that he be buried secretly. Now, he was literate in Arabic. Can you show me his last wishes in writing? . . . No, you cannot, because such a document does not exist. How do you expect us to believe that a man whose fame spread far and wide, who was worshiped in more than twelve of the countries that lie between the eastern and western coasts of the black African continent actually wanted to be buried like a lout who has been banished even by his own family?

Mend your error. The Senior Commandant will never swallow your story, which is far from being a dainty dish. Your inferior roast is in poor taste. You shall consume it alone, and alone you will belch with the consequences of your temerity, of your lack of discernment, if not of your complicity. Do you really believe, Diofo, that the *toubab*[15] drink water through their nostrils,[16] or that they sleep with their ears pressed against the ground and their tongues between their teeth, like hibernating creatures?

"My almighty chief has precise information available concerning the actions and behavior of all the citizens who come under his administration. Do you think that the mysterious iron string that has been stretched across our countryside was placed there with no special reason? Have you ever rested your ear against one of the poles that support that iron string? If you have, you must have heard the vibrations of its continuous, secret whirring. Although you are not aware of it, that is the way the 'spy-string' informs the Commandant of everything that happens in far places. My chief believes that Brildji was murdered. He has sent me to you to find out what really happened, to make inquiries and decide whether a *dogotoro*[17] is to be brought here to carry out an autopsy. The *goforner* and the mighty-mighty chief of all France demand that the reason for the death of their valiant servant Brildji be unequivocally ascertained. I have been ordered to exhume Brildji and to summon a *dogotoro* should his body show suspect marks of violence.

"According to the orders I have been given, tomorrow morning we shall proceed to exhume the body before the imam and local dignitaries. If everything is in order, we will bury Brildji once again and the obsequies will be presided over by Karibu Sawali, his brother and potential successor."

Diofo couldn't believe his ears! Exhume Brildji? How shameful that would be for Brildji and his family!

Diofo and Loli parted from Wangrin with feelings of deep consternation. One by one, all the people present rose and filed out, each wording their leave-taking in a slightly different way.

Wangrin, Karibu Sawali, and his retinue remained under the shelter, lit now by several storm-lamps requisitioned from the village.

Karibu Sawali, who had not anticipated so staggering an event, felt obliged to say to Wangrin: "My good friend, you are a strong and quick-witted man! On top of the hundred bulls I've promised you I'll give you another ten to show you my deep satisfaction." Then he left Wangrin and went back to his lodgings, for he had a private house in Witu just as he did in Guban.

A few of Karibu Sawali's courtiers and griots and some of Wangrin's companions went on chatting under the shelter, listening to Yidi Mama and Idrissa Gadiaga—the two finest lute players in the whole area—play their instruments.

Finally all the stirring of human steps and all noises made by domestic animals subsided, except for the odd, occasional barking somewhere in the distance. The fires went out; the town of Witu was now engulfed in the vast, somber cloak of a moonless night. All living things seemed to have fallen asleep. Only in Wangrin's lodgings were people still awake.

Having sneaked through the town's alleys, a shadow suddenly stopped at the back of the encampment. After a moment's hesitation, the shadow jumped over the low wall that surrounded it and proceeded stealthily in the dark toward the shelter. Was it a thief, or was somebody coming to make an attempt on Wangrin's life following his threat to exhume Brildji the very next day? It was neither. It was simply Diofo in disguise. He was trying to get through to Wangrin and make him a proposal, but didn't wish to be seen by the men who surrounded him. Diofo sat down like one who is certain that he will not lack an opportunity to achieve his self-appointed task. However, after a long wait in the dark, Diofo decided he might as well give up. But just then he heard a voice ask: "Where does one piss in this place?"

Wangrin answered: "Behind the shelter."

As he had just walked away from the light the man didn't notice that Diofo was hidden behind a tree not far from the spot where he had chosen to stop and relieve himself.

Diofo waited for him to finish, then altering his voice he said softly: "Don't be afraid. I am no enemy. Here you are—let me give you this five-franc coin, made of pure white silver in *Franci* proper. Go and take Wangrin on one side and tell him that a friend is waiting for him under this tree to discuss a most urgent matter. Even tomorrow morning would be too late."

Somewhat bewildered, the man took the coin, which, by the way, in those days was no mean tip. Once under the shelter, he called Wangrin, showed him the coin and related the words spoken by the mysterious donor.

Wangrin was as brave as a lioness when guarding her cubs and he proved it by accepting an invitation thrown out in the dark by a stranger who could easily turn out to be a murderer. All he said to his fellow guests was: "I am going to disappear for a moment. Wait until I come back, however long it may take me. If necessary, wait till tomorrow morning."

Then he plunged into the shadows as a fisherman would plunge into a pool. It was only after he had left that his talkative friends began to reproach themselves for having allowed Wangrin to walk all alone into what might easily turn out to be a trap laid with the greatest cunning.

"But who anywhere in this area would dare to touch a hair of the head of the Senior Commandant's interpreter? If the least harm were to come to him, we would all have our heads shaved with pieces of broken bottles and our bodies fried on heat fired straight out of the seventh hell!"

"Enough said!" cried Idrissa Gadiaga. "I don't understand why you want to invoke calamities upon yourselves when we all know that Wangrin is neither stupid, nor paralyzed, nor blind."

"When a man mouths a scorpion," chipped in Yidi Mama with a laugh, "he must have lined his tongue with invulnerability."[18] And he continued plucking his lute.

12 The Ambush

Meanwhile Wangrin had almost reached the tree under which Diofo had been waiting. When he was only a few steps away, he saw that a dark form was breaking loose from the tree trunk and taking a few deliberate but cautious steps.

"Stop where you are," shouted Wangrin, "if you don't want it said that your mother gave birth to a premature corpse! Remain rooted to the spot and tell me who you are. If you are a sucker of that tree metamorphosed into man-demon, I shall destroy you by means of my *Korto*.[1] All I have to do is to propel its deathly effluvia in your direction by uttering these magic words:

Kothiema sunsun
Baathiema sunsun
Sunsun fla ani sunsun.

Diospiros at the center of a lake
Diospiros at the center of a river
The double diospiros and the single diospiros."[2]

Such daring speech, delivered calmly in circumstances which might cause many a brave man to piss in his pants with terror, froze Diofo's blood. But he summoned enough courage to reply:

"Don't do anything rash, Wangrin! If you have brought out your fetish, put it back. I am no demon, or goblin, or devil, or elf, or whimsical creature of any kind. I am your *dimadjo*.[3] I am Diofo."

"What do you want of me, then, that you come here shrouded in the shadows of a moonless night lit by stars that are either pallid or downright livid? Why not come in daylight; why not come at least through the front entrance?"

"A secret is a seed that is likely to rot instead of germinating if exposed to broad daylight. The mighty span of the baobab, king of all vegetation, is held whole within its gemmule, and hidden in the darkness of its seed. Likewise, I hold in my breast a secret greater than the mightiest of baobabs. How, O how I wish you to be the fertile soil into which this secret—which isn't mine, by the way—may be sown!"

"To whom does it belong, then?" asked Wangrin.

"It belongs to the widows, children, brothers, and domestic-slaves of the late Brildji Thiala—a master, father, and husband we mean to mourn until the day when all of us finally join him in the village of flat pedestals."[4]

"Speak, Diofo, I am listening. Night is old enough as it is, and her great age presses on my lids.[5] Make haste!"

"I must ask you first to follow me to our late master's house. There, his eldest son and his widows are waiting to consult you, for all of us still remember the good feeling that existed between you and Brildji when he was alive."

"All right, let's go," replied Wangrin, thinking it unnecessary to warn his friends who were waiting under the shelter.

The two made their way toward the house of the late Brildji Thiala. Like many Africans, Wangrin could see well enough in the dark to guide himself and get his bearings, and he certainly didn't forget to practice this almost elementary skill at a time of hazard and uncertainty!

From alley to alley, careful to avoid all the main streets of Witu, Diofo guided Wangrin to a small, inconspicuous door. This door and a flight of steps led to the first floor of the house in which Brildji Thiala had lived and died. Our two friends went upstairs and walked toward the main entrance, which was kept locked. Diofo let out a hoot like a barn owl. From inside a voice asked:

"Who are you?"

"Crested owl," replied Diofo.

Pushed by an invisible hand, the heavy portal opened a crack. The hall was plunged in darkness. Diofo turned to Wangrin: "Come in," he said. "I will light the room. There is a lamp to the right of the door. Just walk straight ahead."

Trustfully, Wangrin advanced. He took a few steps towards the middle of the hall, then stopped and waited for Diofo to light the lamp. Diofo had taken the precaution of closing the door and wedging a heavy board diagonally across it. He lit three large karite butter lamps one by one. Wangrin found that he was standing in a vast hall, the one Brildji had been in the habit of using for his palavers with the town dignitaries.

Diofo shouted: "Aywa!⁶ Come, Wangrin is here!"

Four slaves, herculean in size, each brandishing a thick *Ngollooru*—a wooden truncheon with a long handle—came in through four different doors.

Wangrin, grasping the situation, burst out laughing and with a voice so firm that Diofo was once again shaken by so much courage said:

"O Diofo! I didn't think that I was in danger of being killed, or there was no need for you to take the trouble of surrounding me with such grim bodyguards, so grim even for the man they are supposed to protect . . . but still! Where are Loli and Brildji's other relatives who sent you to bring me here?"

"Give your bantering a rest, Wangrin! Loli and Brildji's relatives are no more present in this hall than cow butter is present in a stone. You are facing four killers. Since Brildji's demise, four men whom you now behold have committed themselves to a betrothal with death. They are most anxious to consummate the marriage and I happen to share their resolve. When Brildji was alive, we never permitted anyone to look him in the eyes and say 'no.' To us, his wishes were commands. There are three hundred and thirty-three of us, all finely built young slaves, the choicest men among Brildji's two thousand eight hundred and twelve. We were his special guard. We have always struck down those who tried to measure their strength against his; we have always sent to the grave all those who attempted to humiliate or overcome him.

"Since Brildji's death, life stinks for us. It is unbecoming for men so faithful to survive him. Our blood should have helped to mold the clay that covers the hollow in which he is buried. Alas! The Muslim religion which we embraced so as to emulate and please our master forbids suicide and human sacrifice. We are determined nevertheless to smite the man who attempts to discover the whereabouts of Brildji's grave. Those who have not seen his dead body will never see his remains either. While we are alive, it will be easier to resuscitate Brildji than to exhume him. Now you, Wangrin, have told us that you intend to exhume Brildji tomorrow morning. Give up the idea, for if you don't, never again will you contemplate the light of day. And in any case, unless you turn all the land in Witu and Guban upside down—which is hardly feasible—you'll never find his body.

"No *goforner*, no Junior or Senior Commandant, can alter the matter—Brildji will stay on in his secret grave. He won't be made to suffer the dishonor of a shameful disinterment. On the other hand, if you drop the idea and settle the whole unfortunate business, riches await you. I will give you now any sum that you care to ask for, plus a supplementary gift to signify our gratitude for your good will. To sum up, you have this alternative within easy reach; either a vast fortune, or death. It is for you to choose. Do so before the first cock crows in this part of the town. I wouldn't want to hear the first braying of the donkeys mingle with your death rattle."

Wangrin had been lending only half an ear to Diofo's weird mixture of macabre threats and generous offers. His lively brain was busy assessing just how deep was the pit into which he had allowed himself to be flung. Unflappable as ever, he was looking desperately hard for a way out.

Eureka! Wangrin's artful and wily imagination had just laid a very special egg of its own. There only remained for his courage to hatch it and crack it open before the roosters and the donkeys let out their matinal cry.

In Wangrin there was no lack of boldness, spiked with a sort of Machiavellian cunning, and the time had come to exercise them both in order to get himself out of a nasty plight.

"Up to now," he began abruptly, "I had been led to believe—and I believed it firmly—that Fulbe domestic slaves were the most simple-minded and unimaginative of men, not to say outright stupid, even cretinous. And here I am—about to pay dearly for that abominable prejudice. Although I find myself in a desperate situation, I must confess that the enormous contempt I have felt up to now for your caste, O Fulbe domestic slaves, is being replaced by a feeling of warm admiration. As a matter of fact, the hare himself, well known as he is for his slyness, couldn't have trapped me as easily as you, Diofo, have done just now!"

While he was talking, Wangrin took a few steps towards one of the murderers.

"Stop!" shouted the slave. "Another step and your skull will be shattered. Then you won't be able to say another word. . . . "

"You're quite right," replied Wangrin. "It's just that I've lost the notion of what day of the week or of the month we're in and above all of the time of day. Very soon—O father! O mother!—those wretched Witu asses will have a bad dream that will start them braying. Their untimely cries will get the local roosters singing and . . . plif, plaf; whim, wham—the eight bones that make up my skull will be reduced to sharp-edged shards and my poor brain to jam, while my two genital glands will be ejected like stones from a sling. I am beginning to think that in Witu assassins are capable of destroying death itself. . . .

"O my God, how depressing it is to be a descendant of the Bambara. The only skills those rustics teach their children are to hunt termites to feed their poultry, and mice and grasshoppers to amuse themselves. The day they bring back a water lizard or a giant lizard, no less than a drumming session is made to honor the unexpected feast. . . . "[7]

Suddenly Wangrin started spinning like a top. His face contorted by a demented expression, he grabbed his clothes and twisted them around his body with all his strength and began to cry: "Ouch! Help! I am being stung by a scorpion, I am dying . . . !"

Instinctively, two of Diofo's assassins started searching Wangrin's clothes for the poisonous insect. Still spinning, Wangrin maneuvered himself into such a position where he could seize each assassin with one hand. With hawk-like speed he drew them toward himself, knocked their heads together, and threw them against Diofo, who fell and became entangled in his bubu.

With a leap worthy of a leopard, Wangrin landed by the door. He grabbed an oil lamp and threw it at his enemies. Taking advantage of their disarray, he tore away the wedge that held the door fast, opened it, went out, and closed it, making use now of the lock on the other side.

While his kidnappers were busy putting out the incipient fire started by the oil lamp, Wangrin, like the fine athlete he was, jumped from the high terrace on to a lower one and from there to the wide street that led to the encampment. He ran as if the devil were at his heels, allowing himself to stop only when he was quite close to the compound, where his companions were waiting for him in an exhausted stupor. A lamp was still lit, but mouths were idle and lids heavy.

Wangrin took a few deep breaths, as he had been taught to do when he was given lessons in physical training at the School for Hostages in Kayes. His breathing returned to normal, and he arrived looking cool, as if nothing had happened.

"What a lot of sissies you are!" he bawled at his friends. "Wake up! Sleep isn't meant for men with hairy chins and rugged heels,[8] sleep is for women and mediocre men."

They woke with a start. Yidi Mama asked: "Where have you been, Wangrin? We were so worried."

"Go to your beds," said Wangrin, "but before you fall asleep, don't forget to tell yourselves that there are still a few men around who don't allow the night to swallow them up."[9] Then he too went to bed and slept peacefully, in spite of having just lived through one of the nastiest experiences of his whole life.

While Wangrin was enjoying the sleep of the just, Diofo and Brildji's family were in an entirely different state of mind. With their attempt ended in miserable failure, Diofo and the four assassins decided it was best to raise the alarm among the head slaves of the household. Before dawn, they forgathered and held an important meeting, presided over by Brildji's eldest son and heir, Loli, in great secrecy.

Diofo spoke up: "As if our cruel bereavement weren't enough, we are now oppressed by the added weight of two calamities—Brildji's dis-interment and Wangrin's ambush—which has ended in abysmal failure. We were trying to escape from a menacing fate and instead now we are faced with an implacable future. The earth has turned to fire under our feet, yet we cannot climb to heaven. What can we do?"

"Die all together," many people offered.

"What a foolish suggestion!" thundered Diofo. "The more dead there are, the more mounds in the cemetery. The dead can't take revenge, and the problem of our tarnished honor will remain unresolved."

"What shall we do, then," asked Loli, "since Diofo is against all of us dying together?"

"Listen to me," rejoined Diofo, "we are the richest family in this whole area. We have fifty cattle pens with at least fifty thousand fully grown animals. There are two thousand eight hundred and twelve of us, all adult slaves capable of bearing arms. If we were to include our wives and children, we'd be three times that number. If we were to be auc-tioned, we would be worth a sum heavier than a whole mountain. We own at least three million grams of ductile gold mined in Bure. Our lots are full of precious stones, our immense storehouses are cramful of cow-ries; and I know not what else. . . .

"Loli, if we can't achieve our ends with the aid of all these riches, it must mean that our mothers have delivered a lot of despicable skunks!"

Then Loli said: "Diofo, my late father left all decisions to you, al-though he was respected by all the great men of his time and had great erudition, a vast fortune, many people around him. I would be ill-ad-vised, then, not to follow in his footsteps. I know that you love my father and his children even more than they are capable of loving themselves. Give orders, and I'll see to it that whoever disobeys you swings at the gallows!"

"No, Loli, there is no need to hang or even slap anybody. Your slaves recognize no one but you as master, and no one but me as their leader. All I ask you is to let me act in my own way. Get the gunpowder ready by all means, but don't set fire to it unless I tell you to do so."

As Diofo's words were dying down, the muezzin's fine voice rang in the air, calling the faithful to the first prayer of the day.

"Alhamdu lillah!"[10] said Diofo. "This call to prayer is a good omen. By the grace of the Lord, from now on our lives will be nothing but happiness and contentment. Let us banish all depressing thoughts from our hearts. Wealth has a way of saying to her lord and master: 'Express your wishes and they shall be fulfilled even more swiftly than you hoped, and well beyond your expectations!' Fortunately we are not wanting for riches."

"Go," said Loli, "do your best. May God guide your steps . . . !"

"Amen, amen!" replied Diofo, who having asked everybody to disperse was already on his way to the encampment.

As the sun was flashing gold from his immense globe on the eastern horizon, Diofo entered the encampment.

Wangrin, always awake at the first cock crow, was up and about. Diofo found him reclining on a deck chair, his legs stretched out on the folding stool. Five men sat round him in a circle, and appeared to be discussing a serious matter.

Diofo approached and threw out without hesitation:

"Djam-Waali, Wangrin?"[11]

"Djam-Tan!"[12] replied Wangrin.

"I have come to inquire after your health, Wangrin, and to bring you news of Brildji's family and of myself."

"Last night I had a nightmare," said Wangrin. "My ears are still buzzing, my hands and feet still hot with the sensation. Imagine, Diofo, I dreamt last night that I was being chased by five weird hyenas. Four of them had teeth shaped like bludgeons. I was running like a leopard in pursuit of a doe; I was leaping over terraces, high walls, and low walls. I couldn't tell you how my dream ended, but I do find your presence reassuring, for I hope you will have time to take me to a marabout who knows how to interpret dreams."

"As a matter of fact," replied Diofo, "I know an outstanding interpreter of dreams. I have consulted him so often on behalf of my master Brildji, his family, and even myself that in the process I've become a bit of an interpreter of dreams myself, so I can explain at least the gist of your dreams."

"I am listening," replied Wangrin.

"Terraces and walls are symbolical of the financial difficulties that punctuate people's lives. If one can leap over them and land on the other side, an immense fortune is about to come one's way either in the shape of a gift or through one's own efforts. My conclusion, roughly speaking, is that your dream is not all ill omen. Of course, Tierno Taali, who is both a marabout and a skillful interpreter of dreams, will be able to enlarge on the details. I can easily take you to him, if you wish."

"Thank you. We'll think about that when the sun is as high in the sky as the tip of a standing spear," said Wangrin.

Then he added: "What brings you here so early, Diofo?"

"I would like to ask you for some advice in private, if you don't mind."

"I don't see why not, Diofo. If you come with me to my private room, I think we'll be more comfortable there."

Wangrin rose and Diofo followed him to his room. When they were alone, Diofo came straight to the point:

"Wangrin," he said, "you are far stronger than the lot of us and our ancestors put together. You have proved that we are no more than puppets in your hands. But as a noble Bambara and the descendant of a family of chiefs, you will understand that a slave who has enjoyed his master's affection is capable of dying—if necessary—to save his master's life or defend his honor. That was my wretched crime. Now I come to plead with you, appealing to your kindness and to your traditional rank.

"You, Wangrin, as the noble son of noble chiefs, should feel pity for the imbecility of an overfed retainer. I forgot that I am no more than an ugly hyena, and I dared to attack you—a noble lion. Have mercy. Break my bones if you wish; my vanity deserves as much. But for the sake of the respect due to all the *horons*[13] who ever lived, spare Brildji's remains a humiliating exhumation.

"Throughout Brildji's life, his body exuded the sweetest scent. The air through which he walked was impregnated with his perfume. How could you disinter a Brildji whose stench would befoul the atmosphere? If you were to exhume him, the fetid smell would send people running; it would attract evil vultures in search of quarry.

"No, Wangrin. You were suckled on noble milk, and it is noble blood that flows in your princely veins. You would not dishonor a man of your own rank, now rendered defenseless by death. It would be an abominably dirty trick; surely you cannot lack decency to the point of forgetting the proper way for a nobleman to behave when confronted with the dead body of one of his peers. The similarity between your rank and social status and Brildji's places you under some sort of obligation.

"I will say no more, Wangrin, but let me repeat that gold, silver, lovely captive maidens, and boundless quantities of plump oxen and sheep are yours for the taking. Give me your word of honor as a *horon* and tell me what you would have us do to please you. My young master Loli is ready to shower gifts on you. But if you refuse, before you begin a search for Brildji's grave so that you can disinter him you'll have to climb over the dead bodies of five or six thousand men. It is for you to choose. . . . I await your answer. I will take myself away now, but let me warn you that if you turn down my proposal, this will be the last time we'll have shaken hands."

Wangrin was a rogue, true, but his soul did not lack sensitivity. Although his heart was consumed by a desire to make money by any conceivable means at his disposal in order to satisfy his congenital covetousness, there was much goodness, generosity, and even grandeur in his makeup. The poor and the many people who had benefited by his unostentatious help were well acquainted with that side of his nature. Although his behavior was cynical toward the mighty and the favorites of fortune, it was at no time despoiled of a certain elegance.

Diofo's speech, then, had perturbed him deeply. Two large tears rolled down his cheeks. "Diofo," he said, "my dream is forgotten. No disagreeable incident occurred last night. Come back when the sun reaches its zenith and the shadows creep back under the objects that project them. My head and my heart will converse, and my tongue will make their decision manifest. Go, Diofo! Go in peace and take my greetings to Loli and his relatives."

His speech over, Wangrin pulled out of his pocket a piece of white linen, square in shape. First he dried his tears, then he blew his nose. He slipped back into his pocket the square of white linen and shaking Diofo by the hand, he added absently: "Go now, Diofo, go at once!"

"Billayi-Wallayi!"[14] said Diofo to himself. "Wangrin is not just a *horon*; he's also an accomplished 'white-Black.' Look at him, drying his tears and blowing his nose like the 'white-Whites'! That's exactly what I've seen Whites do during the *quatran-juliyet*[15] festivities!"

13 The Calamitous Bird's Egg

Wangrin ate his breakfast. As soon as he had swallowed the last mouthful, he split open a fine, pink kola nut and popped it in his mouth. Chewing it like a ruminating goat, he explored ways of getting out of his plight. With his traveling trunk already laden with twenty pounds of gold—a gift from Karibu Sawali's treasury—it was essential not to make an enemy of the latter and at the same time to find a way of leaving Brildji's grave undisturbed.

Wangrin mumbled to himself: "Here I am, in exactly the same hopeless situation as the man who has happened on the two eggs hatched by the *kilinti-kolonto*, bird of ill omen. Anyone who has contemplated the eggs of this calamitous bird is faced with three equally tragic prospects: either he takes one egg and loses his father, or he takes both and loses his mother, or he takes neither and dies."

With a faraway look in his eyes, he continued the rhythmic movement of his jaws. Then he emptied his lungs with a good deal of noise and addressed to his fetish the following prayer:

Kothiema sunsun
O *Bathiema sunsun*!
O thou who knowest in advance the sex of a fetus
when it is still hidden in its mother's womb!
O thou who recallest all that ever happened
since the beginning of time!
O thou who art present
because thou art sempiternal presence,
O thou who knowest the outcome of events
before they have come to pass—

I am your humble worshiper who never doubted your powers.
Behold me, caught in a trap I myself have set.
Set me free, and with words or by means of premonitory dreams
suggest what offerings you desire of me, where and when I am to
sacrifice to you, and with or without the help of another.
O *Kothiema sunsun!* Speak to me at once, give me the inspiration I
need. I believe in you and I trust you completely.

Although Wangrin prostrated himself regularly in prayer,[1] he was
not averse from time to time to appealing to the traditional gods of his
own country or to the efficacious spirits of his ancestors.

He withdrew to his chamber and ordered Badgi, who was at once his
groom, servant, and bodyguard, to prevent anyone from disturbing him
until the hour when the sun hovers above human heads and treetops. He
also sent a message to Karibu Sawali asking him not to bestir himself
until the first call to prayer in the afternoon.

Total isolation enabled Wangrin to meditate on his problem deeply
and at length. A happy ending was by no means in sight.

Just as Diofo was due to return, he was suddenly struck by an inspiring thought. He exulted in it like the man who—lost in the desert and
about to die of thirst—unexpectedly stumbles on a no longer hoped-for
oasis.

He was stroking his beard contentedly when Diofo made his entrance:
"Salamale-kum! Peace be unto you!"[2] he said.

"Mbaa!"[3] replied Wangrin. "Similla Diofo! Similla!"

"This reception bodes extremely well," thought Diofo to himself,
shaking off his slippers before going in. Then with a respectful bow he
shrank his height and continued to walk—bent double—until it was time
to squat by the deck chair chosen by Wangrin for his hours of meditation. Diofo got hold of a round straw mat that had been left on the floor
and began to fan Wangrin, but first he dropped furtively on the ground a
bundle of kola nuts and a large snuff-box made of leather decorated with
silver.

As he sat up, Wangrin noticed the bundle of kola nuts and the handsome large snuff-box.

"It's the first time I have seen one of these large snuff-boxes chiseled
by the jewelers of Djenne," he said. "What an agreeable surprise. Thank
you, Diofo, thank you from the bottom of my heart."

"It contains an excellent *almundialla*,[4] you'll see. . . . " Wangrin picked
up the snuff-box. It was much heavier than he had anticipated; he had to
lift it with both hands. He opened it and saw that it was full of gold dust
from the Bure mines.

Accustomed as he was to receiving a great deal of gold as well as lavish inducements, he was moved infinitely more by Diofo's gesture and by the deference of his manner—at once elegantly spontaneous and appropriately tactful—than by the contents of the snuff-box.

"Why are you giving me this tobacco made from precious metal powder, Diofo?"

"Since you are as a father to him, Loli, your devoted son, feels it his duty to offer you some tobacco. Accordingly, he sends you this bundle of kola nuts and this snuff-box that you may breakfast a little before your principal meal."

"And what will the principal meal be?" asked Wangrin.

"As regards both quality and quantity, it shall be whatever my master Wangrin chooses to order."

"Wallayi, Wallayi! O Diofo! your hands are as strokes of the hammer on an anvil and the spell of your magical tongue reduces the most obstinate and least ductile of metals to a supple wax which you then fashion at will. You win, Diofo! Brildji's remains will sleep inviolate in the secret niche of his undiscoverable tomb. Only the sound of the trumpet on the day of judgment will raise your master, my late friend, out of his grave."

Diofo took his leave and went off almost at a run. Only his status as supreme head of Brildji's domestic slaves kept him from bounding and capering out of sheer joy. As soon as he arrived home he cried to Loli:

"O Loli! sacrifice everything you can spare to Allah! Your father will continue to sleep peacefully in his grave. He will not leave it until the day of judgment when he will rise among the sweetly scented host of the elect. And so much the worse for those who were looking forward to holding their noses and saying contemptuously: 'Who would have thought that Brildji could smell so foul and revolting!'"

Loli straightened up. "O papa Diofo![5] So Wangrin has really promised?"

"Yes!" he answered. "He said: 'Brildji will not leave his grave until he hears the sound of Azrael's[6] trumpet.'"

"Do you really believe that Wangrin can keep my uncle Karibu Sawali at bay and keep the promise he has made us as well?" asked Loli, breathless with emotion and beset by doubt.

"I am so sure of it that I would let my throat be slit and my innards be unwound rather than disbelieve it!" replied Diofo. "Wangrin is a scoundrel of the first order and a most skillful schemer but paradoxically he is also quite a gentleman. Besides, he is so tough that he fears neither God nor the Devil, no question about that. I trust him, even though I have no idea in what sauce he's going to pickle Karibu Sawali to stop him from ordering Brildji's disinterment. Patience, however! for the object which travels out of darkness into light cannot help but become discernible. I hear that Wangrin has arranged to meet Karibu Sawali this afternoon while the faithful are being called to prayer. That hour cannot fail to come, for time never lies."

Just as Diofo stopped speaking, the sound of "Allaahou akbar! Allaahou akbar!" was heard in the distance. The muezzin in the great mosque of Witu was intoning his song with beautiful ringing tones. From the top of the minaret, his droning voice exhorted the faithful to prepare for the ritual of Muslim worship which strengthens the body, soothes the soul, and brings tranquillity to minds which are oppressed by adversity:

Allaahou akbar! Allaahou akbar! . . .
God is incommensurable,
He is the only God,
and Mohammed is his Apostle. . . .

Diofo turned to Loli and said: "Karibu and his retinue must be just about ready to leave for the encampment. Let's ask one of our men to sneak in among the crowd. He might be able to gather the odd useful scrap of information."

The choice having fallen on Bila Tonel, the latter propelled himself, fleet as an arrow, toward the encampment.

Needless to say, Karibu was convinced that when the prayers were over Wangrin would want to be led to Brildji's grave so that the exhumation could take place.

Karibu's horse Barewal, which was as white as if he had been caressed by moonlight and very richly harnessed, was let out of his stable by a young *dimadjo* who held in his hand a fine Moroccan bridle bought in Fez.

This magnificent animal, rearing to be mounted, stamped the ground and described circles round his groom, who found it very difficult to restrain him. Now Barewal was neighing. Diamburi, as the young *dimadjo* was called, started talking to him as if to a human being:

Keep still, Barewal!
I'll take proper care of you.
You'll drink fresh milk tonight.
If you do not attend,
you will repent,
for Karibu's spurred heels
will not speak so gently
and your two flanks will shed

tears of blood.
You will yearn for my hands
which caress your strong neck,
O great steed!

Karibu appeared, all resplendent in immaculate white, except for his tawny "kola juice" boots embroidered in multicolored silks, and his large, dark blue turban. His Hausa[7] turban had been given a special sheen through a process known to that Nigerian tribe alone, and very jealously guarded. Reflecting the brilliance of the sun like a mirror, it was both royal diadem and headband—a symbol of great riches. Nowadays the Fulbe still use the name *Pilkol-bugue* for this kind of turban.

Karibu advanced on the tide of sound made by his griots, who were improvising praises in his honor amidst the strident yu-yus beating out the motto of the Thiala dynasty, which six griots, three mounted and three on foot, were vying with one another in reciting.

The ease with which Karibu leaped astride Barewal betokened his fine horsemanship. Brildji had been known as the richest man in the area, but there was no doubt that Karibu was its finest rider.

Once Karibu was in the saddle, Barewal knew that the man on his back was his master, and decided that it was wiser to heed the nudging of his hands and heels rather than insist on being restless.

Karibu opened the procession. His horse went forward with a gentle, dancing motion, surrounded by ten other horses and over twenty men on foot. The whole band swayed together toward Wangrin's station.

As he approached, Yidi Mama, a griot of great renown, who was a member of Karibu's retinue as well as mouthpiece for his lord, cried: "Salamale-kum! Salamale-kum! Peace be unto you!"

"Mbaa! Similla—similla!" answered Wangrin. When they had all made themselves comfortable under the shelter, Wangrin turned to Karibu: "Come along to my apartment," he said. "There is something I want to talk to you about, but not in your people's hearing. Chieftaincy business, and therefore of the utmost secrecy."

As soon as they were alone, Wangrin showed Karibu that pick axes, mattocks, and shovels had been piled up in a corner. "As agreed between us," he said, "I summoned the great Imam Suleyman and asked him to hold himself ready for the disinterment. But the imam was so visibly perturbed by my words and looked so haggard and bewildered that I began to think he was about to have an epileptic fit. How intense was my fear, then, when I saw him fall senseless on this very mat—a slimyish liquid oozing out of his nostrils and the corners of his mouth.

"At that sight, for the first time in my whole life I experienced terror, like a man who is about to drown. At a loss as to how to help, I began to apply artificial respiration just as I was taught at the School for Hostages. Mercifully, after some time he recovered his senses.

"When I saw that he was once more in full possession of his faculties, I asked him what might have been the cause of his faintness. Let me tell you what he answered: 'These are the last three months of my eighty-second year, yet never in my whole life have I had to listen to so execrable a proposal as the one you have just made—to exhume a dead body! Even Satan would take great care to do no such thing. It is written in our holy texts that a somber destiny awaits those inhabitants of earth who dare to order an exhumation. It is also written that the seventh hell will host any man who, during his lifetime, will have made so bold as to enjoy this most macabre of spectacles. How dare you, Wangrin,' added the imam, 'suggest that I lend my presence to so sacrilegious an undertaking? You will discover that there is not one single man in our whole community who is willing to help you!'

"With these words Suleyman left me, but his look was one of such contempt that for a moment I thought he was going to spit in my face. In spite of the imam's warning, however, I am quite prepared to defy holy texts and hellfire if you remain impervious to the condemnation of your co-religionists, let alone the implacable retribution foretold in those reliable documents—the holy texts. On the other hand, an idea has flashed through my mind. This idea would be face-saving for both of us and above all it would give a new boost to your popularity. An unpopular leader has no future. If my suggestion is to your taste you'll recover in prestige the pleasure that will be denied you by our failure to exhume Brildji."

"What do you suggest I do?" asked Karibu.

"I could maneuver Loli and Diofo into leading to you a delegation with a public apology on behalf of widows, heirs, and relatives for having buried Brildji's body without your knowledge. They could also be made to ask you to appeal through me to the Commandant and the *Goforner* that they may relent and forgo a request which does such violence to the customs and religion of our country."

Karibu decided that all things considered this solution would be infinitely more viable in respect of his ambitions than the sight of his brother's corpse.

"You are my friend," he said to Wangrin, "from now on I mean to let you act on my behalf in my best interest—whether it be apparent or concealed."

As soon as Karibu had left, Wangrin sent for Loli and Diofo and advised them to compromise with Karibu so that the matter might be settled to everyone's satisfaction. Naturally Wangrin had fabricated the whole scene with the great imam. As soon as Loli and Diofo had left, he sent for the imam.

"O imam," he said, "I must perform an unhappy task. I am ordered to exhume Brildji's corpse to prove beyond doubt that he wasn't murdered. I have never heard of anyone having to accomplish so macabre a deed. No one in the whole of the Sudan, Senegal, let alone Mauritania, would ever think of tolerating an act so sacrilegious as the one I am to perpetrate. Therefore I entreat you to accompany Loli and Diofo, who intend to lead a delegation to Karibu and entreat him to come to me with a request to suspend the exhumation ordered by the white-Whites who rule over us."

"O Wangrin," replied the imam, "exhumation is unheard of in Islam and in our own Fulbe tradition. A double duty, then, compels me to rise in protest against this nefarious deed. I will be glad to escort Loli on his mission to persuade his uncle, as you suggest."

A few hours later, before the second afternoon call to prayer, Loli, Diofo, and the Imam Suleyman led a delegation consisting of Brildji's relatives to Karibu Sawali. They found him sitting in the shade of his vast shelter, surrounded by a large number of dignitaries from Witu and Guban.

When the members of the delegation had been made comfortable, the imam began:

"Karibu Sawali! I am the Imam of Guban and one of the oldest members of our tribe. Loli and Diofo have come to me with a story I had already heard as a mere rumor—a story which I could not have credited until they told me that it was really true. It concerns the exhumation of Brildji's body as ordered by the Senior Commandant and is to be put into execution by Wangrin before the afternoon is out. . . .

"Karibu Sawali! Let me warn you that if this deed is accomplished in your lifetime, although public opinion may well forget that Brildji had affronted you and harbored ill feeling toward you, it is not likely to forget your callousness toward his remains. And some of your detractors—they always exist, no matter who the leader is—will be only too happy to exploit this instance to besmirch your reputation. They will proclaim far and wide that it was you who engineered the whole affair. That kind of publicity will place you at a disadvantage for the rest of your life and will prevent you from participating in any honorable undertaking. You will sink very low in your people's estimation. Remember that our great ancestor Butorin[8] said: 'Let any one of my descendants be cursed should he be willing to honor a member of my tribe known to have dishonored a dead body—be it that of an enemy.'

"Now I can't conceive of any greater dishonor than an exhumation when burial has already taken place. No, Karibu Sawali. You must not allow this to happen. Go and see Wangrin at once. Intercede with him. Explain that to dishonor Brildji's body is to cover the entire Fulbe race with shame. In any case, if you intervene, Brildji's relatives and domestic slaves will be only too glad to offer you a public apology."

Yidi Mama, renowned griot and lute player, one of Karibu's praise-singers and genealogists, rose from his seat. Pointing his index finger at Karibu, he sang:

"Karibu, son of Sawali the gallant and grandson of Mawnde, the brave shepherd who twenty times over in his lifetime set to flight the ferocious lion who wanted to raid his cattle-pen, though he was armed with no other weapon than a flexible branch! Mawnde died an honorable man, free from the stain of iniquity. Although often he inflicted grave wounds on his enemies, and sometimes even destroyed them ruthlessly, it cannot be said of him that he ever treated them dishonorably.

"Would you now do that which another of our ancestors, Boori-Moodi, refused to do?

"The Mossi Prince Bila Wobogo swore to procure for his own wives the milk yielded by the white cows reared for the special purpose of quenching the thirst of Boori-Moodi's wives. Bila Wobogo, whose other name was 'the angry leopard,' pounced on the thirty shepherds in charge of the cattle-pen. Ten were killed, ten wounded, and the remaining ten took to their heels. Outraged, Boori-Moodi jumped on his chestnut thoroughbred. He caught up with Bila Wobogo between Gorongoru and Kumbila, in a spot so lonely that the cry of man could be heard only by birds, and his call answered only by a distant echo. He hailed Bila Wobogo, who responded with a shower of poisoned arrows. Boori-Moodi managed to avoid them by lying flat on his mount, who was leaping about like a wild lion from the Sahel. Before Bila had time to recharge his bow, Boori's horse collided with his and sent them both—rider and mount—sprawling into the tangle of a thorn bush. Before Bila could rise, Boori's halberd was already poised on his chest. 'Boori!' he said. 'Kill me if you wish, but don't dishonor my body by leaving it above ground, a prey to vultures.' Boori did kill Bila, but he also buried him with his own hands. Since it is the blood of so noble a knight that courses in the veins and the arteries of his descendants, in your own arteries, O Karibu Sawali, how could you bear to, nay, how could you delight in dishonoring your dead brother? Remember that your ancestor restored honor to the Mossi Prince Bila Wobogo, an enemy who had robbed him!"

Karibu Sawali exhaled powerfully and said: "Thanks be to God who has placed in my path wise counselors—counselors who know how to prevent me from following the satanic promptings of my heart. O Imam

Suleyman! My brother shall continue to sleep peacefully in his grave. Let my horse be saddled. I will go and see Wangrin. I will ask him to let this matter rest. If need be, I'll even go as far as Yaguwahi and I'll speak to the Commandant. I might even push as far as Gudugaua and see the *goforner.*"

Accordingly, Karibu made his way to the encampment, followed by an imposing crowd. There he had a talk with Wangrin, and pointed out to him just how damaging the operation would be to his reputation in so traditional an environment.

Wangrin raised his arms to heaven and said to Karibu: "I am infinitely happier this way, for now I'll be better able to plead your cause. As a matter of fact, it is as well for you to know that the turban of Witu and Guban is not yet safely poised on your head. One must always reckon with the white-Whites, who are curiously determined to make us vomit our ancient customs at all costs and to ram their own down our throats instead. As you know, they are so partial to those who have been through their own schools and armies that I wouldn't be a bit surprised if they decided to place Loli in charge of this province instead of you. One must remember that Loli served in the army during the Great War, and there he holds a valuable trump card. With their positive mania for preferring the straight line in all things they may well want to replace Brildji with Loli, just in the way that in their country Louis XIV succeeded his father Louis XIII. We'll have to put in some good groundwork so as to avoid disagreeable surprises."

Wangrin had killed not just two, but several birds with one stone. He had exonerated himself from the macabre task of exhuming Brildji's body, and with what financial advantage! At the same time he had managed to hold on to the ten kilos of gold—a reward for that same undertaking! Besides, having sown the seed of doubt in Karibu's mind, he could now be certain that the latter would banish all thoughts from his mind except that of securing the turban of Witu and Guban, which he thought he was in danger of losing.

At last, having appealed in public to Brildji's family to follow Karibu Sawali's counsel and to undertake no action without his knowledge, Wangrin could at last take his leave.

"It is in your interest," he said to Loli, "to be on friendly terms with your father Karibu, rather than to set yourself against him. Anyway, I'd like to discuss with you once and for all the sort of relationship I think you ought to have in future with Karibu Sawali."

Wangrin and Loli detached themselves for a moment from the group of people who were lingering under the shelter with Karibu Sawali.

Once they were alone, Wangrin looked Loli straight in the eyes and

said: "My dear boy, have I quite convinced you that I have more than
one string to my bow and far more ruses in my brain than an old hare?"

"You have," conceded Loli. . . .

"Well, Loli, listen to me, then. I want to speak to you as your father's
old friend. Yes, your father once took me on one side and said, 'Wangrin,
a terrible worry is gnawing at me.' 'What can be worrying you, Brildji?'
I asked. 'I suspect Romo of having already set in motion some machinations,' he went on to say, 'to prevent my son from replacing me as chief
of this province. Tradition prescribes, I know, that my younger brother
be my sole successor and heir, yet this custom goes against Muslim law
on the one hand, and against the law according to which the French
govern us, on the other. Mercifully Romo has been swept out of this area
as if he were no more than a dead leaf. To me your arrival was a good
omen, and I'd like us to become truly devoted friends, but without making a display of our feelings—rather like people who are planning a raid
together. If I were to die while you're still alive,' your father went on to
say, 'I trust you will do your best to help my son receive the turban of
Witu and Guban.'

"Do you remember, Loli," insisted Wangrin, "during the celebration
for the latest *Kattos Suliye*[9] your father took your hand and placing it
within mine said: 'Wangrin, this is my first born. I entrust him to your
care. . . .'"

As a matter of fact, this moving little scene had actually taken place
at the time of the last French national day. Wangrin, who was good at
turning anything in the world to his own advantage, had suddenly remembered it and had decided to exploit it to create dissent between Loli
and Karibu Sawah and elicit yet greater rewards from the existing situation.

"I do indeed recollect everything you have just mentioned, Pa
Wangrin!" said Loli. "I am your son, your protégé, and your ward. I will
be docile and obedient. I will follow unswervingly the path you trace for
me. I will stop whenever you order me to do so. I am sure that under
your guidance I will reach the village of my dream, avoiding the barren
climbs, slippery slopes, and yawning chasms that might otherwise bar
my way. Led by you, Pa Wangrin, I will ride over ruin and disaster."

"Well, my boy, if this is how you feel, let's speak even more openly.
You are a prince. You possess a fortune, that is to say, the most effective
means of making yours the object of your most whimsical desires. Now,
if with that immense fortune at your disposal, with your record as former
tirailleur, one who enrolled voluntarily in the army and moreover for
four years fought the 'pointed helmets,'[10] those fearsome enemies and
former conquerors of the French, if—I repeat—with so many trump cards,

and buttressed by my support which is no mean asset, you allowed the glorious and most majestic turban of Witu and Guban to be snatched from your grasp, you'd be the meanest, puniest little squirt among all of Fulbe princes. Forgive me, then, if I don't mince my words. If that were to come true, the seed that you were might as well have been ejected and wasted in the flux of menstrual blood. That way your mother would have got rid of you discreetly and would have washed away all traces ritualistically, according to custom."

His pride stung (Fulbe people are naturally inclined to overestimate their own importance somewhat), Loli replied:

"If I am to beat stars down from the heavens in order to inherit the turban of Witu and Guban, I am fully prepared to reward most handsomely the stick that causes them to fall!"

"Calm your youthful ardor, my son. Stop bragging. Apprentice yourself to this old chameleon; my steps will be cautious. I shall change hue according to the environment, I shall make use of my very long tongue, but my head will remain inexorably pointed in the direction of my preestablished goal, which is your installation as head of this province."

"How much money do you need, Pa Wangrin, to pull the necessary strings, so that this whole affair may run as smoothly and as pleasantly as milk flowing from a mother's breast straight into her baby's throat?"

"I need a down payment equivalent to the price of fifteen hundred bulls worth three hundred francs each, that is four hundred and fifty thousand francs. Let's say five hundred thousand to make it a round figure. That will enable me to pay the numerous bribes I'll have to deal out to corrupt houseboys, cooks, office cleaners, typists, filing clerks, etc., etc. They alone can slip the carbon paper used for the typing of confidential letters into my hands."

"What is 'carbon paper'?"

"It is paper made out of a magic coloring substance, usually black. This paper is placed between two white sheets and it vomits onto the sheet beneath everything written by hand, or typed, on the sheet above. Besides, this wondrous paper retains all the words it has already vomited. That is its magic quality. All I will have to do is to turn this paper back to front and holding it against the light, read the secrets engraved on it. With that information at my disposal, it won't be difficult to use my knowledge in the pursuance of your interest."

"Five hundred thousand francs is fine with me," declared Loli, in the knowledge that to him such a sum was a mere drop in the ocean.

"You will pay me either with powder, or with rings made out of that noble metal called 'yellow man,' for it knows how to prise open all doors easily, smoothly, and noiselessly."

Loli promised Wangrin that he would dispatch the gold discreetly to Yaguwahi through his dumb Mumal, one of the oldest and most respected among Brildji's domestic slaves. To him had been entrusted the care of the treasury, and accordingly he also bore the name of *Biibaafe*, which means "keys."

Wangrin made his adieus and returned to Yaguwahi after five days' absence. Nor did he forget, on his way home, to assure Karibu once again of his friendship and support.

14   A Cumbersome Turban

Wangrin timed his arrival in Yaguwahi for the late afternoon, after working hours. That would enable him to go straight to the Commandant's residence. There, his chief would be in a more agreeable frame of mind and prepared to listen to Wangrin's report without the irritation caused by continuous interruptions.

As he rode into town, the setting sun cast a golden glow on every living creature. Every compound resounded with the bleating, lowing, braying, and whinnying of all domestic animals, large and small, each one calling for their young, their nourishment, their drink. At intervals, the sound of the pestles slowing down as they finished their work in the mortars mingled with the voices of men, women, and children who were laughing, exclaiming, and chatting with animation. It was as if each voice wanted to be heard for the last time before being smothered by darkness, by the silence that succeeds nightfall.

The branches of the *balanzas*[1] and of the spreading cotton trees were heavy with white egrets who looked like large, stylized pearls set in the pale-green luxuriance of the foliage.

But always last to perch were King Bata Griti's old vultures. They had been used to feeding from the bodies of men executed for some misdeed. Now they had to hunt for carrion themselves. After a great deal of hovering and circling, they would land at random on some terrace, stretching their scrawny necks and bald skulls, and shoot voracious looks below in the hope of spotting the odd piece of rotting flesh or, with any luck, the body of one of the smaller denizens of the farm discarded on a heap of rubbish.

As Wangrin was approaching the area where meat was usually roasted—not far from the slaughterhouse—he saw a cloud of vultures perching on the roof of the butcher's shelter. As he approached, the birds of prey scattered with a heavy flapping of wings and alighted on the large mahogany trees that surrounded the official residence.

This, Wangrin took as a warning. In spite of his immense courage, Wangrin, like most other Africans of his time, firmly believed that one could foretell the future on the basis of certain significant incidents. His mind did not admit of chance or fortuitous happenings. Too bad for those who refused to listen to the warnings of those supernatural forces which govern our universe and sometimes speak to us, however inaudibly. . . .

He blocked his ears with his little fingers, and with his thumbs he stopped his nostrils. The palms of his hands he turned upwards and his remaining six fingers he pressed against the sides of his neck. He closed his mouth with a strong pursing of the lips. He waited in that position for a brief spell, then spat three times on the ground. Afterwards he unblocked his four orifices and listened keenly. He heard a voice say: "Hand over your guinea-fowl. Don't be afraid, nothing terrible is going to happen to you."

Wangrin came to the conclusion that it was opportune to sacrifice a guinea-fowl before making his report. He dispatched at once his faithful servant, ordering him to catch one of the finest guinea-fowls out of his private poultry pen. The bird was to be given to the poor. He waited on the spot for the sacrifice to be performed.

His groom went as fast as his horse could carry him and was back a few moments later. Safe now in the knowledge that he had insured himself against any nasty tricks or disastrous denunciations, Wangrin presented himself before Commandant Gordane.

"Good evening, Sir."

"Good evening, Wangrin."

"Good evening, Rammaye Bira."

"Good evening, Wangrin. Similla."

After the exchange of greetings that must precede all conversation between visitors and visited, Wangrin embarked at once on his report.

"Sir, although I have only just returned from my mission, I thought it was proper to come straight to you and give you a report on the events of the last few days."

"Rammaye! Run to the kitchen and see that little wizened old Noga doesn't prepare yet another *ratatouille* for my dinner."

Rammaye understood that her husband wanted to be left alone with his interpreter. She withdrew, eyeing Wangrin in a way that would be difficult to define. But Wangrin smiled back as cheekily as ever. As soon as she had left them he turned to the Commandant:

"Sir, Brildji's family and the entire population of Witu and Guban wish to express their gratitude to you, in fact both to you and to France, 'motherland to all of us.'

"Unfortunately, since Brildji's death an uneasy and oppressive feeling has spread through the area. Contrary to appearances, no real harmony reigned between Brildji and Karibu Sawali, who were brothers only through their father. It so happens that among Fulbe people this relationship entails a duty of mutual aid, but not necessarily a bond of brotherly affection. They say that blood half brothers are often rivals to the death. A few well-known proverbs illustrate the fact far better than any elaborate explanation. These two, for example. The first says: 'The teeth of your blood half brother may well appear to be white, but don't forget that when he is dealing with you they are ever wedged in bloodshot gums.'[2] And the second: 'It may well be that your blood half brother does not wish you to be covered in shame, for some of it might reflect on him; your death, however, is unlikely to displease him, for it enables him to take your place.'

"Great tension existed between Brildji and Karibu. To find out exactly how matters stood, I took the liberty to suggest to Karibu that he demand Brildji's exhumation,[3] knowing that the latter had expressed a wish to be buried incognito so as to deprive his brother of the pleasure of contemplating his corpse. . . . "

"You actually dared to suggest that, Wangrin? . . . You fool, you idiot!" cried Gordane.

"I beg your pardon, Sir, I am no fool, and even less an idiot. I knew only too well that nothing in the whole world could persuade the dignitaries of Witu and Guban to accept such a sacrilegious undertaking. But Karibu's acceptance, or refusal, would establish the degree of rancor he felt for his brother and consequently for his sons, of whom Loli is the eldest. Karibu did in fact go along with my suggestion, and only Imam Suleyman's intervention could make him see reason. So now we know exactly where we stand politically. Karibu had agreed to smear his brother's honor posthumously, when the worst a blood half brother can do is to wish his brother's death, but without tarnishing his honor, according to the Fulbe adage I have just quoted. This means that Karibu is capable of setting the whole province to fire and sword just to efface any lingering trace of Brildji's tenure. There will be a Fulbe civil war, which may go on and on, causing numerous deaths and a considerable waste of money. The Yaguwahi district circle will be shaken by deep political unrest; secret investigating agents as well as administrative inspectors will descend on us in rapid succession. These will poke their inquisitive noses where their duty directs them, and perhaps also where they ought not to be.

"I myself as your interpreter, your wife Rammaye Bira, and your cook were all great friends of Brildji's. He had regaled us lavishly, according to custom. If a tragedy were to occur, it is conceivable that Karibu, with the help of deft accomplices, might get us embroiled in a situation perhaps not difficult—but rather painful—to explain.

"I would suggest, Sir, that you wait for the period of mourning to come to an end and then send Karibu Sawali and Loli to Gudugaua where the governor, with the help of his Political Bureau, will settle the question of Brildji's succession and proceed to appoint the next head of that province. Coming from Gudugaua, the appointment will carry so much weight that no one will dare to speak out against it, since the weight of decision is felt in direct proportion to the height from which it falls. . . .

"Believe me, Sir, the phrase 'the governor has accordingly decided . . .' will represent the ultimate verdict against which no appeal is possible. It would be really sad if only a few months before the end of your stay you were to be beset by worries that might result in a reprimand or in delaying the promotion that you have so truly merited. In the name of the friendship that ties me to Rammaye Bira and her family and the loyalty that I owe you, Sir, I entreat you to follow my advice, which derives from my profound knowledge of the Fulbe mentality and of the psychological attitudes of the peoples of Yaguwahi."

Gordane stretched his arms forward lazily. With his left hand, he grabbed a tall glass, and with the right a bottle of *labissanti*[4] which he poured generously, adding a little water. Then he went to sit on his large folding chair and leaned back. From this recumbent position, he raised his right hand, almost as if he intended to drink to his interpreter's health.

He looked straight at Wangrin, let out a soft moan . . . then downed the contents of his glass. When he had drained the frail object, he threw it violently against a wall, where it shattered into a thousand pieces.

Wangrin couldn't understand what sort of feeling might have prompted Gordane to behave in such a disquieting manner. Anyway, this was no time to give up or be intimidated. He waited for the liqueur to have effect and plunge Gordane into that ephemeral feeling of well-being, that illusory feeling of satisfaction with one's own existence which alcohol and drugs are wont to infuse in those who take them.

Sure enough, Gordane's eyes soon began to glitter. One could see that they were brimful with tears. He began to stroke his chin and cheeks mechanically, caressing softly his moustache the while. He yawned several times, drew himself up on his chair and said:

"I have no intention of forfeiting my reward for all I've done in this country just because of a stupid business that has nothing to do with me whatsoever, a quarrel between loonies. . . . I am going to think it over. Night brings counsel. Tomorrow I am bound to wake up feeling more alert and serene. In any case let me assure you of this—I will stand by you. If necessary, you have my permission to accept the odd bribe—we know that all interpreters do—and sometimes it does serve the purpose of reassuring the donors. In turn, this reassurance helps our administrative policy. Nevertheless, be prudent and use restraint.

"Here, Wangrin. Take this bottle of syrup. You can serve it to the marabouts when they come to your house to welcome you back." And he handed him a bottle.

Wangrin disguised under a wide grin the heavy sigh which lifted the pressure off his chest and dispelled the anxiety that Gordane's enigmatic behavior had caused him to feel.

Having taken the bottle, as well as his leave, Wangrin returned to his residence, which stood eight hundred meters east of the Commandant's residence. He found it already full of griots, musicians, beggars of both sexes, petitioners and defendants engaged in lawsuits, courtiers, representatives of warrant chiefs, etc. They had all learned from hearsay that the "big cheese" was back; everyone was trying to be pleasant to him, hoping to avoid his wrath, to gain favor with him or simply to ingratiate themselves. It is a fact that everyone who could claim that "the great interpreter of the Senior Commandant was his friend" had attained something equivalent to an aristocratic title and was able therefore to smooth many a rough edge in the day-to-day life of colonial times.

Wangrin nodded briefly to the large assembly. A few minutes later, pleading the exhaustion caused by his travels as an excuse, he dismissed his visitors who on the contrary were all extremely eager to stay on.

The next day, Wangrin went about discreetly distributing gifts, especially to the blind beggars (many of whom were already informers in his pay), then to the marabouts. The elderly and the poor were also remembered as usual.

15   Where Each Gets His Due

Meanwhile, in their territory, Karibu and Loli led lives similar to those of the snake and the snake hunter.[1] Slowly, a month went by. No unusual event came to interfere with the normal run of things, either in the province or in the district.

Commandant Gordane, having conducted a small inquiry of his own alongside the information received from his interpreter, discovered that Brildji's succession wouldn't in fact be as easy to settle as the customary successions. Consequently he decided to wash his hands of the whole affair, lest any rash move on his part earn him a sound rapping on the knuckles.

He convened Karibu, Loli, and Diofo and sent them off to Gudugaua. Wangrin was to accompany them there and deliver a detailed and confidential report to the governor.

Once in Gudugaua, Wangrin called unaccompanied on the governor's chief of cabinet. He handed over Gordane's report and gave him a brief, but comprehensive sketch of the situation that obtained in the Witu and Guban province.

The governor read the report and jotted down:

"Political Bureau—study and discuss with me next week."

It fell to Monsieur Reardris, Chief Colonial Administrator and Director of Political Affairs in the area in question, to study the report. He interrogated Karibu, Loli, and Diofo and consulted all the African dignitaries whose reputation rested mainly on their knowledge of things traditional.

According to Fulbe custom in Witu land, Karibu was to inherit all of Brildji's possessions. He was to marry, however, all the widows of the deceased and adopt his brother's children. This custom did violence to the sensibilities of the Chief Administrator Reardris. He found it bizarre, as well as opposed to the dictates of ordinary common sense.

Wangrin realized that Reardris's attitude would provide ample scope for helping Loli succeed his father. Yet, if Karibu were to come out of this affair totally empty-handed, he might react. Romo, former interpreter at Yaguwahi and Wangrin's sworn enemy, had now been appointed to the Gudugaua District. He of all people was bound to back Karibu. Wangrin might well end up choking on a throatful of lethal fishbones.

Whenever he wasn't needed in the Political Bureau, Wangrin combed Gudugaua, seeking advice, sounding public opinion, and trying to evaluate how much weight each competitor carried. Nearly all the warrant chiefs ruling at the time inclined toward the theory that a son must succeed his father. But since in Bana Griti's kingdom there were chieftaincy titles that traditionally devolved on the brother of the deceased, Karibu too, had strenuous supporters. Several of these were administrative clerks or former non-commissioned officers.

The affair dragged on three interminable months.

One fine day, Wangrin resolved to tackle Reardris. "Sir," he said. "I have become increasingly aware that Brildji's succession is likely to trigger off a mood that in the future might endanger the peace of any province where a chief dies leaving a brother and a son as his successors. It doesn't seem logical that Loli, Brildji's eldest son, should be deprived of both title and inheritance. Loli enlisted as a volunteer, and fought bravely for four years against the Germans. He is a non-commissioned officer of great merit. He has shed his blood for France. France, then, should protect him from a custom which the Muslim religion has rendered obsolete in any case. Both Karibu and Loli are practicing Muslims; therefore it would not be unfair to treat their case according to laws set by the faith they have embraced of their own free choice.

"Yet it would be very bad policy to leave out Karibu altogether. He might escape to the Gold Coast with a large number of followers. In any case, if he is ousted, he is bound to provoke a great deal of opposition; peace within the district would be seriously compromised.

"Bearing all these considerations in mind, I went to consult the venerable Baliba Woliha, who is Chief Counselor for Muslim Affairs to King Romobana. Now he has made a suggestion which—in my opinion—represents an excellent solution to the impasse we have reached.[2] Baliba Woliha recommends that the chieftaincy title be passed on to Karibu while Brildji's fortune is made over to Loli and his brothers. As to Brildji's widows, they should be allowed to marry whomever they wish."

This suggestion seemed most felicitous to Reardris. He decided to submit it to the governor for approval. Meanwhile Wangrin was given the task of persuading the two protagonists, so that the affair might at last reach a happy conclusion.

Off went Wangrin to see Karibu.

"Karibu," he said, "I have come to tell you that I suspect that something extremely serious might be in the offing. Wanorgo Dobuli, Reardris's secretary and interpreter, has told me confidentially that the governor likes things such as military service and a good knowledge of the French tongue to be taken into account whenever a chieftaincy title is in dispute. France wants *her own men* to rule the countries that make up her empire. Now, that suggests that the title might go to Loli, who not only speaks French but did also four years of voluntary war service in the army."

"What shall we do, Wangrin?" asked Karibu. "I trust you! Only you can help me. Suggest something. I am so worried. Act in my best interest. I am prepared to place once again at your disposal the same amount of gold as before. Give lavishly, speak to marabouts, griots, and courtesans who hold sway with powerful people. But act swiftly, Wangrin, whatever you do!"

Wangrin invited seven marabouts and introduced them to Karibu. During a whole week these marabouts engaged in special prayers—for their reward would be handsome!

Meanwhile Reardris had gone on tour for a couple of weeks. This gave Wangrin plenty of time to work on Loli. Accordingly, he went off to see him. He drew him aside and began:

"I have just heard that the governor is not too keen on having inexperienced young men hold important chieftaincy titles. He prefers them to assist with their collaboration for a goodly long while. However much man may voice his wishes, omnipotent Allah's prescripts cannot, alas, be altered! Reardris is to be away for a fortnight. On his return, the matter will be settled once and for all."

Two weeks passed. To Loli and his uncle Karibu they seemed an eternity. As for Wangrin, he made sure that Romo, always on the lookout, didn't discover his reason for being in Gudugaua.

On the day of Reardris's return, Wangrin went to call on him to find out when he was expected to summon Loli and his uncle, who were waiting to be told what solution had been devised for them. Reardris made an appointment for the Friday morning.

Then Wangrin went to Loli and said:

"The appointment is for next Friday. I can let you know the governor's decision in advance: although you won't be appointed head of the province immediately, you will inherit your father's fortune in its entirety. Now, with those riches in your possession, within a few years you will be able to eclipse your uncle provided you know how and to whom to give. Your uncle will be crowned with an indigent turban. As a matter of fact with what he now possesses he won't be able to meet the costs of succeeding your father. Do not refuse the governor's decision. His goal is to prepare you all the better to take over command of the province when the time is ripe. It won't be long before that happens, I shall see to that. We have many effective means that we can bring to bear."

Having now predisposed Loli toward trading his father's fortune against the chieftaincy title, Wangrin set about preparing Karibu. This is what he told him:

"I have spoken to Commandant Reardris, who has let me know in confidence that the governor has finally reached a decision. For some unknown reason, the governor has changed his mind about installing Loli as political and physical successor to his father. When I say 'for some unknown reason,' I am of course quoting the foreigners, for we happen to know that the earnest and pious prayers that were offered on your behalf to Allah, our one and only God, for whom nothing is difficult or impossible, have shaped the governor's attitude and led him to alter his decision. To us, he is governor, but before God he has no more power than a louse hidden in the feathers of a hen.

"Commandant Reardris, then, has let me into the secret. You are to have the headship of the province, but not Brildji's fortune, which will be allotted in its entirety to his inheritors, but will be managed by Loli.

"Should you wish to enforce the application of the traditional law established by the red Fulbe of Thiala,[3] the governor will hold you to the dictates of the Muslim religion—which you have embraced of your own free will—unless you publicly abjure your faith, but that would place you in the worst possible position.

"On the other hand, let's reason out the whole thing. How did Brildji amass his fortune? Wasn't it through his powers as a chief? By assigning to you that same title, I get the impression that the governor is unwittingly placing the source of an immense fortune in your way. The relationship between Loli and yourself—with you inheriting the title and he, the fortune that proceeded from that title—will be that of a man who is given a milk cow vis-à-vis the man who gets only the liquid yielded by her udders. Moreover, you have nothing to fear, for Loli has chosen a very dangerous path. He has given himself over to alcohol like a man cursed by ill fortune, drinks day and night, and makes as many men and women as he can find around town drink as much as himself. And if he limited himself and his friends to imbibing *dolo*,[4] it would take him a good many years to squander his immense fortune. But he drinks only strong European liquor: absinthe, Pernod-Fils, rum, gin, berger anisette, and a raw mint distillation. Every week he orders from the Maison Perysac, which is one hundred and seventy miles away from Witu, one, two or three hundred cases of twelve bottles each.

"And have you heard, by the way, that he lavishes astronomical sums on women and griots daily? Do you know his latest folly? He has decorated every single tree in the native town of Kumba Diallo, his official mistress. Did you know that when this same Kumba went to Guban to have her hair plaited he sacrificed fifty bulls to mark the occasion?

"Burning up his fortune all over the place the way he does, he is heading for the kind of destitution that at some point or other will place him helplessly at your mercy. In view of this, I advise you in utmost earnest to accept the turban rather than the wealth."

Thus neatly prepared and feeling well-disposed, Loli and Karibu presented themselves at the Political Bureau where Reardris communicated to them with great ceremony the governor's decision, inspired by a desire to maintain peace and serenity among the population of the province.

Later, the two protagonists were received by the governor in person. He exhorted them to be disciplined in their behavior and to respect laws and human rights. Besides, he not only congratulated Wangrin, but also bestowed on him an official testimony of appreciation by pinning on his chest the silver medal of honor in recognition of his service.

In this way—Loli rich, Karibu "turbaned chief," and Wangrin displaying a fine medal on his chest—everyone returned to Yaguwahi, where they organized a celebration that went on for three whole days and nights. On that occasion Loli spent over six million francs—a good half of which went to swell Wangrin's existing assets.

16 The Dream of the Fulbe Shepherdess

ntil May 1921, everything proved favorable to Wangrin's multifarious enterprises. His success was so overwhelming that in his heart of hearts he began to believe that no infelicitous contingency could ever come to obfuscate the brilliance of his lucky star, or that any drought could ever dry the abundant spring that fed his profits—as easily begotten as they were illicit.

One day, at the beginning of that very same month of May 1921, just as Wangrin was about to lie down for his siesta, an old Fulbe shepherdess came to knock on his door. Wangrin let her in, muttering under his breath: "Couldn't this wretched old hag have let me finish my digestion? Now there won't be time to rest . . . and my meal is like a boulder pressing on my stomach! Anyway let's see what this elderly descendant of *Illo Yaladi*[1] has to tell. No Fulbe is ever without his genie. He who sees a Fulbe without seeing his double has seen nothing."

Wangrin invited the old shepherdess in and asked:

"How come you have braved the midday sun to come and speak to me, when you could easily have waited for a cooler hour?"

"I have come now, Wangrin, because I wanted to tell you at once about a dream I had early this morning, between the first call to prayer and sunrise. This is it. I saw a vast expanse of water billowing in a storm of towering waves. The storm appeared to be closing in all at once from several directions. From this tempestuous water an immense metal canoe was coming in to land. Out of the middle of this bizarre craft, through a gigantic chimney, rose a puff of black smoke, dense as a *tibaduule krum*— the cloud that announces storms and sudden showers.

"The metal canoe conquered the waves and pulled in to the shore.

Many white-Whites and a few Blacks dressed like white-Whites came ashore. One of the white-Whites was shouting his head off: 'Wangrin! Wangrin! Where are you?' At the same time, I noticed a large sandhill: you were bent double, and were hiding behind it, invisible to everybody, except to a black giant, who swooped down on the sandhill, dealing it heavy blows with a hoe. It eventually collapsed on top of him, but he managed to scramble out, although his hair, his mouth, and his clothes were choked with sand. He bit one of the fingers of his right hand up to the second knuckle, then he threw away his hoe and vanished out of sight. Meanwhile you started running at full speed, just like a hunting dog.

"I woke up dazed by that painful dream, and I was so haunted by it that I couldn't wait to come and speak to you about those phantoms. I left home at sunrise and it is now noon. I think you ought to have my dream interpreted before sundown. That's all I came to tell you. I am going now."

Without any further ado, the old shepherdess gathered the small calabash gourd she had left trailing on the ground. Slipping her feet in her sandals of tanned ox-skin which she had deposited near the door, she vanished as suddenly as she had appeared.

Somewhat taken aback, Wangrin missed his chance of stopping the old woman and asking her a few searching questions. By the time he had recovered himself, she was already out of reach.

Unable to resume his siesta, he sent at once for Mulaye Hamidu, a Moorish marabout who was especially renowned for his extensive knowledge of the occult. As soon as the marabout arrived Wangrin related to him the dream of the Fulbe shepherdess and asked him to interpret it.

Mulaye Hamidu had no need to consult his book of spells, whose contents he carried constantly in his head.

After a moment of reflection, he said:

"Wangrin, black smoke flaring out of a chimney symbolizes problems and obstacles on the horizon of your existence. From now on you will have to put up a hard fight to protect yourself from the many troubles that are going to rain down on you from all sides. A ferocious enemy, powerful, well armed, and absolutely adamant, will attempt to demolish the barrage of occult forces which up to now has supported and protected you. That is the meaning of the attack on the sandhill behind which you were squatting as the white-White who disembarked from the mysterious smoking canoe[2] called out to you. I advise you to mistrust all white-Whites who come into our territory as from next Saturday, for among them is the one who is prepared to get the better of you at any price. Nor would he worry one little bit if in the process you were to lose your life."

"Mulaye Hamidu," replied Wangrin, "would you be prepared to go to work on my behalf and protect me from my white-White, black-White, and black enemies, and if so, at what price?"

"Yes, Wangrin, I am. But as far as fixing a price for my intervention—I am afraid I can't do that. I don't sell prayers to the richest buyer or to the highest bidder. I only pray to Allah; I don't sell his name."

"Well then," rejoined Wangrin, "pray for me, and I'll find a way of rewarding you for your services."

"You must feed for a whole month seven indigent widows and seven orphans. You must also buy them sumptuous clothes. And you yourself must fast for seven days and during that time abstain totally from sexual intercourse."

Wangrin was no faithful devotee. Rather, he practiced a sort of opportunism that enabled him to embrace without scruples the religion of those whose assistance or silence he needed for his own ends. But he did it quite openly, so that his attitude was totally free of hypocrisy. In any case he followed the marabout's advice to the letter.

While Mulaye Hamidu was still busy praying, and Wangrin feeding his widows and orphans, one morning towards the end of May 1921 a large steamer from Marseille sailed into the port of Dakar. Aboard this steamer was a new assistant colonial administrator, who was just at that moment getting ready to disembark. As etiquette demanded, he was in full dress. On the cuffs of his white drill jacket he made proud display of several gold stripes set against a background of black. His peaked cap looked exactly like that of a general. He sported fine gold epaulets, and a slender sword with an elaborate hilt.

Paradoxically, his smiling face wore a look of vague sadness. In his right eye lodged a silver-rimmed monocle, which added a certain sternness to his expression.

He proceeded slowly down the gangway. An Administrator who was his equal in rank and had been detailed to officially welcome him was waiting for him on the pier. The new man introduced himself:

"Jean-Jacques, Count de Villermoz, Assistant Colonial Administrator, Grade One."

Upon which the man who was welcoming him extended his hand and intoned in turn: "Paul Louis Vincent Casse-Carreaux,[3] Assistant Administrator, same rank. How do you do?"

The two colleagues, surrounded by some friends in the same corps, exchanged a few conventional phrases, then made their way toward a cab that awaited them at the exit of the docks.

Count de Villermoz was taken to the "transit house."[4] This was a rather fine apartment, always ready for any colonial administrator who might chance to pass through Dakar.

On the very next day, Villermoz showed up at the G.G.'s[5] office. He was received by the chief of cabinet, and then, almost immediately after, by the G.G. himself.

He was to spend a week in Dakar before being posted. According to a ritual that had become *de rigueur* he was to pay several calls, in the following order:

—on the S.G. of the G.G. (the Secretary General of the General Government of West Africa);
—on the Representative of the Members of Parliament for Senegal;
—on the Governor of Senegal;
—on the Chief of Staff of the French West African Army;
—on the Inspectors of Administrative Affairs;
—on the Directors General of the various departments;
—on the Mayor of Dakar;
—on the President of the Chamber of Commerce and Industry;
—on the Bishop of Dakar; and lastly,
—on the Secretary of the Syndicate of Colonial Administrators in French West Africa

During his visit to the Personnel Department, Villermoz took advantage of the opportunity to find out in which area the interpreter Wangrin was currently employed. This he found out without difficulty, since all one needed to do to discover the whereabouts of any employee was to glance at the rolls compiled in alphabetical order and divided into cadres.

The Count bit his lower lip lightly—one of his old mannerisms. Was it an expression of pleasure, or spite? . . . Whatever the answer, he exerted himself so as to be appointed to the area where Wangrin had been working the last few years. Nothing stood in his way. It was a territory of fairly recent date, far from the sea, and still short of the many amenities which a European who lives in Africa is likely to find indispensable. To be given a post there was considered a sort of mild punishment. Only volunteers or civil servants under discipline in some way were sent to that area. It is only fair to say, however, that thanks to the administrative skill and the humane attitude of the first governor, assisted by an excellent secretary general, little by little the territory became a small paradise. Between them, those two men transformed the colony into a place where it was a joy to live. So much so that the inhabitants of that zone, and especially the griots of *Diorogurku*,[6] used to sing:

She is mysterious indeed
Our mother country.
Far from the sea
She is like a jewel
Hidden in the land.
She makes visitors from afar
Shed tears twice over:
The first time apprehensively,
The stranger weeps, when he is told:
"Go to that country!"
But he weeps inconsolable tears
When he is told: "Go away!
Leave that land where every man
Lives in his own field
And where every head of a family
Is revered as a king."
Our country is a hidden paradise;
One must see it to believe it.

Following the governor-general's decree, Count de Villermoz was placed at the disposal of the governor of that territory. He left Dakar and spent thirty-five days traveling to Gudugaua. He had been appointed Commandant to Danfa Murga.

Romo heard that the Count had arrived. Knowing that he had had a quarrel with Wangrin, he did his best to arrange a meeting with him. He told the Count what dirty tricks Wangrin had played on him as repayment for his generous hospitality in Yaguwahi and without any further preamble went on to say: "Alone, I'll never be able to avenge myself, but if you were to give me some support I could easily slip you a lot of information (on the quiet) about Wangrin's malpractices during his years in Yaguwahi. I already have proof in hand, and could provide even more if I were re-appointed there, or at least attached as interpreter to the inspector who once a year carries out an administrative inquiry in that district."

"Give me time to get acquainted with the area and with my colleagues," said the Count, "and then we will return to the subject. Let me warn you in any case that Wangrin is a hard nut to crack."

"Placed between the two of us, Sir, he will be like a nut in a nutcracker. We shall reduce him to smithereens."

Romo took his leave. Villermoz hadn't expected to find so easily an ally who actually wanted to help him destroy Wangrin. Nevertheless he felt that it was essential to find out first a little more about Romo and so he began a little inquiry of his own. All the information he gathered turned out to be excellent. He was even told that Romo had been a great scrapper during his years of service under Gouraud.

Meanwhile Wangrin had finished feeding and clothing the widows and orphans according to Mulaye Hamidu's prescriptions. Yet his mind had not been set at rest either by his offerings or by his self-denial. He had an uneasy feeling that something intangible was haunting him, but as soon as he tried to identify it or to define it, this indefinable shadow vanished from sight.

One morning he found among the weekly correspondence the official bulletin for the first half of July 1921. After looking through the mail, Wangrin glanced rapidly at the new appointments and postings. Suddenly, he spotted these few lines: "Jean-Jacques Count de Villermoz, Assistant Colonial Administrator, Grade One, recently placed at the disposal of the Governor of the Territory, has now been appointed Commandant to Danfa Murga, replacing Fernand Edouard Quatrebras[7] who is to be repatriated on sick leave."

This paragraph had the effect on Wangrin of a violent, albeit invisible, electric shock. He heard a ringing in his ears as though he had hit his head on an iron bar. He saw sparks all around him, as if a cloud of tiny, shimmering worms had just sprung up from under his feet. His eyes opened wide, his nerves contracted, and his blood rushed from his toes to his skull. He tried to react by stiffening his muscles. No good. The mysterious blow he had been dealt was not something one can either dodge or deaden in any way. It was one of those shocks that strike as unexpectedly as lightning itself, a blow both hard and noiseless, one that destroys ruthlessly, felling the victim and leaving him gasping for breath on the ground for hours, days—sometimes forever.

Wangrin collapsed as if he had been struck by an epileptic fit. The orderly rushed toward him and shouted for help: "Come quickly, O sons of my mother! Wangrin is shaking all over! Hurry up, he's dying!"

Gordane came out of his office. Seeing that his interpreter was seriously ill, he forbade anyone from touching him and sent post-haste for Captain Lelamentin, the army doctor.

The latter came running to the office. At first he leaned over Wangrin, who was stretched out on the floor and listened to his heartbeat.

"It is nothing serious," he said, getting up, "but it's hard to conjecture how it came about. I suppose his fainting fit was caused by some sort of physical shock or by an unexpected emotion."

Still senseless, Wangrin was carried to the dispensary and finally came round, thanks to Doctor Lelamentin's able ministrations.

His senses fully recovered, Wangrin went home and used the three days' rest the doctor had prescribed to round up without fuss Mulaye Hamidu and a few other marabouts for consultation. To these he promised all the rewards they might want in exchange for prayers. Then he turned to Mulaye Hamidu:

"My mortal enemy Count de Villermoz has returned from France. He now has a far more powerful job than in Diagaramba, where the whole terrible business began. Our case was heard in the white-White High Court at Dakar, and the Count turned out to be the loser. A shameful thing for him! If he hadn't been 'Count de Villermoz,' the affair would have cost him his career."

"Mulaye Hamidu!" continued Wangrin, "with the exception of Tierno Siddi of Diagaramba, you are the most veracious and the most powerful marabout I have ever met. I trust you absolutely. It was you, after all, who interpreted the old shepherdess's dream. . . . I am still extremely perturbed by that prophetic vision. Ever since I've heard of it, my mind has been unhinged. I see now that the white-White who called out to me in the dream can be no one but Villermoz. This is confirmed by the fact that he has had himself appointed to this territory so that our necks may be stuck in the opening of the same bubu,[8] as the Fulbe say. As to the lumpish fellow who attacked the dune that protected me, it can only be Romo Sibedi, that misshaped ruffian with limbs swollen by elephantiasis; his hideous hoe represents the slanderous rumors he will spread against me. A dream where Romo and Villermoz appear together can only mean that my two enemies are going to try to get me. But they will not . . . ! Your prayers will protect me, and God's reward for what you are doing will be even greater than mine."

The marabouts agreed to help him and when they returned home, they began to pray at once. Wangrin placed himself on the look-out . . . and Count de Villermoz traveled to his new post.

17 Pretty Much in the Lion's Jaws

anfa Murga could boast, among other things, of beautiful women—particularly those of Fulbe extraction—thoroughbred horses, a special breed of imposing racehorses with an exceptionally fine coat, and an abundance of livestock. In fact, that territory would have been a real paradise if it hadn't been plagued by the most ferocious of all breeds of lions—black lions with huge manes—"man eaters," as they were called. Unlike tawny lions who never set out to attack men or devour them unless provoked, black lions pursue them as far as and into their very homes.

Around Danfa Murga, black lions were so ferocious and aggressive that the administration had been forced to build shelters in the branches of the largest trees to ensure protection for travelers caught unaware by darkness, as villages in that zone were very widely spaced.

Count de Villermoz's first priority was to undertake an epic campaign which he christened the "delionization of Danfa Murga." Accordingly, he sent a detailed report to the governor, requesting that his patrol[1] units be reinforced with drafts consisting exclusively of *bons-tir*,[2] the appellation most commonly used for indigenous veterans renowned for their marksmanship.

Governor Bernard Linguet was most appreciative of Count de Villermoz's initiative. He commanded that the best *bons-tir* in the whole territory be sent off at once to Danfa Murga. He also arranged that Sourgens, a warrant officer in the colonial infantry, be placed on the Special Duties List and posted to Danfa Murga as Chief of the Military Bureau, which would have the job of administering the special delionization task force.

Who, then, was this Sourgens?

He was the best shot in the Sudan, the Ivory Coast, and Upper Volta, and had won five of the most coveted prizes for marksmanship in French West Africa.

For him, there were no hobbies or forms of amusement more enticing than riding and shooting. It was rumored that he owned more guns than clothes and that he felt greater affection for his weapons than for his *musso*.

As soon as he was installed in his new capacity, Sourgens was instructed to select twenty-five *bons-tir* to reinforce the existing squad in Danfa Murga. He consulted the files of all the patrolmen serving the district and chose twenty-five men whom he regaled with the epithet of "bottleneck shooters"; nothing could have expressed more adequately the consummate quality of their skill.

Sourgens and his squad set off for Danfa Murga. The day of their arrival sounded the death knell for the black lions. Within three months, the feline colony was inexorably decimated. The bag consisted of a hundred and ten lion skins, one hundred panthers, two hundred hyenas, and ten boa constrictors. Besides, twenty lion cubs were captured and sent to various zoological gardens in Europe, West Africa, Morocco, and Algeria. Count de Villermoz alone had killed eight lions, and Sourgens twenty-three! This cleansing operation did much to enhance the reputation of Count de Villermoz and his assistant.

Meanwhile life continued much the same as usual in Yaguwahi, Gudugaua, and Danfa Murga.

Although Wangrin had somewhat recovered his spirits, he continued to wonder whether the count's silence did not resemble that of a loaded gun. . . . As we shall see later, his apprehension was quite justified.

Unfortunately Gordane, who had become Wangrin's greatest supporter, was nearing the end of his colonial assignment. Accordingly, he left Yaguwahi and was replaced by colonial administrator Hubert Leon Jacques, Count du Pont de la Roche.

On taking up his appointment, the latter used Wangrin as his sole interpreter for no more than a week: just time enough to find his way about his new station. Afterwards, contrary to all colonial administrators' common practice, he employed indiscriminately Metiogo Makara, assistant interpreter, Suyufi Kadjite, chief clerk, and Wangrin—in that order.

"Water can change only through the influence of a foreign element," thought Wangrin. And he was right: the silence he so dreaded was loaded, but the explosion had been delayed until Gordane's departure, his presence being the safety catch that prevented a shot from being fired.

The colonial administrator, Count du Pont de la Roche, had arrived in the colony at the same time as an old colleague, Georges Sauvage, who in the event was appointed in Gudugaua to the post of Director of Personnel.

As they were both contemporaries of Count de Villermoz in the Colonial Administration, they were well aware of the amount of distress the latter had had to endure as a result of Wangrin's machinations.

The Director of Personnel was quite free to indulge his whims in reshuffling indigenous civil servants, subject of course to the exigencies of the service. So it came to pass that two months after his arrival in Yaguwahi, Count du Pont de la Roche received a confidential letter from his friend the Director of Personnel, inquiring whether he might have any objection to having Romo Sibedi re-appointed in Yaguwahi in place of Wangrin, who was due for a transfer.

Count de Villermoz wrote personally to endorse the request. As was to be expected, du Pont de la Roche reacted favorably to the proposal.[3]

Wangrin, who had many informers in the personnel department, heard that a comprehensive reshuffle of interpreters was about to take place and that he himself would not be spared. He wasn't surprised by the news. It was far better for him to leave Yaguwahi than to have to endure a treatment which any Commandant's interpreter could only regard as both a lack of trust and a mark of contempt. Just like a monogamous husband, a truly respectable Commandant could have one interpreter only. Wangrin, then, was ready to be transferred; in fact he was almost impatient for the change.

A week later, as he was sitting musing on his bench, fairly close to the Commandant's door, he heard a shout of: "Orderly!"

"Presensa, Oga Commanda!"

"Ask Wangrin to come in."

"Wangrin! Oga Commanda I sey mek you enta."

Wangrin, according to time-honored custom, ran towards the office. At the door he stopped and said: "Here I am, Sir."

"Come in," said du Pont de la Roche in a commanding tone.

Wangrin stepped inside. The Commandant handed him an official telegram, the usual yellow piece of paper. Wangrin took it and read the following message:

From Governor to Commandant of Yaguwahi. By decision of to-day's date official interpreter Romo Sibedi transferred Yaguwahi and official interpreter Wangrin transferred Danfa Murga Stop Send Wangrin immediately to new station via Ayka.
Bernard Linguet

The shock that had floored poor Wangrin when he discovered that Count de Villermoz was appointed to a post within his same territory seemed now a gentle caress compared to the blow administered by this latest piece of news, which amounted to a death sentence. Nor was there any hope of a reprieve, not even from heaven above. Oddly enough, and for no reason that Wangrin could ever explain, this new catastrophe left him as unmoved as if it had hit someone other than himself. As a matter of fact, he managed to muster up enough strength to say with an aplomb that du Pont de la Roche found totally disconcerting:

"Well! It looks as if at last I am going to have a chance of renewing my acquaintance with my dear old friend Jean-Jacques Count de Villermoz! With any luck, we'll be able to talk once more about those fine bulls who laid gold coins!"

Count du Pont de la Roche struck the table with his fist:

"You old son of a bitch!" he shouted. "You dare to speak to me that way once again, and you'll spend whatever is left of your nasty life in jail. Bugger off! If you spend the night in Yaguwahi I'll have you dismissed for disobedience and insubordination! . . . Sergeant!"

"Presensa, Oga Commanda!"

"If Wangrin hasn't left town by 4 P.M., you will arrest him, take him to jail and leave him there until further orders."

Wangrin left the office and went to call on the Reverend Father Superior of Meba Catholic Mission. He told him that Count du Pont de la Roche intended to arrest him arbitrarily. Then he went home and waited calmly for things to happen.

When the sergeant turned up at 4 P.M., Wangrin not only was still there, but he also refused to budge in spite of the command, initially, and later the pleading, of the wretched non-commissioned officer. In the end the sergeant had no alternative but to obey orders. He arrested Wangrin and led him to the Yaguwahi jail.

As soon as he was consigned to the cells, Wangrin sent a message to the Reverend Father Superior of Meba Catholic Mission, letting him know that he had actually been taken to jail, so that the fears he had expressed earlier that day had proved totally justified.

The Reverend Father Superior left home at once to plead Wangrin's cause with the Commandant, but discovered that the latter was going to be out of town for the rest of the day. Du Pont de la Roche returned late that night and the sergeant who had waited up informed him of the events of the day and of the Reverend Father Superior's visit.

The Commandant was extremely vexed. He was well aware that his decision had been arbitrary and consequently he feared the priest's testimony. He ordered that Wangrin be set free without delay. Wangrin, however, refused to be released. He had taken the precaution of bringing along a revolver and now he threatened to blow out the brains of anyone who attempted to winkle him out of his cell before morning.

The next day, the reverend Father Superior made another call on the Commandant, who readily confessed that his idiot of a sergeant had applied to the letter an order he had given in a moment of anger. He was deeply sorry about the whole thing and entreated the reverend to calm down the outraged Wangrin.

Accordingly, the priest went off to the town jail and asked Wangrin to drop the matter. Wangrin consented, but felt bound to add: "I promise not to turn this story to my advantage only so long as it does not become indispensable for me to do so in order to survive." Then he began his journey to Danfa Murga by way of Ayka just as he had been ordered to do. This itinerary had been prescribed so as to prevent him from passing through Gudugaua and to deprive him of the chance to appeal to the few well-disposed, kindly souls he knew in the capital.

As soon as he got to Ayka—halfway between Gudugaua and Danfa Murga—Wangrin stopped at the local administrative encampment and settled his family in. The following morning he jumped on his bicycle and charged toward Gudugaua, but before leaving he gave his senior wife the following instructions:

"If I am not back by tomorrow evening, go to the Commandant and say: 'Last night my husband went off on a hunting expedition. He knows that we are due to continue our trip to Danfa Murga yet he hasn't come back. I am terribly afraid that he might have met with an accident!'"

Wangrin pedaled like an escaped convict, reaching Gudugaua that same afternoon, before closing time. He went straight to Robert Rando, Inspector of Administrative Affairs, who was known for his integrity and courage, and deposited in his hands a detailed report on the Diagaramba cattle affair. He also protested against his transfer to Danfa Murga, where he would be at the mercy of Count de Villermoz, his sworn enemy.

Later he deposited a copy of the same report at the office of the Gudugaua Public Prosecutor, indicating that his transfer was the result of machinations set in motion by Count de Villermoz and his two friends, du Pont de la Roche and Georges Sauvage, Commandant at Yaguwahi and Director of Personnel for the whole territory respectively.

André Cols, Public Prosecutor, warned Wangrin against the danger of leveling formal accusations at three administrators all at once. "But I have proof, Sir," replied Wangrin.

Robert Rando, Inspector of Administrative Affairs, went to the governor's office and placed before the governor Wangrin's report. Having read it, the governor sent for Georges Sauvage, Colonial Administrator and Director of Personnel, and asked him to explain the reasons for Wangrin's transfer to Danfa Murga. No doubt the reasons offered by the latter did not meet with the governor's approval, for Wangrin's family and luggage were ordered out of Ayka and brought to Gudugaua.

Several days went by.

At Ayka, the Commandant had organized a hunt, not in search of game, but rather of Wangrin, who was thought to be lost somewhere in the bush. How amazed must he have been, then, to receive a telegram from the governor ordering him to send Wangrin's family and luggage to Gudugaua. However, he complied at once.

Wangrin was kept at Gudugaua for three weeks at least, awaiting orders. During that time, he had more or less nothing to do.

Meanwhile, du Pont de la Roche and Villermoz were summoned to Gudugaua. What happened during their interview with the governor is not known, for no word of the interview ever leaked out. Off they went again, back to their stations. But a few days later, a new decision, this time from the governor himself, rescinded the previous decision ordering Romo to Yaguwahi and Wangrin to Danfa Murga. Instead, Romo was sent to Danfa Murga and Wangrin was appointed to the District of Gudugaua.

Thus, once again, Wangrin's skill and audacity had saved him from a really serious threat. Yet the outcome was not a happy one. In Gudugaua, Wangrin felt like a caged lion. "I must find a way out of this dungeon," he would say to his friends.

Unfortunately, soon after these events, Governor Linguet, Inspector Rando, and Public Prosecutor Cols left on prolonged leave of absence.

Count de Villermoz was appointed Commandant at Gudugaua and Wangrin could not help but be once again under his authority. It was extremely difficult, of course, for an African civil servant—even for a European—to hold out against colonial administrators. It was with good reason that they were called "gods of the bush," being the most powerful among all white-Whites in the colony and holding as they did unimaginable rights over the Africans.

Wangrin asked for a transfer, using his report as a strong reminder and invoking the rescission of the first decision, which had placed him under Count de Villermoz's order. But Georges Sauvage lent a deaf ear and didn't follow up Wangrin's application.

Came the day when Count de Villermoz arrived in Gudugaua and assumed command of his new post. Wangrin wished to avoid at all costs an encounter with his new chief and long-standing enemy. He went to see a healer. For one franc, he bought a little sachet of powder which would simulate the effects of an attack of enteritis, and another which had the advantage of causing a temporary lachrymation and disfiguring of the face.

Wangrin swallowed his enteritis powder and waited for results. It worked without delay. He went off to the dispensary, taking along a stool sample to Dr. Victor Diabade. Just before walking into the consulting room, he sniffed a pinch of "disfiguring powder."[4] His face ravaged and his eyes brimming with tears, Wangrin walked in and said to the head physician:

"Sir, I have had a pain in my bowels for the last five days. I am suffering from gripes and diarrhea. I've brought you a stool sample. Here it is. My belly feels as if it were on fire. . . . I am in terrible pain. . . . "

Dr. Diabade was the only European medical officer in a dispensary that dealt with between one hundred and one hundred and fifty patients a day. He cast a brief glance at Wangrin's offering, then:

"With this sort of enteritis, you can call yourself lucky that you could stand up at all and get this far from your house on foot," he said very naturally.

"I also have a headache, and a burning sensation in my eyes and my nose," added Wangrin.

Dr. Diabade examined him. "You must be a real bull of a man to be as fit as you are, with two fires burning away inside you—one in your head and one in your belly! Unfortunately I haven't got time to take care of you personally, but I'll have you undergo proper tests."

Armed with an admission card, Wangrin presented himself at the main hospital. He was taken in and entrusted to the care of Assistant Medical Officer Sanaye Biamdu. Like Wangrin, he came from the Sudan. Wangrin was placed under observation.

Wangrin decided to take Sanaye Biamdu into his confidence. Since the three assistants who worked in the hospital laboratory were devoted to him, he was in a position and willing to use his authority effectively to shield a fellow countryman from Count de Villermoz's dangerous clutches. In great secrecy, he said to the laboratory assistants:

"If Messrs. Sauvage and du Pont de la Roche are determined to join forces to deliver our Wangrin into Count de Villermoz's clutches, why can't we Sudanese get together and come to the rescue of our fellow countryman? This is a case where professional integrity comes into conflict with compassion. We must give precedence to compassion. We will be saving a man from certain death and our gesture will be consistent with, rather than alien to, the medical ideal which strives to liberate human beings from the onslaught of death."

These three laboratory assistants, all of them Sudanese, felt boundless admiration for their chief. They were all the more impressed in that Samaye Biamdu was known to be a very honest man who never sold his services. They were delighted, then, to be able to help Wangrin. Through their tests, they contrived to prove that his enteritis was of a kind that would require long hospitalization. Wangrin, of course, no longer needing to pretend, had thrown away the remainder of his potions in his bedpan. . . .

From the hospital, Wangrin wrote a letter to the acting governor and managed to have it delivered to him through the latter's head steward. In his letter, he drew attention to the special circumstances that had induced Linguet, the substantive governor at the time, to rescind the original decision. In view of his situation, he was applying for a transfer to avoid being at the mercy of Count de Villermoz. For his part, the doctor in charge of the hospital wrote out a certificate stating that Wangrin's physical condition made him unfit for service in Gudugaua.

So Wangrin was transferred once again, this time to Diussola. He packed his bags and moved to his new post without having set eyes one single instant on Count de Villermoz.

In any case the latter had adopted a contemptuous attitude toward him, and tended on the whole to ignore him. He hardly ever mentioned the subject. All he deigned to say about Wangrin was invariably: "Wangrin is the worst possible swindler, and a damned cheeky fellow to boot. It's a real pity that a man of such exceptional intelligence and courage should have such dubious ethics. . . . "[5]

Wangrin too, recognized the Count's noble nature. "The Count finds it repugnant," he would say, "to grapple with me publicly. He is against me, but his behavior never lacks dignity."

But of the Count's associates—Commandant du Pont de la Roche and the administrator, Sauvage—he spoke very differently. They were his most ferocious enemies. Du Pont de la Roche seemed to fear a denunciation from Wangrin regarding his arbitrary imprisonment. Sauvage worried in case the reprimands he had wished on himself came out into the open and jeopardized his chances of promotion. In any case, he was no longer able to transfer employees at random. Now it was the governor's chief of cabinet who supervised all appointments and decrees relating to personnel.

18 Where Wangrin Is Off Once Again to a Good Start

The District of Diussola, Wangrin's new post, was run by Baron Arnaud de Bonneval. The local inhabitants had nicknamed him "Commandant Piff-Paff," for he was wont to crack his whip with great abandon on any human being or animal who happened to come too close to his restless hand.

Immediately after his arrival, Wangrin reported to him at the district office and was ushered into a spacious office. Wangrin couldn't help noticing a horsewhip lying across the desk, and another alongside the portrait of the French President, as though these corrective weapons had been an integral part of the coat of arms of the Third Republic! "Good morning, Sir!" came Wangrin's greeting.

"Ah, there you are! You must be the new interpreter. Come and tell me what you've got in your nut, and what you imagine you're going to be up to in Diussola."

Long experience had taught Wangrin that first impressions often determine the quality of the relationship that will be established later on between a colonial administrator and his dependents, especially his interpreter. He also knew from information he had been careful to gather that in his heart of hearts Baron Arnaud de Bonneval was a neurotic rather than a nasty man. Army life had soured him. He had enlisted in the hope of re-gilding his faded family crest and restoring his sadly depleted finances. Alas, his military career had been ruined by a superior officer who felt an aversion for men whose names began with a *de, du,* or *de la* and the unhappy Baron had never got beyond the rank of captain, while his ambition and scholarly attainments had marked him for a fine generalship.

Wangrin made a deep bow and replied to his new Commandant in the following manner:

"Sir, I am Wangrin, your new interpreter. As for my nut, you may think of it as a bowl carved out of brand new wood, therefore completely unseasoned, empty, and ready to be filled with whatever ideas you yourself may choose to put in it.

"I have come to serve you in any manner in which you may desire to be served. My duty is my only religion. To please my Commandant is to please the superior force in heaven above. I am a Muslim, but not a bigot. I dislike chauvinists; I am in favor of civilization and I am a particularly enthusiastic admirer of French civilization, the mother of human rights and the enemy of slavery!"

"I say!" broke in the Commandant. "Where did you learn to speak such faultless French?"

"In the School for Hostages at Kayes, and by dint of reading over and over again Dumas, Lamartine, Victor Hugo, Leconte de Lisle, Voltaire, La Fontaine, Alfred de Musset, and Boileau. I also know by heart Victor Hugo's celebrated phrase, which provides a mnemonic means of holding in one's head the list of one's favorite authors."

"What phrase is that?"

"Here it is, Sir: *Corneille, perché sur les Racines de La Bruyère, Boileau de La Fontaine Molière.*"[1]

"Well, I'll be damned! You're a lot better than an ordinary interpreter. . . . I've heard that in the past there's been some unpleasantness between you and a certain Count de Villermoz."

"No, Sir, I couldn't really say that he's been unpleasant to me. Rather, he forced me into a situation that made it impossible for me to have a proper relationship with my Commandant. Count de Villermoz put me in charge of certain operations which, although not altogether dishonest, were incompatible with our respective jobs."

"What sort of operations were they exactly?"

"Sir, I know you will understand that the oath I have sworn never to reveal to anyone the operations carried out through me by my superiors, especially my colonial administrators, forbids me from repeating what I was ordered to do by Count de Villermoz."

Arnaud de Bonneval started drumming on his desk with the fingers of his right hand, looking intently at Wangrin, as if he were trying to hypnotize him.

Wangrin looked back calmly, with the air of one who has nothing whatever to be ashamed of and is not easily put out of countenance.

"How many languages do you speak, Wangrin?"

"I speak fluently Bambara, my native tongue, Fulfulde, Dogon, Mossi, Djerma, and Hausa, and reasonably well Baule and Bete."

"You will be my own private interpreter. You needn't worry: you won't be involved in anything irregular. The only thing I care about deeply is to have my orders carried out punctiliously. I am used to giving orders. I don't fear responsibilities and I stand by my decisions at all times. . . . "

"Sir, I am your man. I have never allowed sentiments to interfere when it comes to carrying out orders. One day, long ago, my mother, holding out her breast in her right hand, said to me: 'My son, life is a city from which no one can escape alive; to fear death, then, is useless cowardice. In that knowledge, free your soul from all fear of death. Face danger like a man and always keep your promises. Respect your elders. Assist the poor, even if it requires depriving the rich of their fortune.'"

"Your mother must be a good Christian, then."

"My mother is a good Animist, Sir."

"Courage and morality are beyond the boundaries of race and religion, my friend. Go home now, Wangrin, and come back on Monday to start your new job. You'll find plenty to do!"

Having dismissed Wangrin, de Bonneval unhooked his whip from the wall, stuck his large pipe in his mouth, and went out. He mounted his fine stallion and began his inspection, followed by his corporal, also on horseback. Every morning, he spent at least two hours visiting every establishment in town before starting work in the office. His management of the district would have been a blessing if he hadn't had the unfortunate habit of cracking his whip across the backs of a couple of people and taking two or three others to jail who were guilty of the terrible crime of not having saluted their Commandant from a distance of twenty-five yards. For a Commandant on horseback must be just as noticeable as the sun at its zenith! Very bad French subjects indeed they must have been who didn't acknowledge his presence from a distance of twenty-five, fifty, or even a hundred yards!

Some colonial administrators punished this misdemeanor with a fortnight's imprisonment. That was one of the many advantages that accrued when one was blessed with the status of Commandant, whether senior or junior. These sentences came under the Native Code and so did not merit the fuss and bother of a trial.

One must say in defense of Baron de Bonneval that he did not abuse his prerogative to punish according to his whims. He never inflicted more than two days' punishment on any French subject who had neglected to salute him—the Commandant!—or the hoisting of the flag, since this operation was marked by a blaring of trumpets and could not, therefore, go unnoticed.

Wangrin used his three days' holiday to make dutiful calls on all the local dignitaries: the warrant chiefs who happened to be in Diussola at the time, the managers of commercial firms, the Catholic bishop, and the marabouts—beginning with the chief imam—and later the indigenous dignitaries and civil servants.

The townspeople gave Wangrin the sort of reception due to his rank. He was offered several home-fed sheep, bulls, millet, and a number of large bucketfuls of rice.

In his turn, Wangrin distributed various "souvenirs" he had brought along from Gudugaua. He went to the holy river that crossed the town and fed the fish as a sacrificial gesture. It was a thought that deeply touched the hearts of the town elders, who assured Wangrin that from that moment he could count on the cooperation of the inhabitants.

Wangrin and his family settled in. Wangrin was profoundly affected by the beauty of the town and the environs. The garland of hills, with their tapestry of green, was interspersed with ridges of reddish yellow soil, which the sun caressed with gold and sprinkled here and there with luminosity, as if an immense green carpet had been flecked with dots shaded by the varying hues of trees and grasses. The beauty of this landscape quickly dispelled his sad recollection of Gudugaua's implacable flatness.

Diussola was not only the commercial capital of the area and a center for exchange between several countries, but also an extremely fertile zone inhabited by industrious and hospitable people.

After having called on everybody who mattered and having gathered ample information on all parties and on the traditional local taboos that must never be violated, one evening Wangrin decided to unfold his deck chair on the terrace of his house, where one could enjoy to the full the coolness of the night. He asked not to be disturbed. Stretched out on his chair, very relaxed, and lost in contemplation of the immense celestial vault studded with stars, he began to meditate.

With lightning speed, he mentally reviewed his past. His whole existence unfolded rapidly within the recesses of his mind. At first he saw the little pot-bellied Bambara child, his naked body covered in grey dust, with a little rectangular double bag made of cotton strips dyed a wishy-washy yellow worn as bandoleer. The little devil ran like one possessed, after a mouse, or a lizard he'd wounded with pebbles, or a squirrel who was dragging across the tall grass the trap that had caught him, trying to break free. He saw the young recruit in the School for Hostages, dressed in grey shirt and shorts, a little red round chechia with a blue silk pompom on his head, and bare feet.

He saw the circumcised youth who had lived three months with forty-five companions, dressed in a seamless yellow bubu and a cap shaped like a caiman's head,[2] who had listened to the teaching of his Sema,[3] singing and dancing long hours around a holy fire.

He saw the young schoolmaster dressed in European clothes, always sporting a pencil behind his ear.

Then he saw all the remaining episodes rolled into one: Racutie, his first rival and aggressor, Commandant de Brière, who had made him his first political gift, etc. He allowed his wandering thoughts to linger on Count de Villermoz and his two friends, du Pont de la Roche and Georges Sauvage, and on their hefty bloodhound Romo Sibedi. Yes, it was true that for Wangrin those four wretched acolytes did represent a heavy stone suspended above his head by a spider's thread. Suddenly he shivered without knowing whether he was afraid or simply indignant.

He breathed in deeply the cool night air, further refreshed by the gentle breeze that was blowing across the terrace and the unbroken stillness of the sleeping town. Then he exhaled noisily. He felt much better. He grimaced to himself, sneering at his morbid fears.

"Have I not," he said to himself, "aided by Allah, my two begetters, and my marabouts, especially Tierno Siddi and Mulaye, have I not, I repeat, sent packing and nearly driven out of their minds all Whites and Blacks who tried to stand in my way? Now that I am in a sort of paradise on earth, instead of having morbid thoughts, shouldn't I rather offer my thanks to the powers above, comparing myself to the frog in the fable?

"One day, according to the tale, Niedjugu the termagant found a poor, thirsty little frog who was striving ineffectually to get water out of her brimful pot. The poor animal was hoping that a few drops might spill over and dribble into his throat. Instead Niedjugu grabbed the little frog, lashed it with the evil ejaculations of her cutting tongue, and sent him flying, closing her rosary of insults with the words: 'Go to the devil, and burn forever in hell with your unquenchable thirst, you horrible batrachian!' But you see, the termagant had cast away the frog with such violence that he had ended up in a large pond afloat with juicy aquatic leaves from which sprouted yellow, white, and blue flowers. In fact, that pond had insects enough to feed a whole colony of frogs.

"Hasn't the very same thing happened to me?

"To have had a chance to leave Yaguwahi just as I was beginning to fear some denunciation after having accepted so many bribes must be seen as a piece of good luck!"

The following day, refreshed and happy, Wangrin donned a white percale shirt and a long-sleeved Moroccan felt waistcoat, embellished with silk braids intertwined in a most effective arabesque. On top of the waistcoat, he slipped on an ample bubu made of bombazine, with a design of bamboo leaves woven into it. Then he pulled on baggy trousers cut out of a printed fabric called *limeneas*, whose edges were trimmed with narrow bands of white silk.

To complete this fine attire, Wangrin chose a beautiful pair of embroidered boots and a brand-new colonial helmet. In his hand, he flourished a walking stick of sculpted ebony. He had forborne from wearing any scent as he didn't know whether Arnaud de Bonneval was one of those administrators who can't bear African spices, even when they release the sweetest aroma.

He climbed on his horse and with his faithful groom in tow made his way to the district office. He had left a little earlier than necessary with the idea of having a chat with the orderly who stood outside the Commandant's door and—if he had the opportunity—with a few civil servants.

As soon as he had made his entrance into the courtyard through which one acceded to the various offices, he dismounted and handed the reins over to his groom. He strode forward with the majestic gait that befitted his rank and made his way under the covered verandah. There he met some civil servants, some patrolmen, and a few representatives of warrant chiefs. Having heard that the mighty new interpreter was about to take up his duties, everyone had made a point of coming to greet him and to demonstrate—either sincerely or hypocritically—their friendship.

The clerk, Tiombiano Treman, was the first to shake hands with Wangrin, reciting in the white-White manner his name, surname, and position. After that it was lance-sergeant Thie Sarama Uattara's turn and then, jockeying for position, came all the others. . . .

Wangrin understood that in Diussola, as everywhere else, the chief interpreter was a top citizen. He modeled his behavior on the kind adopted by great white-White chiefs when civil servants are introduced to them—shaking hands rapidly and smiling more or less warmly according to the status and the cadre to which the person in question belonged. Then he asked a few laconic questions. These were followed by little explosions of laughter—the politician's laugh, which does not originate from the heart but from somewhere between the uvula and the tip of the tongue! Wangrin played his part in masterly fashion. An excellent mime, he could reproduce faithfully and at will any gesture, sound, or cry. Apart from that, he had always enjoyed a bit of leg-pulling.

"Permit me to leave you," he said to his new colleagues. "Let me go and stand outside the Senior Commandant's door. If he finds me in this midst he'll think that I can't wait to pump you full of subversive ideas against French security. . . . "

They all burst out laughing. Wangrin joined them and said: "Let's all laugh together. Laughing is the most reliable thermometer of good health and happiness."

Then he went to the comfortable chair that had been reserved for him. Immediately, he was joined by the orderly, who stood to attention, his little fingers poised on his trousers' seams, his head carried high and his body straight as a rod. The orderly recited: "Me Bila Kuttu, I be lance-corporal, regimental roll 73. Before I be infantry corporal inside class of 1912, regimental roll 903; I be orderly for ma commanda."

Wangrin inclined his head sarcastically first to the left, then to the right. He looked at the ground as if he wanted to examine Bila's feet. Meanwhile Bila hadn't moved a muscle. Wangrin let his glance wander slowly upwards and when their eyes met, he looked intently at Bila and said: "Stand at ease! Dismiss!"

As soon as Bila had complied Wangrin said to him: "Between us there is to be no question of orderly and interpreter. We'll be like identical twins. We must swear to each other loyalty and mutual assistance and each must act for the other in the other's absence. There must be no secrets between us. If the idea appeals to you, I suggest that you come to my house tonight, after the Saafo prayer."[4]

While Wangrin and Bila Kuttu were chatting, somebody noticed that the Commandant was returning from his morning inspection of town and works in progress.

Baron de Bonneval was a good town planner. From time to time he'd say: "Oh, if only the governor could force the hand of Mister Nolira, that Scrooge in charge of treasury, and provide me with the necessary funds . . . I would do for Diussola what Baron Georges Haussman did for Paris!" Alas, Bernard Linguet was no Charles Louis Napoleon! Too bad that a Bonaparte could not be placed in charge of the territory!

The Baron dismounted and let go of the reins, knowing that the lance-sergeant and the groom would take care of his horse. He crossed the courtyard with bowed head as if he didn't want to see what was going on around him. Rapidly he ascended the flight of steps that led to his office and went in. He sat down and called:

"Orderly!"

"Presensa! Oga Commanda!"

"Call in the new interpreter."

"Here I am, Sir," replied Wangrin, who had taken the precaution of placing himself within earshot of his chief. Was he not after all an old fox who knew all the ways and idiosyncrasies of the gods of the bush?

Wangrin went in and "took over" from the Commandant himself instead of dealing with his predecessor, who had already left before his arrival.

Wangrin began by inspecting the files concerning warrant chiefs and village heads, marabouts, town dignitaries, chiefs' representatives, *porsantants*,[5] intelligence agents, rich traders, and lastly sorcerers who were officially recorded as such and were watched as closely as marabouts.

Helped by all this information, within a very short time he was able to spread a new net, a veritable cobweb in fact, far wider-reaching and far more solid than those he had spun in Diagaramba and Gudugaua.

It wasn't long before an opportunity to make a mint without incurring any serious risk presented itself. The government of the colony had sent special instructions to each district with a view to giving impetus to the "produce-picking" campaign, as it had been called. It was needed for industrial expansion in France.

Of course it fell to the indigenous population to provide karite nuts,[6] gum resins, vegetable silk fibers (especially kapok), and various other products under ill-disguised conditions of forced labor.

Each village was to supply the quantity determined by the territorial government on the basis of the requirements stated by the Chamber of Commerce and Industry. Each family residing in a village was expected to send off adults and children, men, and women, indiscriminately, through brambles and sharp-leaved grass to gather nuts and husks from one tree to the next, to bleed fig trees and then load on their heads the gross pickings and take them home. There, they would spend interminable nights sorting and cleaning, with the aid of primitive winnowing baskets or blowing with their own exhausted breath.

The trimmed products were then to be sent on their way, carried either on heads or on the backs of beasts of burden, to markets sometimes more than twenty-five miles away. These markets were always situated on inter-communicating routes—whether it was by land or water—so that the traders could easily dispatch the products they had acquired at a ridiculously low price, a price determined by the Chamber of Commerce, and unfortunately endorsed by the local government, which had no power to alter it.

Wangrin knew what was going on and suffered in his heart. His inexhaustible and innate greed, which he acknowledged impudently but also sincerely despised, without, however, being able to subdue it, did not prevent him from being a sensitive creature who inclined toward helping the poor. True, to make money, he was ready to play the most outrageous tricks, but always to the detriment of colonizers, local chiefs, or rich traders, for he considered them exploiters of the peasant masses.

19   A Profitable Pledge

Wangrin had turned his terrace into a veritable bower of meditation, not the purely spiritual exercise practiced by the Sufi,[1] but rather that of a fighter who has engaged in hand-to-hand combat for wealth. What he wanted was to make a fortune without getting hurt in the process, and it was no mean task.

Ready to enter the arena once again, Wangrin now needed to make a strategic plan. After a very frugal evening meal, he went up to his terrace where his comfortable deck chair awaited him. As on other similar occasions, he asked not to be disturbed. It was a beautiful, cool, tranquil night. The sky, intensely dark and dotted with glittering stars, resembled a ceiling of ebony studded with large pearls of silver.

To which powers would Wangrin address his prayers, alone with his thoughts under such a sumptuous vault? To his ancestral forces or to those of some alien creed? Whichever he was going to choose, his request would be the same as usual—that they might inspire him to make vast amounts of money, and protect him from his enemies, both white and black.

Reclining on his deck chair as if he were recovering from a long illness, Wangrin addressed himself silently to the spirits of his forbears.

"O spirits of my ancestors," he called. "O you who are in the kingdom of power, do come once again to my aid. My blood is the very same blood that coursed in your veins. From your arteries it flowed into my father's and from his into mine. Whether you think me worthy or unworthy, I belong to you. Breathe into me the ability of the chameleon to change color according to his environment, that he may wander about unnoticed. Endow me with the tender gentleness of the lamb, that I may be loved by everyone and be all the more successful in my dealings.

"But, O great ancestors! O ferocious warriors! endow me also with lions' and leopards' claws that I may tear to shreds ruthlessly and unhesitatingly all who try to stand in my way, or seek to divert the course of my riches toward someone else's coffer. . . . "

Wangrin was not able to finish this unusual prayer. Sleep, always stronger than man, overcame him and carried him off to the kingdom whence people return with an unpleasantly dry mouth.

It was only in the early hours of the morning that, feeling cold, he suddenly woke up. He went downstairs and continued to sleep in a warm and comfortable bed. There, he dreamt that his wife had given birth to a girl with a silver head and golden hair cascading down to her hips. He inferred from this that he was on the threshold of financial affluence.

He went on to work out how he could best exploit the produce-picking campaign to his own advantage. Money attracts money, he concluded. To ensure a large profit, one must invest some funds. Yes, the timely planting of a millet seed in fertile soil reproduces a thousandfold. But first of all it must be planted. . . .

Wangrin quietly convened ten experienced produce buyers who until then had been working for important European commercial firms. This is what he said to them:

"My dear friends, I have just realized that your white employers have been exploiting you for years. So I have decided to find you a white employer who will pay you fifty centimes per kilo over what you are earning at present, plus a bonus, yet to be fixed, at the end of every picking season.

"Monsieur Louis Rameau is a rich merchant in Marseille; he doesn't want to appear on the scene because he might incur the displeasure of his compatriots. Therefore, each one of you will have to sign a promissory note for the money that Fabukari, his representative, who will shortly be here from the Ivory Coast with the necessary funds, will advance you. In this business my role will be to open wide to you the roads to all the villages who contribute produce, and to recommend you to the administration and to the indigenous chiefs. But I am telling you quite openly that I don't intend to work out of pure love for Monsieur Louis Rameau! He will of course recompense me. I have insisted however that my reward must not be taken out of your salary, and we have managed to agree on a suitable sum.

"From now on," Wangrin added, "the fruits of your own labor will be yours. You will cease to be intermediaries who toil and sweat in the heat of the sun and get soaked in the thundery rains all for the benefit of some fine gentlemen who wait indolently under their mosquito nets—a glass of iced vermouth within reach—for you to turn up with the tonnage that will add to their already abundant harvest. Up to now, your labor has brought you only the dubious pleasure of being able to manipulate hundreds of thousands of francs for five months as if they were your own. At last, this Monsieur Rameau will enable you to earn something of your own. He is a French white-White trader; he is different from those colonial white-White traders who are not ashamed to deceive an African—first when they buy from him the raw material of the land and once again when they sell back to him the very same stuff after it has been manufactured. Nor will you have Monsieur Rameau come here and trouble you for days on end putting diabolical accounts under your nose and inevitably concluding: 'You still owe twenty-five or fifty thousand francs,' which is tantamount to saying that you must go on working without pay for the same firm another whole year. The fact is, at the moment you are no more than retrievers kept on a tight leash. A few administrators, Commandants, and magistrates are positively revolted by the way most white-White merchants behave in the colonies. And they do want to help the African buyers and small traders. But the Chambers of Commerce are on the lookout both in Bordeaux and Marseille. Unfortunately, they are more influential than the Syndicate of Administrators, than the gowns, caps, and arm-bands worn by magistrates and lawyers. In a few days from now, Monsieur Louis Rameau will send us his representative—a fellow countryman of ours called Fabukari. He is a man who did his national service in the French navy. He knows Marseille and Bordeaux like the palm of his hand. There are few stretches of water he hasn't crossed. He has visited every land from the East to the West, from the frozen waters of the distant North to the lands lost in the immense oceans of the distant South. He speaks French, English, Spanish, and Arabic, and seven African languages, as well as the Bambara tongue, which he sucked from his mother's breast. He understands the ways of man, whether he be white, black, red, or yellow."

Who would have failed to be convinced by a proposition delivered so dithyrambically! Of course, the ten buyers agreed to switch masters.

Always cautious, Wangrin made the ten swear that they would stick to Fabukari come what may, and that no one was to be told of the agreement that had just been sealed. Then he produced a calabash full of fresh milk. "In order to survive, every one of us," he said, "has drunk his mother's milk. Milk, then, is the holiest of all forms of nourishment; that is why it feeds and quenches thirst all at once. Now we will let a drop of our blood fall into this milk, and then we will drink it. In this way neither I, Wangrin, will ever be able to betray you, nor you, my associates, me, without incurring a violent and ignominious death. When Fabukari arrives, we will renew this oath in his company."

Wangrin's proposal was enthusiastically accepted.

Two days later, Fabukari arrived from the Ivory Coast. First of all he went to the district office to be introduced to the Commandant with whom he had already made an appointment. Having announced him, Wangrin took him in.

Fabukari, an old sea-dog, stated his case before the Commandant:

"I have been a gold-miner in my own country in the Nubigu and Bure regions," he said. "Sanu[2] has bestowed on me his godly favor. So far, I have managed to extend my trade as far as the Ivory Coast, where I have bought a vast plantation which I manage profitably. But I'd like to work in your area too, and I'd like to employ about ten, or perhaps a few more, buyers of local products."

"What you say is very fine indeed, but first of all you must fulfill all the legal obligations of a trader. Form a limited company, take out and pay for a license, register your company, and post a bond as surety."

"Actually, I don't need to form a new company, because the one I have in the Ivory Coast and in the French Sudan is entitled to operate in the whole of French West Africa. All I need do is to buy the general wholesale first-class license required by law."

De Bonneval couldn't believe his ears. . . . An African, a French subject, buy the general wholesale license which up to now had been a privilege reserved solely for the most important commercial firms? It was almost unbelievable!

He let his glance rest on Fabukari for a few moments, then he said: "You astound me. . . . By Jove, you deserve to be encouraged, it's high time Africans broke free and secured the position which is theirs by right in the trade and industry of their own countries!"

Then he turned to Wangrin: "Take care of Monsieur Fabukari, Wangrin. This African deserves to be called *Monsieur*. It's a title I am only too happy to bestow on him. Too bad if Monsieur Bodressoul, President of the Chamber of Commerce, isn't going to like it!"

Thus, Fabukari's name in all his papers was preceded by the title of *Monsieur*—a highly honorific title—for in documents concerning French subjects a man was invariably referred to as "One such-and-such." As a matter of fact, the title of *Monsieur* was only given to Europeans, or to Senegalese who were citizens of the four Communes of Dakar, Goree, Saint-Louis, and Rufisque. These enjoyed the same civil status as French citizens.

At nightfall, Wangrin and his ten employees met Fabukari in the large house which the latter had already bought in a crowded part of town called *Koo-ko*. The same oath was sworn anew, but this time Wangrin added to the milk three grains of rock salt, which gave even greater force to the pledge and bound the conspirators together even more indissolubly.

Who were Louis Rameau and Fabukari anyway?

The former had never existed except in Wangrin's prodigiously fertile imagination. As for Monsieur Fabukari, he was Wangrin's younger brother and a former sailor. He was prepared to do anything on earth to please his elder brother, whom he worshiped as a god. Fabukari was as proud of his brother as if he had been sired by him.

On the other hand, Wangrin realized that his younger brother was a godsend. It was only thanks to his intervention and his polyglot sailor's experience that Wangrin was going to be able to camouflage his illicit dealings.

Every buyer received from Fabukari the sum of five hundred thousand francs and signed a promissory note for the same sum. That was yet another of Wangrin's Machiavellian brainwaves.

A fortnight before the official date for the beginning of the campaign, Wangrin sent his ten bonded buyers into the most fertile regions of the "produce-picking" scheme. Incognito, they bought almost a quarter of the year's harvest in advance, paying one half of the total amount due and promising to pay the second half when the campaign was officially inaugurated and the goods delivered at the market.

Needless to say, the warrant chiefs and village heads had been bribed into a discreet silence.

On Wangrin's advice, Fabukari had given his suppliers a means of recognizing his people. He would place near his scales either a drum or a balaphon player. The suppliers simply had to walk toward those particular scales, have their merchandise weighed, and received in exchange a bill of payment, to be settled later, when every activity in the market came to an end.

In each market Wangrin would change the identification sign. In this way he was able to foil his competitors' attempts to imitate him.

It is easy to imagine with what astonishment the representatives of the large commercial firms contemplated the sudden rise of an upstart nigger who cornered almost a quarter of the total Diussola harvest to his own profit. Moreover, this same nigger was able to carve out a special place for himself within the markets of the neighboring districts. "Something fishy is going on," they thought. "We must get the Chamber of Commerce to intervene as quickly as possible."

The merchants suspected de Bonneval; some of them positively took to hating him. As for the Lebanese and Syrian traders, at this point they were prepared to sacrifice half their capital to get rid of him. On the other hand, Romo Sibedi had never ceased to spy on events in Diussola, always in the hope of catching Wangrin out and succeeding at last in denouncing him to the authorities. He had already got in touch with Monsieur Bodressoul, who was president of the local Chamber of Commerce, and had offered his cooperation in uncovering the scheme that had thwarted the agricultural operation in the Diussola district. He boasted publicly of his unshakeable conviction that Wangrin must be connected in some way or other with the affair.

20　The Reconversion

While all these things were happening, Arnaud de Bonneval concluded another tour of duty and returned to France for a year's leave. Bodressoul and the big merchant mafia took advantage of his absence to apply to the territorial government for Wangrin's transfer and replacement by Romo Sibedi. Meanwhile the latter had become the right-hand man to the Chamber of Commerce.

So Wangrin was transferred once more, this time to Dugotenku.

Henri Tolber, the new Commandant, who had taken over from Bonneval, had already had occasion to notice that Wangrin was a first-class assistant. In the event, he couldn't make out what was going on. He conjectured that the Chamber of Commerce had mounted a plot against him and he had good reason to believe it, for his predecessor had warned him against that organization, or for that matter the Lebanese and Syrian traders. "So long as you have Wangrin as your interpreter and direct informer," Bonneval had told him, "you have nothing to worry about. You will be let into every secret. He will help you to unravel the most complicated political entanglements. With a smile on his lips, he will foil any nasty trick, whether it's the doing of the Church[1] or of the Chamber of Commerce."

Henri Tolber, then, wrote to the governor asking that Wangrin be kept on. In reply, he received the following official telegram:

"Wangrin's transfer unchanged. Stop. Very experienced interpreter Romo Sibedi will take up post. Stop. Ensure Wangrin's dispatch immediately after handing over to successor is completed."

Wangrin disclosed to Tolber who Romo actually was and why he was so keen to come to Diussola. "Sir," he said, "Romo is backed by three administrators. Besides, he is in cahoots with the Church and with the Chamber of Commerce. He is bound to bring along with him a packet of trouble."

Like his predecessor, Henri Tolber was not overfond of priests. Moreover, he heartily disliked the European merchants who, in his opinion, took advantage of the administration to make illicit profit.

He confided to Wangrin that he was going to ask for a transfer for himself, as a sign of protest.

"Leave it alone, Sir," replied Wangrin. "Let Romo come. We know each other very well. Once we are here together, it won't be difficult for me to neutralize him."

"How can you possibly do that if you are to rush off to your new job as soon as you have handed over to him?"

"I will hand over to him, but I have no intention of leaving Diussola. In fact, I intend to submit my resignation to you the very moment I've finished handing over to Romo. I mean to set up in business, and believe you me, I am going to be like a fishbone in the throat of both Romo and the Chamber of Commerce. Between you and me, I have no intention of going to church on Sundays to confess and receive holy communion. I have no desire whatsoever to place myself at the mercy of the 'flowing beards' and 'rosaried necks.'[2]

"I don't know exactly which plotters are busy pulling strings in this affair, but I do know that their schemings and intrigues will not bear fruit. In order to be successful, however, I need your trust and your support. Within his district, a Commandant is a very powerful man. Yet, he too, to thwart his enemies' machinations, needs reliable and intelligent agents. I will find you some, and I'll be their adviser. It goes without saying that all this must be unofficial and strictly between ourselves, otherwise our plan won't work."

Henri Tolber shook hands with Wangrin. "You can count on me," he said.

Eventually Romo appeared before the new Commandant and was well received. Wangrin had counseled this attitude as politic.

"Your colleague is going to hand over to you," Tolber said to Romo. "I hope everything will proceed smoothly, without fuss and without delay."

"Certainly, Sir," replied Romo, inwardly pleased at having been spared the scowls and rude language many administrators used on first meeting their African employees. For some, it was a way of putting them to the test; for others, it was simply the outward manifestation of a cantankerous disposition further aggravated by the intensity of the tropical heat.

Henri Tolber called Wangrin and introduced him to Romo. The handing over took place in an atmosphere of painful suspicion, for Romo was suspicious of Wangrin, and Wangrin mistrusted Romo. The nasty designs that each was hatching for the other were expressed in uncouth whisperings that would have astonished the audience had they been spoken aloud. But Wangrin and Romo knew how to quarrel on the sly and without attracting attention.

As he entered the office that had been Wangrin's, where all the archives were kept, Romo said softly, so that Wangrin alone could hear:

"This is the office which you thought you could use as a center for your deceiving and embezzling, you rotten bastard, cursed even by your own mother. As it so happens, I'm throwing you out instead; as soon as I've settled in I'm going to make public all the intrigues that only the son of a shameless hussy like yourself could have engineered. After that, I'll send you off to rot in jail. Come on, rascal, hurry up and hand over, and shed tears of blood in the process!"

Wangrin burst out laughing with gusto, as if Romo had just finished singing his praises. Then he too, spoke in low tones: "To you, this offiice will be hell's seventh chasm. In it you will live out such torture that you'll invoke death, be it a violent and ignominious one, in order to be relieved of your suffering. Your mouth will taste bitter and your behind will sizzle without cease. Come forward, you aging son of a bitch! May the dust from these archives blind you before the floor sets fire to your feet and the ceiling collapses on your head."

They went on in this vein for two whole days, without anybody suspecting what vicious thrusts were being exchanged between the two antagonists during the handing-over operation. Outside the office, they greeted each other politely, smiled, and even went as far as talking in familiar terms, just like affectionate old friends. Finally Wangrin and Romo went to Commandant Tolber's office and let him know that the handing-over operation was at an end.

"Have you been through all the papers?" the Commandant asked.

Romo replied truthfully: "Yes, Sir, my colleague has shown me all there was for me to see and has explained everything in great detail."

"Very well. In that case," replied Tolber, "there only remains for you to settle in and get down to some good work."

Then, turning to Wangrin as if he had known nothing of his plan, he said:

"Now that you have handed over to Romo, he will assign to you the porters and mounts needed for moving your family."

Romo's face lit up with malicious pleasure. Without giving Wangrin a chance to reply, he cried out cheerfully: "Very well, Sir. I'll see to it that my colleague is properly taken care of."

In reply, Wangrin pulled out of his pocket a sheet of paper and handed it to the Commandant with these words: "Would you be kind enough, Sir, to forward this letter to the governor? It contains my resignation from my job as interpreter."

Then, turning to Romo, he said in Bambara: "Your mother has aborted once more the bastard she conceived to help you destroy me!"[3]

Romo saw red. Losing control, he began to tremble. He shouted: "You son of a bitch! Just see if you won't go to Dugotenku! The governor is not going to accept your resignation!"

Taken aback by Romo's outburst, Tolber called him to order. "What has Wangrin's resignation got to do with you? How do you know that the governor will refuse to accept it? Why are you insulting him?"

Romo realized his mistake and thought to save himself by saying: "Wangrin has used our Bambara language to insult my mother."

Wangrin replied with a smile: "Romo is lying, Sir. I'm sure he's incapable of repeating what I am supposed to have said to him in Bambara."

Henri Tolber turned to Romo. "Tell me what Wangrin has said about your mother, so that I can judge whether it is an insult or not."

Shaking with repressed and indignant fury, Romo replied: "No Sir! Don't ask me to desecrate my mother's name!"

Wangrin, always more astute than Romo, had been playing on a custom. He knew that, according to tradition, to repeat an insult was tantamount to uttering it. Now, not for all the riches in the world could a son bring himself to insult his mother. That would have been the vilest abomination.

Not knowing this custom, Henri Tolber felt certain that poor Romo's accusation was prompted by jealousy—that he might even be something of a stool-pigeon. He gave his new interpreter a sound reprimand.

Romo brought a hand to his face, bent his head and with very slow steps walked back to his seat on the verandah.

Wangrin also made his exit, stopping a moment on the verandah to take his leave of the African staff of the district office.

"When do you plan to leave Diussola?" asked a *porsantan*.[4]

"I am not going to leave," replied Wangrin. "I have resigned. I'm going to stay right here with you. I am setting up in business and hope you'll all be my customers. I'd give you all easy terms for payment."

Romo sat stricken in his chair and listened to this exchange without looking up. His head was bent very low, resting almost on his knees. He wasn't actually weeping, but the large beads of sweat on his forehead bespoke his suffering.

Wangrin shook hands all round, but to Romo he said: "I would have shaken hands with you if just now you had had the courage to repeat to the Commandant what I had told you in an aside. But since you didn't dare do so I'll use my hand for a different purpose, and you'll find out what that is at your own expense. . . . "

Romo rose to his full height and thrust out at Wangrin his fat right arm. The palm of his hand was wide open and turned upward. Imitating the flourishes of a swordsman, he threatened Wangrin. Then he said: "Wangrin, I knew that your parents were people of loose morals. What I hadn't realized up to now was that both of them were incestuous too! I renew before you the pledge I made long ago not to allow myself either rest or respite until I am in a position to arrest you with my own hands and send you to die in a lugubrious dungeon. That day is drawing near. Get out of here now!"

Wangrin burst out laughing as usual: "Romo, if you'd like one promise in exchange for another, I'll renew my own as well. Here it is, in case you've forgotten it. On the day you come to arrest me, I'll play a trick on you that is extravagant enough for the lute players to want to set it to music."[5]

At last the African personnel, who up to that moment had not suspected any feeling of enmity, realized that contrary to appearances there was no love lost between Wangrin and Romo.

"There'll be some mighty drumming among the drunken hunters,"[6] said Tiombiano Treman. Wangrin walked away, humming the coarse refrain of the *korojuga*, buffoons at the court of Segu. Here it is:

Korojuga Zanke! ee Korojuga Zanke
I baa bonona wolo-la
Denin kelen soroba o keera Korojuga ye
I makkun de ndowani i makkun de ndowani
I ba keera to so Jo-ye
ee na kee o nan so Jo-ye

O Zanke the buffoon! O Zanke the buffoon!
Your mother's labor has been worthless
Her only son has become a buffoon.
Be quiet, my brother, be quiet, my brother.
Your mother gave herself to pay,
Now you will give yourself to pay.

21   An Elephant's Tale

Within a few months, Wangrin's affairs were in perfect order. He had acquired several warehouses all over the territory, with headquarters in Diussola.

Six months later, he merged with Fabukari. They called their enterprise the Bany Import-Export Company. It is worth mentioning in passing that Fabukari had made a net profit of fifteen million francs out of the famous "produce-picking" operation.

The new company became known by the acronym CIEB. It had a paid-up capital of ten million francs—a fabulous sum in those days—the same capital as CFAO, one of the largest French commercial enterprises in West Africa.

Wangrin assumed the title of Director-General and bought himself an open sports car which sped along at 60 miles an hour—at a time when a Delahaye lorry couldn't be pushed faster than 20 miles per hour.

With his "torpedo," Wangrin could get anywhere in no time at all. He scoured the countryside from west to south. He never missed a market. His company began to tender right and left, robbing the largest firms of several important contracts, particularly by supplying provisions and meat to a wealthy railway company which was laying tracks at that time.

Wangrin had undertaken to contribute a certain amount of venison to the total quantity of meat required by the company. Accordingly, he engaged about twenty hunters and supplied them with licenses and modern weapons.

Wangrin owned a rifle gun—a firearm French subjects were forbidden from using. This he gave to Soridian, one of his hunters and a great elephant killer.

"Elephant hunting is forbidden," Wangrin told him. "Nevertheless, if you do come across a herd, kill as many elephants as you can and let me know about it as quickly as possible."

To save time, Wangrin had placed a bicycle at Soridian's disposal, complete with spare parts.

But Romo was watching. His men spied on Wangrin's every movement. Having heard that Soridian was shooting elephants for Wangrin, he asked Sanun Wattara to keep watch over that area. Accordingly, Sanun Wattara approached Soridian and offered him tobacco and kola nuts in exchange for shooting lessons. There was nothing unusual in this; no reason why Soridian should suspect anything fishy. The scheme would have worked to perfection if Wangrin hadn't taken the precaution to warn Soridian against anyone who made advances of a hospitable and friendly sort, however benevolent and spontaneous they might appear to be.

"I know my dear compatriot Romo—that old elephant. He spies on me day and night. No doubt he's heard that I'm paying you to shoot elephants because of the high price of ivory. He's sure to have you shadowed or to lay a false friend in your path. I advise you most strongly to let me know at once whether anyone gets in touch with you and whether, intentionally or by chance, you happen to make new friends."

Sanun Wattara's approach to Soridian had been as follows:

"I am an apprentice hunter, which is the same as saying that I am very clumsy. What I badly need is an instructor, and who could help me better than you? There can be no doubt of your reputation. I would very much like to be taught by you. I promise to be a good pupil: I'll follow every bit of advice you give me. I hope it won't be too long before I am accepted in the hunters' brotherhood, where you are a great master. I'd like you to be my sponsor."

Sanun's frankness and lack of affectation were so engaging that Soridian forgot his master's warning. He accepted Sanun's gifts and promised to take him along on his beat across the bush.

Employing as he did people who kept him informed on the migrations of "hefty meats,"[1] Wangrin heard on the sly that a considerably large herd was advancing slowly toward the north.

He jumped in his car and drove at once to Ranfabo where Soridian had pitched his camp. He took him aside and said: "I've brought you a box of ammunition. I have a sizeable order for ivory tusks, and it so happens that a vast herd is making its way toward the north. Go down to meet them. You know what do to. Don't waver!"

As he got ready to return to Diussola, having instructed Soridian on what course to follow, he noticed Sanun walking toward them.

"Who is that?" asked Wangrin.

"It's one Sanun. He wants me to teach him to shoot 'hefty meats' and 'deer.'"

"Where is he from? Ranfabo?"

"I don't think so. He seems to have come in search of a master hunter who is willing to train him and be his sponsor when he's ready to join the hunters' brotherhood."

Wangrin drew Sanun aside and said to him: "Soridian doesn't understand what you're doing here," he told him, "but I do. However, I don't go in for striking an enemy in the dark. You are one of Romo's men. You've come to collect proof that Soridian is shooting elephants for me. Now that you've seen me here there will be no doubt left in your mind that he does work for me. You have two alternatives then: one is to stay in Romo's service and be my enemy, in which case I will crush you without mercy; the other is to change sides and earn three times as much as you are earning at present. If you stay with Romo now that you've been discovered, remember that in the course of a hunt, a stray bullet is a most plausible and acceptable eventuality. I leave it to you to choose. Let me know your reply through Soridian no later than three days from now."

Sanun was frightened beyond description. He had heard from Romo that Wangrin was a demon in human flesh. He turned his heels and almost ran.

Seeing him decamp, Soridian asked Wangrin what was the matter.

"That's an apprentice spy, not an apprentice hunter," replied Wangrin. "Romo sent him after you hoping to catch me. I think, however, that he'll come over to our side. And until he's found out, I'll make use of his services against Romo."

That same night, Sanun went to Soridian. "Your man, Wangrin is a devil," he said. "I owe you a confession and I beg you in advance to forgive me. I was originally recruited by Romo to spy on your movements, from near or far, and supply proof that you are shooting elephants · for Wangrin. Now I've been unmasked in the most unexpected way. Wangrin suggests that I go over to his side, else I must be prepared to have him on my back. To think that all I wanted out of this thing was to make money enough to feed and clothe my vast family! I have therefore come to ask you to tell Wangrin that I accept his proposition. I am waiting for his instructions."

It was then that Soridian realized how difficult it was to deceive Wangrin. He lost any desire he might have had to fool him or try and lead him astray with lies.

Soridian sent word to Wangrin that Sanun had capitulated. The next day, Wangrin went back to Ranfabo to meet Soridian and Sanun secretly.

He said to Sanun: "You will go on feigning loyalty to Romo. You will let him know Soridian's movements and the elephants' present trail. I will also give you a certain amount of information on myself, which you will then pass on to Romo. He will continue to reward you, while I give you three times as much."

At the appropriate time Sanun went to report back to Romo. As he was waiting in the courtyard to be received, he came across one Karim Traore. The poor fellow seemed to be in a state of utter bewilderment. So troubled was he that he couldn't resist confiding in Sanun.

Apparently, he had just offered Romo a hefty bribe to ensure his support at a trial in which a great deal of money and cattle would be at stake. Now, instead of taking the bribe, which amounted to a hundred thousand francs, Romo had asked Karim to drop the money in a bag and deposit the latter in the pot that lay buried in the ground under a tree in a field of his, two miles from town.[2]

Still perturbed by this bizarre request, Karim was leaving Romo's courtyard when Sanun stopped in to submit his report to Romo, just as Wangrin had asked him to.

In the dead of night, Sanun slipped across to Wangrin's house and related the details of his meeting with Romo, as well as Karim's secret.

At sunset the following day Karim was to deposit in Romo's field the sum he had agreed to pay. Romo had told him not to worry—the money would be perfectly safe.

Wangrin called his groom and asked him to go off and hide somewhere near the edge of the field: "A man will come to drop a bag in a pot sunk in the earth near a tree trunk. As soon as he leaves, you will fish out the bag and replace it with this one"; and Wangrin handed him a bag which he had filled with pebbles, enclosing a letter.

Karim turned up punctually. He advanced steadily toward the tree, found the mouth of the pot, slipped through it the bag containing a hundred thousand francs in coins and covered the hole with a lid he found lying close by.[3] Karim felt certain that no one, except perhaps a relative of Romo's, could possibly come to the field till the next morning. All the farmers had already gone back to their villages for the night. So Karim returned quite happily to town.

As soon as he had disappeared in the bush, Wangrin's groom leapt out of his hiding place and ran toward the pot. He seized the bag deposited by Karim and replaced it with the one he had been given by Wangrin. Then he made off with the stolen bag and delivered it to Wangrin.

After dinner, Romo sent a trusted man to fetch the contents of a certain water pot, explaining carefully where it could be found. The messenger did in fact find the bag lying snugly in the pot. He lifted it out and took it back to Romo.

The latter unfastened it with impatient movements, but all he could find was a heap of pebbles and a letter. He tore the envelope and read: "Go to the bank and cash your hundred thousand francs' worth of pebbles. Each time a son who's been cursed by his mother reaches out for some fruit, the son of a mother who's showered blessings on him gathers it instead—Signed—You know who."

Romo's heart almost failed him. There was no doubt in his mind that Wangrin had had a hand in this, but how to establish his guilt? He called Karim and questioned him closely as to the people he might have taken into his confidence. Forgetting his brief encounter in the courtyard, where he had spoken in a state of distraction, Karim replied: "Apart from my relatives, no one knows about this. None of my relatives has any reason whatsoever to betray me."

While poor Romo, sick at heart, pursued his investigations, Sanun continued to and fro, keeping his foot in both camps, with Wangrin's consent.

Meanwhile the elephants' herd continued its slow climb toward Ranfabo. Soridian went south to meet the animals head on. He shot three grown males with the largest and most beautiful tusks of all. Soridian and Sanun rooted out the tusks from the heads of the pachyderms and then buried two of the carcasses in deep graves. Soridian sent Sanun off to apprise Wangrin of their success.

Sanun arrived in Diussola at night, around eleven, and went to knock on the small door which Wangrin kept camouflaged specially for his secret interviews. As soon as he was let in, Sanun told Wangrin with what incredible swiftness and skill Soridian had shot the three enormous beasts.

"What did you do with the bodies?" asked Wangrin.

"We followed the instructions you'd given Soridian and buried each animal in the very spot where he had fallen, except for one, who has been left exposed to the open air."

"All right. Spend the night in town, and tomorrow as the muezzin is calling the faithful to prayer, go to Romo and tell him that Wangrin's hunter had shot three elephants somewhere near a village in the Ranfabo area. Romo will be delighted with you; moreover, you'll be telling the truth."

Sanun went home, and promptly fell asleep. Meanwhile, Wangrin zoomed off to Ranfabo in his car, arriving there before sunrise. He arranged to have the tusks of the two already buried male elephants hidden in a grove, and loaded those of the third elephant in a lorry which delivered provisions to the laborers.

Taking with him his precious spoils, he returned to Diussola and went to the district office, where he asked to see the Commandant.

Meanwhile Romo, armed with Sanun's news, had hastened to submit a report to Tolber. The latter was about to send an agent from the Forestry Commission to make a check on the spot and draw up a report of the infringement, when Wangrin walked into his office.

"Sir," he said, "I have come to report that a little while ago my hunters were attacked by one of those herds of elephants who are always stomping about destroying our plantations. One of my hunters, by name Soridian, killed a big male in self-defense. I have brought you the tusks, which belong by right to the government rather than to me."

"Romo tells me that your hunter has killed three males, not just one," replied Tolber.

"I am astounded that Romo, who doesn't even know what happens in his own field two miles out of town, can get hold of such detailed information as to what goes on in Ranfabo. I imagine he's been led up the garden path once again. Villagers are very fond of improving on figures and embroidering the truth. Do send an agent from the Forestry Commission, Sir; then you'll know which one of us is lying. And allow me to remind you, Sir, that although Romo is my compatriot, his feelings for me are none too affectionate."

Tolber sent the tusks to the Forestry Commission Office, where they would eventually be sold in a public auction. He was convinced that Wangrin had spoken in good faith and that further inquiries were totally unnecessary.

On the day of the auction, Wangrin was among the bidders. With a frenzy that astonished everyone present, he propelled the starting price to astronomical heights.

"You're crazy, Wangrin!" whispered a friend. "At the sort of price you're bidding, what margin of profit will be left for you when you come to resell?"

"The pleasure of having annoyed my elder brother Romo, who will be furious when he sees that I'm actually getting these tusks. You must bear in mind that if on returning from the market a farmer orders his harvest to be burnt, it means that he's discovered that he can make a higher profit from the sale of ash than from the sale of his cereals."

Wangrin's bid got him the pair of tusks. On the way out, walking past Romo, he let slip in Bambara: "Another bitter pill for you to swallow! I am going to pay for this ivory with the money I found in your water pot. . . . Greetings, elder brother."

Romo was so stricken and bewildered that on the way home he started talking to himself. Up to then, he had only suspected Wangrin of having stolen his hundred thousand francs. Now there could be no doubt left.

Suddenly, a thought flashed through Romo's mind. He remembered that on the day of Karim's visit, Sanun had been in his house as well and he inferred that in one way or another Sanun must have got wind of the affair.

He sent for him and said: "A transaction between Karim and myself has misfired badly. Karim tells me that imprudently he let slip to you the information that he had been given a bag to be deposited inside a water pot in one of my fields. Now things have not worked out well at all, and although I repose great trust in you, I have every reason to believe that you have in fact stolen the bag and substituted it with another."

Sanun swore upon his ancestor's spirits and his mother's breast (an oath considered absolutely sacrosanct) that Romo's bag had never been in his possession and that he didn't even know the whereabouts of Romo's field—all of which was strictly true.

"Are you sure that Soridian is not aware that you are working for me?"

"I have earned his complete trust. He has even introduced me to his employer who comes to see him and other agents he employs every three days."

"Has Wangrin spoken to you?"

"Yes, he has."

"Has he asked you anything about me?"

"Yes, in an absent-minded sort of way. He asked me whether I knew you. 'By name,' was my reply. After that, he let the matter drop, but he did look at me intently, stretching out to me a packet of cigarettes. But since then he hasn't spoken to me at all."

"I am sure that Wangrin is up to something. He will probably try to use you in order to get at me, and if you refuse he won't hesitate to wipe you out. I had better find some way of sheltering you. But before I do that, since you've told me that Soridian hunts with a rifle gun, you must note down and let me know the serial number. It won't be difficult. You are a scalesman and know perfectly well how to read numbers."

Sanun returned to Ranfabo and during one of Wangrin's visits related the conversation he had had with Romo.

"We're going to give ample satisfaction to our big brother," declared Wangrin. And he gave Sanun the serial number, the address of the makers, and the year of manufacture.

Once he possessed this piece of information, Romo told Sanun: "You are going to lie low somewhere for a few months, else Wangrin will have you done away with."

Sanun was quite ready to comply with this piece of advice, but on that same evening he reported it to Wangrin, who was willing to let Sanun follow it. Sanun made himself scarce, only too relieved to be able to escape so cheaply from the jaws of two fighting caimans.

22 A Disquieting Arrival

As time went by, Tolber too, completed his statutory three-year stint in the colony. M. de Chantalba, a friend of Villermoz's, was appointed in his place. During the interval between Tolber's departure and Chantalba's arrival, the administration was entrusted to the Junior Commandant.

Romo's situation was now bound to improve, for although Tolber had been using him from time to time, his trust in him had been very limited. From now on, with Jacques de Chantalba in charge, things were going to change drastically. Romo had been warmly recommended to the new man by Villermoz and his two friends who, needless to say, had also warned him against Wangrin.

As soon as he heard that Jacques de Chantalba was going to be transferred to Diussola, Wangrin began to gather information on the new Commandant. His friends in Gudugaua helped him. He found out that Chantalba was a close friend of Count de Villermoz's and that they had been seen together, day and night, during the whole week preceding his appointment. Wangrin came to the conclusion that Chantalba would become no devoted friend of his, that in fact he would try his best to "squeeze" him. One way or another, he would find a way of making things awkward for him. That meant yet another battle.

How Wangrin regretted the absence of Tierno Siddi and Mulaye Hamidu! At least they would have prayed once more to shield him from the new Commandant's unpleasant attitude. Wangrin, however, had never been the devotee of one god alone. Rather, he acknowledged divine power anywhere it chose to nest. . . . In the absence of his miracle-working marabouts, he decided to turn to his personal god Gongoloma-Sooke and invoke his protection against the evil that might emanate from the new Commandant. The battle would be strenuous, for Romo could be counted on to do his best to stir things up. And Wangrin knew that a war, however trifling, must be carefully planned. . . . So he pulled a small, bloodstained pebble out of the bottom of a bag made of black catskin. It was the little stone which symbolized his link with Gongoloma-Sooke. On it, long ago, Wangrin had sacrificed the fowl that betokened his alliance with, and allegiance to, the god. Then he bought two chickens, one black and one white. He returned home, laid down the small pebble, grabbed the black chicken in both hands, and said:

"O pebble! You symbolize the first force in the whole cosmos.[1] You contain iron, and iron contains fire.

"The spirit of my protector god, Gongoloma-Sooke, inhabits you, O pebble. A storm of ill fortune is gathering above me. My soul is parched. Soon there will be no cooling breath left in the air either for my heart or my mind.

"A new Commandant, Jacques de Chantalba by name, is due in Diussola. He cannot fail to be my foe, for his friends are my sworn enemies. He will weigh on my peace of mind like the smothering heat of the midday sun. My deep double[2] is already beginning to sink into the darkness of despair.

"And this is why, o pebble, abode of Gongoloma-Sooke, I command you, in the name of *Koo ceema sunsun* and *Baa ceema sunsun*,[3] to open wide the minute orifices of your petrified skin, that the blood of this black chicken, symbol of the night of distress that is about to engulf me, may seep into you.

"Gongoloma-Sooke will come and drink this blood. Then he will tell me how I can triumph over my enemies."

Before sacrificing the black fowl, Wangrin added:

"The white chicken, I will keep until the dark night that threatens me turns into a bright day of happiness. Only then will I sacrifice it."

Then he cut the throat of the black chicken and let a few drops of blood fall on the pebble, leaving it exposed to the sun until it was dry.

But Wangrin had no intention of limiting himself to this animist ceremony. "If you haven't got your mother's breast you must make do with your grandmother's," he thought. Since he couldn't consult Tierno Siddi and Mulaye, he felt it was indispensable to make do with the services of any old marabout he might come across.

So he sent for several who lived in the neighboring towns.

Within a few days, he had set up a real arsenal of occultists of every kind and caliber: geomancers, magicians, interpreters of dreams and animal cries, diviners of animal tracks, etc., etc.

Like the practical fellow he was, Wangrin realized that this occult intervention would not suffer in the least if it were complemented by some assistance from some district officials. Thus, he got in touch with Tiombiano Treman, the chief clerk in charge of correspondence. In his capacity, he was the best possible person to keep Wangrin informed of whatever news the Commandant might receive and dispatch in the mail. For if, according to the saying, an interpreter was the Commandant's tongue and ears, then a clerk was his pencil and his pen.

Wangrin was on excellent terms with Tiombiano and got him to agree without difficulty to pass on to him all information regarding the administrative correspondence. To Bila Kuttu, the unbudgeable orderly of all Commandants past and present, Wangrin offered a high reward in exchange for all the scraps that were likely to be thrown away in the wastepaper basket and subsequently burned by Bila himself. Bila gratefully accepted the offer, but not without saying to himself:

"Wangrin must be nuts to want to buy worthless pieces of paper. If they were worth anything, can you imagine a shrewd white-White tearing them up and having them thrown away on a heap of rubbish? I'm going to be in the fortunate position of the groom who's found a buyer for his horse's dung. . . . "

One fine day, as he was sitting in his usual place on the verandah, Romo was visited by a special messenger from Gudugaua who gave him a letter. Romo read it avidly. It must have brought him good news, for his lips stretched in a happy smile and his face lit up with joy. He looked like a man who, having been sentenced to death, has just been told of his reprieve. He spun around several times and tucked away the letter carefully in his pocket. Then he returned to his bench and contrary to his habit began to exchange pleasantries with the *porsantans* who surrounded him as if he'd been chatting to his *sanankuns*.[4]

The unwonted elation caused great astonishment. The *porsantan* chosen by Wangrin as the daily reporter of Romo's doing and moods was careful to signal this happening.

Wangrin sent at once for his *Gurmantche*[5] geomancer Kalalempo Kompari. He requested him to "consult the earth" and foretell what would happen to Romo and himself in the next few weeks. "If Romo rejoices like a newlywed who's discovered that his bride is a virgin after all, it must mean that the old vampire's ears have been tickled by some agreeable disclosure. No . . . since Romo's pleasure is necessarily my sorrow, I'd like his joy to subside in his breast and rot like a grain of millet that has dropped in a pool of water."

"When the sun has closed his fiery eye and night has enveloped all things in her somber mantle," replied Kalalempo, "I shall come to you. The earth cannot speak properly when the people who inhabit her are vociferating."

Night descended. Men and diurnal beasts returned to their shelter and lay down to rest. A time came when only the barking of dogs, answering one another here and there, was heard. Then, silence.

Kalalempo Kompari took his geomancer's gear, which he kept in a satchel made of civet's skin, left his house, and glided toward Wangrin's through deserted, dark alleys. He hooted like an owl and knocked on the secret door. Wangrin was expecting him, and opened at once. Kalalempo stepped inside and settled down comfortably. From his civet-skin bag he let some very fine sand fall on a piece of tanned leather. He took a fistful and handed it to Wangrin, asking him to concentrate and think intently of what he wished to know, and then to stare unblinkingly at his fistful of sand and blow on it. In this way, Kalalempo said, his thoughts would infiltrate the sand.

Wangrin did as he was told. Then he handed back the fistful of sand, now supposed to be impregnated with his thoughts, to Kalalempo who mixed it into the heap which he had piled on the piece of leather, then smoothed it all out into an even surface. Using tiny fox bones, he drew on the sand sixteen geomantic patterns. He pondered on them a goodly while, then said to Wangrin: "Your double is twice as strong as Romo's. But a great white-White chief will be here within the next ten sunrises and sunsets. His fondness for Romo will be such that they will drink from the same calabash. And his hatred for you is so virulent, each time he'll see a dung heap in the road he will exclaim: 'Look, Wangrin has relieved himself again!' As his friend's double, which is exceedingly ill-disposed towards you, will be lodged in him, he will hate you unto death."

"Is there no sacrifice I can offer to counteract the great white-White chief's evil designs?" asked Wangrin.

"If on his arrival you could manage to make him swallow a potion I'm going to prepare . . . if you could find some way or other of smuggling this liquid into his entrails, he would no longer be able to conceal his designs from you and as you know, forewarned is forearmed. Besides you must feed for a whole week five indigent families, providing one measure of millet or rice for each person and a hunk of sheep for each family."

Accordingly, Wangrin singled out five indigent families. He weighed for each of them the stipulated amount of rice and promised to send them a quarter of sheep each day of that week.

Jacques de Chantalba had sent his steward and his cook ahead to Diussola. They preceded their master by five days and, according to his instructions, went to stay with Romo—a token of the good relationship that would exist between the Commandant and his interpreter; for at the time, white-Whites' stewards and cooks, especially those who served in high spheres, by no means mixed with ordinary people: they were much too closely connected with their employers; it would have been easy to use them to deal out potions to the white-Whites that induced love or hatred, even slow poisons. . . .

Kalalempo's prediction was coming true. Wangrin saw that he must intensify his vigilance.

23   Pretty Doe of the Markets

There lived in the town of Diussola a girl called Tenin. She was extraordinarily beautiful, but possessed of a vivacious personality as well as a quick tongue. She went by the nicknames of "Pretty Doe of the Markets" and "Comely Egret of the Caravanserai."[1]

She had always refused all offers, however alluring, to be led to the altar. How many white-Whites had yearned for her! How many had been prepared, if necessary, to go through a French registry office ceremony! "I am not so foolish as to let myself be done in by one man," she would say laughingly, "when thousands of them are ready to die for my beautiful eyes and exquisite mouth!"

While she was still a child, her father had entrusted her to Wangrin's care. The latter had brought her up, made of her an able seamstress, and introduced her to the business world, where she was a great success. She modeled for him the fabrics and some of the feminine items of wear he marketed. If she happened to wear a bubu made of unusual material, the next day every woman in town would try to buy that same material in Wangrin's shop.

Tenin felt for Wangrin a filial devotion that bordered on worship. Although every month he provided her with fine fabrics and handsome suits of clothes, he never demanded payment, either in cash and certainly never in kind. According to the Fulbe adage: "If you want the respect a woman feels for you to wane or vanish altogether, just make love to her and you'll be amply satisfied."

On the eve of Jacques de Chantalba's arrival, Wangrin sent a messenger to Tenin very early in the morning asking her to come to him that same night when the sound of human voices and steps had died down in the streets.

At first, Tenin doubted the authenticity of the message. Never before had her gentle benefactor asked her to visit him at the hour of lovers, thieves, and plotters, as it was commonly called. She felt all the more perplexed in that Wangrin expected her to knock on the secret door, which led straight to his private apartments.

The young woman immediately called Niele, who had been her confidante for so many years, to her side. "My dear old mother," she said. "I badly need your counsel. Wangrin, who has been both a father and a most generous benefactor to me, suddenly asks me to visit him at the hour when both town and nature are enveloped in silence . . . what do you suppose he wants? I confess that I feel apprehensive, for I know that the human heart is a labyrinth inhabited by a thousand passions. Which of Wangrin's passions may be trying to break loose? What makes him ask me to visit him at such an unseemly hour? Could you go to him and find out whether the message I got this morning really did come from him? That's all I want you to do."

Old Niele covered her head with her white wrapper and went out. Avoiding all main thoroughfares, she succeeded in getting to Wangrin's house as inconspicuously as she had left Tenin's.

She found Wangrin reclining on a deck chair, in front of his shop, in the shade of a mango tree. He was lost in a reverie that had led his thoughts far, far away. He was so deep in thought that he neither heard nor saw anything around him. His features were drawn, he looked exhausted, spent, as though he were dead to the world.

"Good afternoon, Wangrin!" came Niele's greeting.

As if rudely awakened from a deep sleep, Wangrin started slightly and replied:

"Forgive me, old Niele, I must have been sleeping with my eyes wide open, just the way certain animals do. Peace be unto you. Make yourself entirely at home and be so kind as to sit next to me and tell me to what I owe the pleasure of your unexpected visit."

"O Wangrin! I do not bear you unhappy news; I have but come to ask if you can help me set someone's mind at rest. According to the proverb: 'When an animal whose anatomy is unknown happens to die and is ready for a skinning, the men who are to do the job don't know where to begin.' In other words, when one is faced with a somewhat unusual task one feels perhaps a little perturbed, a little uneasy, one might even say, a little irresolute."

"Come out into the open with what you have to say, old Niele; not everyone is able to separate the crocodile's tears from the water in which he is swimming. A thought expressed through allusions or parables is not altogether dissimilar from the crocodile's tears that have fallen into the water," added Wangrin.

"The trouble in my poor old heart, the trouble that has guided my steps to your house concerns neither me, nor you, but your protégée, Pretty Doe of the Markets. This morning, just as the children were getting ready to guide their goats to pasture, she was visited by a messenger who claimed to have been sent by you. He actually said to her: 'O Comely Egret of the Caravanserai, Wangrin will be expecting you very late tonight. . . . ' Now Pretty Doe of the Markets would like to know whether it was really you who sent that message."

Wangrin looked pensively at Niele: "Heavens above!" he exclaimed. "So there are already four of us who know my secret!"

"Don't worry about me," protested Niele. "I'll be as silent as a grave."

Wangrin crisped his mouth in a grimace of doubt. "An old woman full of discretion and silent as a grave? If anything, she's more likely to *go* into a grave!" he was thinking to himself. But aloud he said: "All right, Niele. Since you promise to be as silent as a grave, I promise to give you a suit of new clothes for the next festival, and enough francs to fill both your palms if you really are able to control your tongue. But if you don't, instead I promise you a very sharp blade to shave your head with and every hairy spot on your body as well before I cut your tongue as far down as your uvula and slit your throat all the way to the neckbone!"

Instinctively, the old woman brought a hand to her throat, as if she were trying to protect it from that hypothetical knife.

"No, Wangrin!" she said. "I know that you are a man of your word, but still. . . . You won't slit my throat, will you?"

"It will all depend on you, my good woman. I don't want to keep you too long now. Go to Tenin Pretty Doe and tell her that the message did come from me and that I expect her at the time and place I mentioned. She is very much at home in the dark, moreover this week the moon is not flooding us with her indiscreet glow."

Niele was about to leave when Wangrin slipped in her hand two hundred-franc notes. "So that you can buy yourself some fresh milk, my good Niele. . . . "

The old woman drew strength from this gift. Baring her teeth in a smile like that of a boiled sheep's head, she returned to Tenin Pretty Doe's house in a third of the time it had taken her to come.

Seeing such a cheerful expression on her face, Pretty Doe of the Markets thought that Wangrin had denied having sent the message. . . . Alas, the old woman undeceived her at once. The message did come from Wangrin. "He expects you without fall tonight. Make sure you get there," she piped cheerfully instead.

Pretty Little Doe pouted sadly, as if she'd just heard news of her mother's or her maternal uncle's death. Having repeated word for word her interview with Wangrin, Niele tried to give her some good advice.

But Pretty Doe, suddenly lost in a daydream, was no longer listening. Instead, she was mentally exploring a vast city of her imagination, and searching for someone who might tell her how to conduct herself during the forthcoming interview with her adoptive father. But all the city gates remained impenetrably closed. Like one electric discharge following another, her mind began roaming rapidly all the streets and alleys of her chimerical city, but none of the doors opened, none of the inhabitants peered out. Pretty Little Doe came back to her senses.

"Sheathe your tongue properly," she said to old Niele. "You know that Wangrin is very good at making other people laugh while he himself remains in dead earnest. If you were inadvertently to drop one single hint of what passed between you two this morning, Wangrin would make such a gash in your throat that his knife would split even the soil beneath you.[2] If on the other hand you keep your mouth tightly shut, he'll dress you to the nines and he'll put plenty of good money in your basket."[3]

"I'll try not to emulate the man who kept trying to fish for sardines while a caiman was already busy chewing one of his feet!" replied Niele.

The old woman left Pretty Doe deep in thought. Like a crazed little bird, her mind fluttered between two alternatives: whether to keep her nocturnal tryst or stay at home. Finally she decided in favor of the former.

The young woman supped without enthusiasm. All she could get down was a small mound of rice and three little gulps of milk.

As time drew near, she bathed and decked herself in her best finery. Scented like a flower, she set forth toward Wangrin's house. On the way there she didn't meet anybody and didn't even notice that a shadow was following her at some distance, choosing the same alleys and bifurcations as herself.

Pretty Doe knocked on the secret door. Five minutes passed without a soul showing up. She was about to turn back, when a man swathed in a dark cape came out of the shadows and said: "You are impatient, my daughter. Wait, the door is going to open." The girl thought his voice familiar, but she was too frightened to incline her mind to any kind of careful listening.

The masked individual came forward and to Tenin's surprise pulled a key out of his pocket, opened the door, drew aside and said: "Go in."

Paralyzed with fear, Pretty Doe took a few steps, followed by the masked man, who then proceeded to open the door leading to the private apartments. She slipped like an automaton into the darkened room. The man struck a match and lit an acetylene lamp that had been left ready on the table.

As the flame dispelled the darkness, Pretty Doe, who was at last recovering her spirits, exclaimed: "Who are you? Where is Papa Wangrin?"

Without answering, the man tore off his mask and said: "Here I am!" It was Wangrin.

The young woman drew back a few steps, her eyes and her mouth wide open with astonishment. Then she said, "O Pa Wangrin, you are a real devil! You nearly frightened me to death."

"I walked behind you in case any vampire nesting in that old haunted cotton tree that is Romo might try to intercept you on the way here and consign you to the night, which knows how to swallow with impunity any passerby. . . . "

"Thank you, Pa Wangrin."

"On the contrary, it is I who must thank you for consenting to come to me at this unusual and seemingly libidinous hour of night."

"What do you want your daughter to do?"

"I want my Pretty Doe to do me a favor which is both easy and difficult, yet something that a beautiful girl can manage with a minimum of effort."

"Come straight to the point, Pa Wangrin, I am in agony lest you ask me for something that I am not able to offer you. I am well aware that you have given me unstintingly—your protection, your kindness, and your generosity have bred in me an attachment and a feeling of gratitude so deep that nothing could eradicate them. But what is it you want from me?"

"I want you to help me to get a magic potion stirred into the stew that is going to be fed to the new Commandant. He will be here in a few days. You'll have to ensure the complicity either of his cook or of the steward who will serve him at table."

Pretty Doe raised her arms in a joyful gesture. "Maa-Ngala!"[4] she said, "thank you for having prevented my father from asking me something that a girl, however wanton she may be, cannot give her father. . . . "

Deeply moved by her words, Wangrin said: "What did you think I was going to ask you, my child?"

"I thought you wanted me to surrender my body to you. That's why I got myself so dressed up and scented."

"And if it had been that?" asked Wangrin.

"I would have let you take me, but afterwards I would have drowned myself in the old ancestral well which has never regurgitated any living soul!" Wangrin pressed the young woman against his breast.

"I am no old libertine," he said. "I know that you consider me your father, and my wives your mothers."

Pretty Doe drew herself up and spoke with great determination: "I don't quite know how I'm going to set about it, but I assure you that the new Commandant will drink your potion as many times as you wish him to!"

Wangrin saw her safely home.

The night continued to cradle gently all sleeping things till dawn. Then the first crowing of the roosters woke the housewives, who began to pound millet for the first meal of the day. The first strokes of the pestle woke the muezzins, who climbed their minarets and threw out their call to prayer. This, in turn, woke the faithful. Sounds of human voices began to be heard, mingled with animal cries. As the sun rose, so, gradually, did the uproar.

Later that day, around three in the afternoon, instruments began to play all over Diussola. Improvised, made-up songs rose from every quarter, while a human throng emptied itself onto the road that led to the Residence. The new Commandant was expected between five and six. All the inhabitants of Diussola in their Sunday best, whether they felt like it or not, were expected to form rows along the sides of the main artery that crossed town and led to the Commandant's residence, then shout their welcome, and wave hands as well as handkerchiefs. On no account must the representative of France discern traces of sadness in the features of the inhabitants of his jurisdiction, for this would suggest a lack of enthusiasm on their part! Decidedly, Jacques de Chantalba was not to be insulted in that way. His good friend Romo, who was about to become the "demigod" of the district, would see to it that his deity was suitably honored.

Around 5:45 P.M., a car flourishing the French flag appeared on the main road and nosed its way into town. At once the sound of drums, balaphons, castanets, flutes, trumpet-horns, the clapping of hands, the griot women's yu-yus, and the vociferations of wags redoubled in intensity, as if each group were vying for first prize. For a Commandant is the microcosm of French authority. Jacques de Chantalba was seen to rise, and from a standing position wave right and left in the same way as the governor was wont to do, and the governor-general, and the minister of colonial affairs, who was the greatest of all colonial masters and responsible for all administrators, who, in turn, feared him and him alone.

Romo, astride a superb mount, escorted the car as if he were the defender of the Commandant's very life.

Wangrin was seated among the managers of the largest firms in town. A dais, situated in front of the residence, had been reserved for officials, missionaries, and managers of big businesses. Thanks to his license, Wangrin had been given a prominent seat.

As soon as Jacques de Chantalba had done with the African crowd, he proceeded with great ceremony toward the dais where the men who went by the name of "constituted bodies" but whom an indecorous joke had re-christened "constipated bodies" were awaiting him.

He shook hands with some, others he regaled with a smile, while a few got no more than a quick, absent-minded glance. With the bishop, he lingered longer than with most.

When he came to Wangrin, Jacques de Chantalba shook hands in a distant sort of way, saying: "I've heard a lot about your doings. I would like to get to know you."

"Thanks to France, Sir," replied Wangrin, "my business is positively flourishing. I am entirely at your disposal as far as making myself known to you is concerned."

With the official introductions over, the crowd dispersed while re-freshments and a variety of drinks were being offered to the officials. Wangrin contented himself with a glass of lemonade.

The day after his arrival, the Commandant sat down to work with Romo as his closest assistant as had been expected. From the word go, no effort was spared to confound Wangrin and eventually destroy him.

24   Two Birds with One Stone

Chantalba had a cook by the name of Burabura. One day, this same cook went to the market to buy some meat. All of a sudden a sweet, feminine scent wafted over to him. He turned round, and found himself face to face with the most beautiful creature he had ever beheld in his whole life. Very perturbed, he drew aside to make way for the girl, for she must be a queen, or at least the bride of a great chief!

Tenin Pretty Doe parted her lips in a beautiful smile. "Brother!" she exclaimed. "Why are you shying away? You are running from me as if I were a *touch-and-perish* woman![1] But if you're really afraid of me, run away by all means like a scared little rabbit!"

A descendant of the Gurunsi dynasty of Leo, Burabura had royal blood flowing in his veins and a heart full of dignity. The nobility of his double heritage surged within him. Recovering himself, he replied: "Little sister, tell me where I can find you and you'll see whether I am a coward or not."

"It's up to the thirsty man to look for the limpid stream that will refresh him," she replied. "So long, brother. . . . "

Burabura watched her graceful gait as she drew away from him. He finished his shopping, paid, and returned to the Commandant's residence. Thereafter his mind was besieged by her image; he yearned to breathe again the scent that had so excited him the moment the entrancing goddess had made herself manifest to him.

While cooking, Burabura started humming the tune *denin cee kanyi,* which means: "The girl is lovely. . . . " He was so unmindful of what he was doing that in spite of his reputation for being—second only to the famous Biga—the best cook in the area, he was compelled to start all over again, for in all his concoctions there was either too much or too little salt while some were even burnt.

When the cooking was done, instead of tidying as usual he left dirty pans and utensils scattered all over the kitchen, and returned to town to look for the girl who had obsessed him all day and whose name he didn't even know. He was hoping to overhear some conversation or to meet her by chance, as he had done earlier.

But he walked in vain all over town and didn't get home till very late. Romo was beginning to worry. He had seen the steward Zumana return before Burabura, which was extremely unusual.

Romo asked a few questions, but was unable to get any clear explanation. He decided not to plague the cook who after all was a grown-up and did not have to account for his comings and goings.

He decided to warn him, however, against keeping bad company in Diussola. . . .

Burabura continued his search for Pretty Doe ten whole days. Then he thought: "I must open my heart to an old woman. She might be able to help me track down the girl who has made me lose my sleep and appetite, or perhaps she can prepare a potion that will make me forget her."

Now there was an old woman called Vassa Wattara, who sold little rice puffs near the meat-shop where Burabura took his custom. She could be found there every morning of the week.

Burabura went up to her and said: "My good old auntie, would you sell me ten centimes' worth of rice puffs?" Then he threw a fifty centime coin on the palmyra leaf winnowing-fan that old Vassa had placed before her. The old woman shook with laughter: "Where do you think I am going to find forty centimes' change? You are my first customer of the day."

"You needn't give me any change. I am looking for a mother, and if you consented to become a mother to me, you could keep the forty centimes as a gift from your adopted son."

"Well, my dear boy! I don't know whether I'll make a good mother or not, but there are ways of giving that are most compelling, so I can hardly refuse to act as your mother. May the spirits of my ancestors guide me, that I may not disappoint you. . . . What is your name?"

"My name is Burabura, the Gurunsi. I am the Senior Commandant's cook."

Vassa gave Burabura her address and invited him to lunch. Around one in the afternoon, his work all finished, Burabura jumped on his bicycle and went to old Vassa's house, where a savory dish of rice and fish was awaiting him. He had found himself a mother whom he could trust with secrets of the sort he could not have brought himself to confide to Romo.

"Mother!" he said. "I am sick with love for a girl I saw in the market." And he went on to describe the girl of his dreams with such precision that Vassa was able to recognize Tenin Pretty Doe of the Markets without effort.

"O my son!" she cried. "Avoid her like the plague. The salary you earn in a whole year wouldn't buy the amount of scent she used in one week. Rather, she would be a choice morsel for your Commandant, if he didn't already have his own French wife."

"Mother, could you arrange for Tenin to come and see me, either here or at the Residence, where the Commandant has set up lodgings for his steward Zumana and myself?"

"I will try," she promised.

That same evening Vassa went to call on Tenin Pretty Doe, and spoke to her of Burabura.

Contrary to her expectations, Tenin announced:

"Burabura is a very handsome young man. He has struck a chord in my heart. I love him for his fine body, fashioned by God with so much art and symmetry, but I'm afraid I might cause him a good deal of unhappiness. I will think about it, anyway, and in a couple of days I will come to inform you of my decision, Mother Vassa."

That same day, Jacques de Chantalba, on horseback, accompanied by his lance-sergeant and his favorite interpreter Romo, inspected the Lartawa district. This happened to be the area where Tenin Pretty Doe was living at the time.

Very provocatively attired, Tenin came to sit in the doorway in front of her house, so that she was in full view. As Jacques de Chantalba drew near, Tenin rose from her seat and began waving her beautiful hands in a joyful gesture, as if she were searching for a suitable way of greeting the Commandant. The latter appreciated enormously being applauded by one of the most beautiful women he had ever seen in the whole of Africa, but even more than the applause, he appreciated Tenin's magnificent curves.

Like the old fox he was, Romo understood perfectly well what was going on. He saw that Tenin had made a deep impression on the Commandant and that before long she would be mistress of his heart. This was most unfortunate for him since Tenin, as the whole town knew, was Wangrin's adopted daughter.

Romo thought it over. If Tenin did manage to steal the Commandant's heart, wouldn't that be a valuable card in Wangrin's hand?

It was essential, then, to prevent it from happening; it was essential not to let Wangrin put a foot in the door. He knew only too well that if Wangrin could do this, very soon his whole body would follow.

Only two days had elapsed since the inspection of the Lartawa district, when Jacques de Chantalba asked Romo to come to his house after office hours. He offered him a huge glass of lemonade and for himself he poured an inch or so of Pernod-Fils diluted with water.

The two companions emptied half their glasses, set them down on the table, and waited. Romo suspected that they were going to discuss a personal matter, since official business was always dealt with at the office, regardless of the time of day.

Looking intently at Romo, Chantalba very carefully wiped every trace of drink from his lips with his tongue. Then he began:

"Old Romo, although here in Diussola you know me only as your Commandant, I am also a man, subject, like any other, to all the frailties of human nature. Now, I want to let you into an important secret. Since I've set eyes on that lovely creature in the Lartawa district, I have had no peace of mind. You must find some way of bringing her to me in strict secrecy. . . . "

Romo felt a cold shiver run down his spine. All his fears were becoming reality.

Somehow, he managed to control himself and to reply:

"Tenin is a beautiful girl, Sir, most beautiful I'd say, but very forward and immodest. If I were to ask her to come to you secretly, she'd be quite capable of blackmailing us. In my opinion, the best way to go about this is to discover some peccadillo of hers, then summon her to your office, where you can speak to her in all discretion and offer to save her from a prosecution that might easily end in a prison sentence. Among our people, a prison sentence is the most infamous thing in the world. Every single one of our dignitaries would willingly renounce his entire fortune to avoid even one day in jail."

Jacques de Chantalba gave the matter some consideration, then he sucked in his lips as if he were trying to swallow them. At last he said: "Let's try your peccadillo idea. We'll see what happens."

Romo went home as preoccupied as the Commandant was enamored. He sent at once for the agent in charge of hygiene and cleanliness in the town and gave him the following instructions: "This is a confidential order issued by our Commandant," he said. "Tomorrow morning you will inspect the Lartawa district. You will post yourself outside Tenin Pretty Doe's house. As soon as her servant throws a bucket of dirty water in the street,[2] you will draw up a report against Tenin accusing her of sullying a public thoroughfare with dirty water and household refuse."

The next morning at eight-thirty the report was ready on the

Commandant's desk. At nine o'clock Romo prepared a summons against Tenin Pretty Doe. Toward ten, an official paper was delivered at her door, ordering her to present herself before the Commandant at eleven over "a matter which concerned her directly."

Panic-stricken, Tenin ran to Wangrin. She showed him the summons and told him her story. Wangrin was silent for a few minutes, then he said: "I'd be very surprised if they summoned you before the Senior Commandant over a pail of dirty water emptied on a public thoroughfare. It is a minor offense—one that usually comes under the Junior Commandant's jurisdiction. I get the impression, rather, that Jacques de Chantalba wants to take a good look at you from close quarters. . . .

"Has Romo ever asked you to do anything for him?" he questioned her.

"No," answered Tenin. She felt bound to add: "They say that Romo's 'huge nerve' has been smothered by fat."

"Don't you believe it," answered Wangrin. "Romo is a perfect bull, as virile as they come. But he's faithful to his wives as the angels are to prayer.

"Whatever happens, you will get a chance to see the Commandant in person, perhaps you'll even see him alone. Fortunately you speak French. However small a dent you make in his heart, it will counterbalance Romo's influence on him, and that would suit me fine. So play the innocent, coax him, but don't let him take you on the sofa right there in his office. On your way back, come and tell me what happened. And above all, beware of Romo. He may be big and fat, but he's far from being stupid."

Stimulated by her dear papa's good advice, Tenin went home, dressed to the nines, scented herself, and set off for the Commandant's residence.

As soon as she had set foot on the verandah, her perfume wafted into every corner. An intense murmur rose, ricocheting from mouth to ear: "Look at Tenin!" Within a few minutes, half the office staff had come out to take a look at the lovely woman who drove most men crazy without, however, surrendering herself to them. As a matter of fact, her bad reputation was due to her free ways and cutting tongue rather than to any real depravity.

Romo went toward Tenin. Lowering her lids as a sign of respect she handed him the summons.

"Follow me," he said.

Once they were in the office, Romo announced Tenin and then disappeared.

With the arrogance she reserved for a certain kind of man, Tenin looked straight at the Commandant and said: "Here I am, Sir."

He let his glance rest on her. Then, hoping to intimidate her: "So you don't think that the hygiene of this town matters, do you?" he said. "You are indifferent to the fact that flies will multiply and mosquitos will swarm? Our doctor has advised me to send you to jail for a couple of days for having violated our hygiene regulations. In France, I will have you know, doctors are as powerful as healers are in your country. One dare not contradict them without risking a jail sentence. They are responsible for public health, and they care for human lives and animals as well."

Tenin, smiling, replied: "If your doctor wants to punish me because he's more powerful than I am, let him do so. But to accuse me of all people of not respecting hygiene is an insult, and I am exceedingly surprised at him for behaving in this way."

It didn't take Chantalba long to realize that Tenin could not be frightened easily. That meant that she couldn't be taken in by his little trick.

"Give me the summons," he said, extending a hand, "and sit down a moment."

Tenin sat on a chair close to the desk and leaned on it with both elbows, holding her face between her hands.

With a smile, the Commandant said: "I'm going to ask our doctor to forgive you this time. I haven't forgotten how nicely you clapped your pretty hands for me when I made a tour of your district. It would be a pity for a beautiful girl like you to have to go to jail."

"Thank you, Sir. You are very kind."

"Are you married, Tenin?"

"No, I haven't come across quite the right man yet."

"Would you like to be my wife?"

"Oh no! I've heard that white-White women are in the habit of shooting their rivals. I have no desire whatsoever to be shot by your wife."

"My wife lives in Bordeaux, in France."

"Yes, but your telegraph wires have a very indiscreet way of passing on news."

"You have absolutely nothing to fear from her. You could visit me twice a week."

"I'm going to think it over and I'll let you have a reply through your cook Burabura, whom I see from time to time at the meat-shop, which is fairly close to my house."

The Commandant rose and went to his cupboard. He pulled out five hundred-franc notes and handed them to Tenin. He stroked the young woman's chin and cheek. Tenin, who was playing the prude, remonstrated faintly, without however pushing away Jacques de Chantalba's nervous hand.

"Sir, if your interpreter, Pa Romo, got to hear of this," she protested, "I'd feel terribly ashamed. I'd lose face if you told him of what may be happening between you and me. Can I count on your discretion? More-over, the old man hasn't been particularly fond of me since I turned down an offer of marriage from a white-White who was using him as his go-between. I don't mean to say that old Romo is a bad sort, it's just that in our society elderly people disapprove of us if we don't submit to their every wish. They take it as the kind of rebuff that might lessen their prestige in the eyes of others."

"All right. Although I always confide in Romo, I won't tell him about our arrangement. Where do you come from, Tenin?"

"I was born in Leo, in Gurunsiland," improvised the young woman.

"What a happy coincidence. My cook comes from the same part of the country."

As soon as Tenin had left the office, Romo went in.

"Is she toeing the line, Sir?" he asked.

The Commandant shook his head. "Not yet," he said. "It isn't going to be easy. I'll have to think of another approach. For the time being, let's forget Tenin and turn our minds to more important matters."

Romo felt a new awkwardness in the air. He went back to his seat and plunged himself in meditation. What had really happened between Tenin and the Commandant? What could she have told him? What might be her reasons for refusing him, or her conditions for accepting? Romo smelled a rat. He was almost on the point of advising his superior to mistrust Tenin because of her close relationship with Wangrin. But at the last moment he hesitated: "I'd better wait till I have some more plausible reason for damaging her in the eyes of the Commandant." However, he resolved to stretch a powerful network of spies round the young woman.

Immediately after her interview with the Commandant, Tenin went to see Wangrin, related to him what had happened in detail, and offered him the five hundred francs.

"You've handled him extremely well, my child!" exclaimed Wangrin.

"The master stroke was to say you were born in Leo. It will come in very useful later. But from now on you'll have to stay home most of the time and watch all your male and female visitors closely. Fearing that I might try to use you to win Chantalba over to my side, Romo will cast his net about you and do his best to report any gossip that concerns you to the Commandant. We must act quickly, and get Jacques de Chantalba to swallow the potion while the going is good, for Romo is bound to find us out sooner or later."

On her way home, Tenin called on old Vassa and said to her: "When your son Burabura comes to visit you, tell him that I'll be happy to see him at my house as soon as he can get there, that I must speak to him about an extremely important matter."

Burabura never let a day go by without calling on his old mother, whether in the morning or in the evening. That particular day he arrived in the early afternoon. At once Vassa said to him: "Tenin was here two hours ago. She would like you to call on her before you go back to work. She has something very special to tell you."

Burabura couldn't get over his astonishment. He burst into a joyous monologue: "Me? Invited by Tenin, after I've tried so long to find her. . . . I can't believe it. . . . I'm dreaming. . . . No! I'm not dreaming, it's true. My mother Vassa has told her about me. She did say that Tenin finds me attractive, that she would think it over and let me know her decision. No doubt she wants to give me an answer, and I fondly hope it will be favorable. . . . and where does she suggest seeing me . . . ? At her house, yes, at her house! . . . *Wallayi!* At her house! . . . May God change me into a gorilla if it's not true that I'm prepared to spend five or ten years in jail in exchange for a night with Tenin!"

Carried away by his rapturous transport, Burabura went out, forgetting even to say good-bye to Mother Vassa. He ran like a squirrel all the way to Tenin, whom he found seated on a Hausa mat, wearing an informal gown that showed with delicacy the admirable proportions of her figure.

Excited beyond description, Burabura greeted her with the words "Happy New Year," instead of "Good day."

Mockingly, Tenin replied: "You must have an entire army of archers at your heels that you've lost your composure to the extent of confusing a whole year with one day!"

"Something far more powerful than an army has thrown me into such a state of confusion: it is your invitation together with my desire to see you. I have been calling you in vain for so long that the tears have dried in my eyes and my saliva in my mouth. Oh Tenin, how can I possibly continue to be the man I used to be when I am ready to become anything you choose. . . . "

"You speak like God,[3] I declare, brother Burabura! But I must ask you to follow me to my room, where no indiscreet ear can perceive what a brother and sister may have to say to each other."

"You are right, Tenin. The vestibule of a house represents not only a public place, but also an ear that knows not how to keep to itself what it has heard."

Tenin rose, Burabura followed, and together they entered Tenin's private apartment, which consisted of three large rooms, some smaller rooms for washing and dressing, and a box-room.

A huge gilded bed, resting on tall legs and adorned by four mosquito netting holders, stood at the center of one of the three rooms. Beautiful, framed portraits hung on the walls of the reception room, which was lined with long, upholstered seats reserved for visitors. The floor, although cemented, was covered all over with colored mats.

Never had Burabura set foot in an African house so clean, so tastefully furnished, so fragrant as this. He didn't know what to do next. Was the proper thing to sit down without waiting to be told? Like a master who returns to his own house after work, or an acknowledged lover? Or was it better to await a sign from Tenin? He opted for the latter. "Let's be patient," he thought, "for the midwife who hurries the labor risks getting hold of something other than the baby's head."[4]

While Burabura was deliberating, Tenin watched her prey. Like a rabbit who comes face to face with a python, Burabura, mesmerized by her scent and her beauty, was waiting to be swallowed without attempting to defend himself.

Tenin sat down on one of the sofas and drew Burabura to her side. When Tenin touched his hand, the youth felt a shock, as if he'd come close to Ntiguin, the electric fish. He began to tremble.

"You are trembling, my brother," said Tenin.

"Yes, my sister; not with fear, but with desire. I love you. I feel that I will love you always, come what may."

Tenin saw that she could ask, and obtain, anything from Burabura.

"Rest your head on my knees,"[5] she said to him, "and control your emotion for the time being. I couldn't give you better proof of my feeling than this. But now you must recover your composure and listen carefully to what I have to say."

"I am listening, Tenin," replied the youth.

"This morning around eleven, the Commandant, your master, summoned me to his office. He wants me to become his wife, or his mistress. . . . This complicates my life and will not make yours any the easier. . . .

"Now I have an adopted father who is extremely knowledgeable in African customs and equally well informed on the ways of the white-Whites. I have gone to him and confessed that I feel attracted to you. I have also told him of my interview with the Commandant.

"Although my father is well-disposed towards you, he has warned me of the risks we might incur if the Commandant were to hear that you stand in the way of his desire. As he is friendly with all the marabouts, magicians, rope-knotters, and wizards of the region, he has asked them to prepare a potion whose effect will be to neutralize any harmful ideas the Commandant might have about us. If he swallows this potion, he will be as helpless against us as a python who's just swallowed a doe.[6] All you'll have to do is to mix a few drops of the potion in his soup or in the water you use for cooking. If you keep on doing it for a period of seven days or so, he'll have had enough for the potion to be effective."

"Tell me about your adopted father, Tenin."

"My father is disliked both by Romo and by your master. But thank God, they are powerless against him. He is formidably well protected by occult forces. Besides, he's immensely rich and most generous with his friends. On the other hand, it must be said that he's harsh—extremely harsh—with people who try to stand in his way. It is always advisable to have him as a friend rather than as an enemy."

"It wouldn't be Wangrin by any chance?"

"That's exactly who it is. But how did you guess?"

"The Commandant and Romo talk about him often. Zumana, the steward, and I too, have been ordered never to have anything to do with him or with any member of his family, and to avoid his friends."

"Fate is mocking Romo and the Commandant, then!" exclaimed Tenin, laughing. "For it has ordained that both you and the Commandant fall madly in love with Wangrin's daughter. But tell me, can you still love me, now that you know of my relationship to him?"

"Yes, Tenin. I would love you even if you were the daughter of the most dangerous vampire or criminal in the world!"

"Thank you, my brother," cried Tenin, and in so saying, she bent so low over Burabura, who was lying on his back with his head on the lap of his beloved, that her breasts brushed his cheeks.

This unmistakably intimate gesture assured Burabura once and for all that he occupied a very warm place in Tenin's heart. For him, the best way to reply was to swear to Tenin that from now on he would share with her both friends and enemies.

Taking him at his word, Tenin added: "Romo is my enemy, and also Wangrin's, while Wangrin is my father, therefore your father too. This is what I propose we do," she urged on. "Let us go at once to Wangrin and ask him what steps we must take to ensure our safety against Romo and the Commandant. It is a most valid and indispensable precaution. In relation to Romo, we're like two small pigeon eggs lying close to a large stone. It wouldn't take him long to reduce us to smithereens. But if we place ourselves under Wangrin's protection, the protection of a bold father with an infinity of means at his disposal for neutralizing the enemy, things will take on an entirely different complexion. He will help us with advice, money, and the prayer of his occultist friends."

Burabura shot up as if an invisible spring hidden between Tenin's legs had suddenly thrown him forward. He stood as straight as a young palmyra tree and said:

"I would wage war on the whole world, should it attempt to come between you and me. I would take the devil for an ally if I thought that was the way to triumph over my enemies. Let's not waste a single minute, then, let's go at once to Wangrin. . . . "

"Gently!" cried Tenin. "My house may be closely watched by Romo's people. His spy, if he's clever, could follow us unseen and discover that we've gone together to see Wangrin. Let me go there on my own. As I visit him at least twice a day, no one will think anything of it. But you must wait for me here. I'll send someone along to tell you what to do next."

"Run along, and be as quick as you can, for to me, minutes will resemble long days with neither breakfasts nor lunches to punctuate them, or those long nights without supper, when mosquitos feast on one's flesh. . . . "

Pulling on a vast bubu over her head before going out, Tenin answered with a laugh: "I'll go as fast as a spark bouncing off a lightning rod, and my messenger will be as intent on his task as the thoughts of a lover."

Then she was off to see Wangrin. Her adopted father was reclining as usual on his deck chair, in the shade of his mango tree. He seemed beset by a consuming worry, although his features remained unaltered.

"Good day, father," greeted Tenin.

"Good day, my daughter," replied Wangrin, attempting with some difficulty to extricate himself from the depths of his low seat. Tenin sketched in with a few rapid strokes the miraculous change she had wrought in Burabura. He was actually ready, she said, to come before Wangrin, ask for his advice, and place himself under his protection.

"*Wallayi*, Tenin! Maa-Ngala and his intermediaries are on our side. Thanks to you, my daughter, I am going to have not one, but two eyes constantly trained on Jacques de Chantalba as well as my cordial enemy and pathetic compatriot, Romo."

Followed by Tenin, Wangrin went to his private apartment. He opened a large wooden trunk and pulled out an outfit consisting of baggy trousers, long-sleeved top, flowing *turti*, vast bubu, bulging turban, and heavy leather bag supposedly filled with sachets containing medicine. It was the attire worn by itinerant Hausa dealers who by preference sold medicinal powders and healing herbs. He handed everything to his servant Maatemimbo, saying: "Run faster than a cheetah to Tenin's house. In her room, you will find a man named Burabura. You will ask him to dress up as an itinerant peddler and to join me at Nieba Sanun's tavern."

Wangrin and Tenin went to Nieba Sanun's, a neighbor who was very devoted to Wangrin and his family, ahead of Burabura. The latter, disguised as a Hausa merchant and led by Maatemimbo, joined them very soon after. Nieba Sanun left them alone, so that they might be free to converse undisturbed.

Wangrin turned to the youth:

"I am happy to hear that you have decided to trust me and place yourself under my protection. I will watch over you as carefully as I watch over my very dear daughter Tenin, and I'll ask Maa-Ngala to watch over us all. With Romo as enemy, one can't be better protected! You see, Burabura, if Tenin refuses to yield to the Commandant, before two weeks are out she'll be in plenty of trouble, and so will you.[7] Control your jealousy, then, and accept the fact that you have no rights over Tenin just yet, although she has confessed to me that she is in love with you. Endure your sorrow patiently. Soon the Commandant will leave the country.[8] Meanwhile, even if he is the least bit suspicious, he won't be able to harm you provided you follow my instructions to the letter. Here they are: First of all, Romo must never get to know that any accord exists between us. You will visit him all the more often and if by chance my name comes up in conversation, whether it is Romo or anybody else who mentions it, you will speak of me with as much spleen as you can manage. Secondly, you will tell the Commandant that Tenin accepts his proposal but as she has just begun a period, which usually lasts five to six days, she will let him know where and when she can meet him as soon as she feels better. The Commandant won't be surprised when you deliver this message, as Tenin has warned him that she will use you as her messenger. Thirdly, while Tenin is supposedly menstruating you will empty this potion into Jacques de Chantalba's every meal. It's important that within seven days he swallows the contents of this half bottle. Here it is. You'll always be able to meet me here, at Nieba Sanun's, between two and five in the afternoon. Don't forget to wear your disguise."

Their interview at an end, Burabura changed into his ordinary clothes and returned to work, clutching the precious bottle with the magic liquid.

Burabura felt supremely happy and gave vent to his joy by declaiming the songs of his native land. The steward Zumana came to ask him what sort of rapture had caused him to break into song. Instead of replying, the youth intoned:

That which my ears have perceived.
My tongue is unable to express.
The damsel whom everyone chases
Has chased me,

Saying, "Wait!"
I thought I had misheard,
But my heart said: "She's calling. . . .
She, whom everyone calls,
Is calling you now."
I answered reeling with joy.
Her lovely lap became my cushion,
My body at rest,
My imagination feverish.
Inebriated by her scent
Which filled my nostrils,
My right hand wished to caress.
My left hand said "No! Wait!"
My heart danced the rumba.
Ah! Zumana, son of my mother,
If you only knew what has happened to me,
You'd say: "Elder brother, sing,
Sing till flowers and leaves float to the ground,
Sing till the city walls crumble and fall!"
Death can take him who is beloved
Death can take even himself
But death can never take love.

That same evening, the Commandant's tea and soup had already been copiously seasoned with the potion.

After dinner, while Zumana was washing up, Chantalba motioned to Burabura to come to him. Before the Commandant had time to open his mouth, Burabura was already reciting: "Sir, I have a message for you from my cousin Tenin. She is more than willing to keep you company, but she's just 'entered the moon!'⁹ As soon as she comes out of it, that is in another five or six days, she will give you some sign of life."

"What, what?" exclaimed Jacques de Chantalba. "Tenin is your cousin?"

"Yes, Sir. During a conversation and a genealogical exchange we were able to establish the exact degree of our family relationship."

"That is a most happy coincidence, Burabura, provided you don't make me a cuckold. . . . "

"Never you fear, Sir! I wouldn't want you to cut off my tool. Besides, sexual relations between Tenin and myself are strictly forbidden, unless in a marriage sanctioned by our elders while they are gathered in the ritual vestibule."

He had learned his lesson well. In fact, Burabura had just delivered to his master a tirade perfected by Wangrin in the course of a previous conversation and destined to dispel all suspicion.

Within six days, Burabura had managed to dose the Commandant with the entire contents of the bottle.

Every night, he went secretly to Tenin who for him was neither in nor even near the moon. On the contrary, she was a most passionate lover, for she had genuinely fallen in love with the young man.

But six days later Tenin had to make up her mind at last to become Chantalba's mistress.

Now Wangrin felt sure that, thanks to the potion, the Commandant was inhibited by occult forces, so that no undertaking against himself could ever be crowned by success.

The Commandant may have been swallowing a potion, but as for Romo, he was wide awake and sought more avidly than ever to catch Wangrin red-handed, especially after hearing that Tenin went, according to the saying, to Jacques de Chantalba's "couch" two or three times a week, and that Burabura was their liaison agent.

The only element Romo found reassuring in the whole affair was that the Commandant was obviously still very inimical toward Wangrin and that Burabura himself seemed to be itching for an opportunity to send off Wangrin to be roasted in public in the main square of the town.[10]

Indeed Burabura, on whom Wangrin lavished clothes, provisions, money, and other small pleasurable objects, was playing his part to perfection.

25 A Narrow Escape

Determined to corner Wangrin, Romo had set traps in all directions, but unfortunately his only catch consisted of whatever little scrap of information Wangrin was prepared to surrender. At nightfall Romo's hunters would return always with less in their bags than on previous evenings.

One day, however, Tontori Mapa, a former *tirailleur* whose pension was too exiguous to support him, came especially from Neduna to inform Romo that the man who ran Wangrin's shop over there was selling spirits without a proper license. Romo's joy knew no bounds. He gave Tontori Mapa a handsome reward and took him at once to the Commandant to denounce Wangrin.

The latter registered the denunciation, intending to send a process server on the following day to make some discreet enquiries first and, if the situation warranted it, to draw up a report.

That evening at dinner time, Romo called on his superior with a little more information. Burabura was in the verandah. Suddenly he heard Romo's voice. "Sir," he was saying, "your process server would do well to leave very early, and be there at opening time. That way, it will be easy to catch Wangrin's shopkeeper by surprise. . . . "

Burabura, pretending not to have overheard the conversation, went into the dining room, asked for some shopping money for the following morning, said good-night to the Commandant and to Romo, then left and made his way toward town, to Nieba Sanun's tavern. Almost immediately he was joined by Wangrin, to whom he related the scrap of conversation he had managed to overhear so unexpectedly.

"My shopkeeper has been found out," rejoined Wangrin, "but I am reserving some bitter juice from my mahogany trees[1] for Romo who has detected him. All his charlatans and wizards will have to count many moons before he can rid his palate of that disagreeable taste."

Wangrin decided not to wait until the following day. An hour later he was already at the wheel of his sports car, which he had christened "the shooting-star of the bush."

At nightfall he took every single case of spirits out of his shop and warehouses, leaving behind only syrups and lemonades, for which no license was needed. He sent three cases of aperitifs to the Moboro market. These were to be left with the caretaker of the administrative encampment until further orders. Then he drove on to Gudugaua, arriving there toward seven in the morning. He paid a visit to Sergeant Bourgeois, who was in charge of the non-commissioned officers' (NCOs) canteen, and asked him whether he might be interested in buying three cases of aperitifs such as Pernod, rum, etc.

"I can let you have them at cost price, provided you ante-date your order by twenty days, to help me straighten up some records. And by the way, you could also help me to cut my loss by giving me a contract, starting this month, for part of the supplies of foodstuffs to your battalion—as well as drinks for your mess—until the canteen is officially open."

Convinced that he'd found a nice person as well as a shrewd trader, Sergeant Bourgeois wrote out an ante-dated order for three cases of spirits, and gave him the supply of provisions to the battalion.

In the afternoon, Wangrin left Gudugaua and without deigning to stop in Neduna returned straight to Diussola as if nothing had happened.

Meanwhile the process server commissioned to draw up a report had been searching shops and warehouses without being able to spot any of the cases mentioned by Tontori Mapa. During the two days he spent in Neduna he did gather information according to which Wangrin was in fact selling liquor to former *tirailleurs* through his shopkeeper, but as to laying hands on any incriminating evidence, that he was not able to do.

Back in Diussola, he submitted a report to the Commandant who saw that Romo and himself had gone to a great deal of trouble for nothing.

Wangrin, on the other hand, had been busy writing a note in *forofifon naspa*, and after a schoolboy had copied it, he had had it delivered to Romo. This is what it said:

"Ma dea Romo,

"In dis ma leta, ah wan tel yu somtin wey de for insaid ma beli. Yu put ma secret in Commanda ear. Wisie I don gon for Neduna for faind wishk aind ogogoro Wangran I dey sel cash cash for dia. Bat Wisie's aye no clear clear. Wangran I bad laik di fox o! Him sabi cona cona job pas yu, even pas wisie sef. A bin carri ogogoro boku na cam Moboro. Ah mek mit den boks ful ogogoro laik mama pyssycat I do mit I on pikin. I haid am here, I haid am die, I haid am op an don an efriwa. Na hia ah go stop dis ma leta. Na mi, you fren, Buguri ken Nyeenan."

When Romo read the note, he couldn't help biting his lips with frustration. Of course he wasn't taken in. Buguri ken Nyeenan had never existed. It could only be Wangrin who was pulling his leg yet again. As a matter of fact in Bambara *Buguri ken nyeenan* means "throw dust in my eyes."

Romo was careful not to show this letter to the Commandant. Instead, he sent off one of his men to the Moboro encampment to ask whether it was true that Wangrin had deposited there some cases of alcohol. The answer was positive. Having been informed at once, the Commandant sent his deputy to interrogate the caretaker and to draw up a report accordingly. This preliminary investigation over, the Commandant ordered Wangrin to be charged with having sold spirits without a license.

Fortunately for him, Wangrin was summoned before the French court. If his case had been heard in the indigenous court which was presided over by the Commandant or his deputy, his goose would have been cooked.

He admitted to having deposited three cases containing aperitifs at the Moboro encampment, affirming however that they did not belong to him. He had bought them at cost on behalf of the NCOs' canteen in Gudugaua. Then he exhibited the correct order, duly ante-dated.

"I have every right," he declared, "to buy as much alcohol for private individuals as they wish me to. What I am forbidden from doing, on the other hand, is to make a profit by reselling, or to display bottles containing spirits in my shop. But I am not guilty of either."

Wangrin was acquitted. As he was leaving the court, he glimpsed Romo, who had turned up in the hope of seeing him sentenced.

With his customary laugh, Wangrin muttered to Romo: "Your ears are disappointed, and your evil heart deceived after a long wait. You've heard the exact opposite of what you wished to hear, haven't you, you great lump of swamp flesh?"

"Mother's manure!" replied Romo in the same tone of voice, "Let me remind you that the snake and the heel, keeping close to the ground as they always do, are bound to meet sooner or later, and the day they do there will be a corpse."

"There might even be two," replied Wangrin, "for often before dying the one who's been bitten may well kill the one who bit him."

The day after the trial, Wangrin went to the district office and asked to see the Commandant but the latter, with the excuse that he was extremely busy, refused to receive him.

Wangrin, then, wrote a little note, and asked the orderly to take it to the Commandant:

Sir,

I am a duly registered and perfectly honorable businessman. If you insist on believing Romo's slanderous accusations, you will continue to commit errors which might lead to a regrettable miscarriage of justice.

This morning, I registered with the Special Agency[2] so as to be able to sell as much alcohol as I may wish. I am now in possession of a General Wholesale License.

Assuring you of my great admiration for France, a country to which I am utterly devoted, I raise my voice in the cry 'Hurrah for the French, who always operate in a spirit of justice!'

Signed *Wangrin Gongoloma-Sooke.*

Jacques de Chantalba was not at all enchanted by this letter, which he saw as the expression of a somewhat jaundiced irony.

For his part, Wangrin did not open a mere shop for the sale of alcoholic beverages, but a proper commercial establishment where customers could come and drink.

26 ... In Which Romo Keeps His Promise ... and Wangrin His

A few months later, Romo heard that Wangrin's hunter Soridian was still shooting elephants. As he was mentioning the fact to the Commandant, he remembered all of a sudden that Sanun Wattara had given him the particulars of a rifle gun, a war weapon for which Africans who were not French citizens could not obtain a license. He knew that Wangrin was a "French subject," but not a citizen. Chantalba jumped at the chance and summoned Wangrin.

"You are in possession of a war weapon, and what's more you use it regularly, Wangrin," he said. "Do you have a gun license?"

"No, Sir," replied Wangrin. "I was given that gun by my uncle, who was a provincial chief. And he had been given it by the Governor-General's office as an honorary gift."

"Where are the papers?"

"I never thought of looking for them."

"In that case, bring me that gun. As from today it is confiscated, and henceforth consider yourself liable for arrest."

This time there was real danger. In the colonies, any irregularity in respect of firearms was considered a very serious offense. Out of bravado and an exaggerated belief that luck would always favor him, Wangrin tied the noose by which he could be hanged. For once his mind felt inert, empty of resources. He had no idea what to do . . . so he surrendered his gun to the Commandant.

The Chamber of Commerce, Romo, Chantalba, Count de Villermoz— all of them swarmed in every direction and agitated in high places to ensure that Wangrin was arrested and tried for the serious crime of owning a war weapon without a license. Finally, Chantalba was authorized to arrest Wangrin and lock him up until such time as the preliminary investigation into the case would open.

But Burabura had overheard a conversation in which the Commandant mentioned that Wangrin was to be arrested and tried without delay. Wangrin was informed and set about at once putting his affairs in order. Two of the lesser European traders, Tronedon and Gourbidan by name, were trusted friends of his. The former, once an administrator, had resigned from the colonial service and set himself up in business. A doctor at law and practicing barrister, Tronedon was fond of pleading for Africans. This inclination had rendered him undesirable within the colonial establishment, which was the reason why he had resigned.

Wangrin went to see his two friends and explained his tricky position. He gave Tronedon power of attorney for his defense and asked Gourbidan to watch over his business.

Four days after receiving the order for arraignment, Chantalba finally made up his mind to arrest Wangrin. He called Romo.

"This morning at nine I am going to have Wangrin arrested," he said. "Do you think he'll come along quietly or will he try to put up some resistance?"

"With Wangrin, one never knows. One must be prepared for anything. But at last the day of Wangrin's arrest, the great day I've been waiting for all these years, has come."

Romo fell on his knees as if he were about to offer a prayer to God. He joined his hands and with a quavering, tearful voice, he said:

"Commandant, my dear Commandant. I implore you in the name of what you hold most sacred to allow me to arrest Wangrin. I will take along as many security guards as you think necessary. I will do a trim and tidy job and feel that I have been revenged into the bargain. So will Count de Villermoz and all those who have suffered from Wangrin's infernal schemes. I beg you, Sir, don't deprive me of the honor of arresting Wangrin!"

The Commandant was profoundly moved. With a feverish hand he filled the warrant for Wangrin's arrest. Handing it to Romo: "There you are! Take fifteen men with you and go and get that rogue!" he said.

Romo ordered the lance-sergeant to equip fifteen men in battle order. "Tell them to wait for me near Wangrin's house," he said. "I'll meet them in a quarter of an hour."

A battle between two sorcerers[1] bears no resemblance to a wrestling match in the market square; rather it is fought with occult practices, which release effluvia that blind the opponent, drive him insane—at times even kill him in cold blood! Now—and Romo knew it well—Wangrin was past master of the art, having frequented and employed the greatest exponents of Bambara, Fulbe, Dogon, Marka, Yarse, Samo, Bobo, Mossi, Gurma, Gurunsi, and Pomporon sorcery, and a few others besides. Consequently, Romo could not think of facing Wangrin in his house, on his own ground, without first undergoing some ritualistic preparation. Therefore, after receiving instructions for Wangrin's arrest, he decided to go home for a moment.

Once he was alone in his "man's apartment," he moved to one side his large water jar and dug the soil on which it had been standing. He unearthed a box made of lead. He opened it and drew out a copper key of African make. The key had seven teeth, two of black iron, two of red copper, two of silver, and one of gold.

He advanced toward one of the doors of his room. This door gave access to a more secret repository, where he kept his fetishes. Using his left hand, he introduced the key in the lock, which had the shape of a statuette. With his right hand, he drew to himself the door, whose face consisted of three wide mahogany boards.[2] Then he entered the room walking backwards.

Once inside, Romo plunged a small calabash into seven different water pots buried in soil up to the neck and drew out enough water to wash himself. Each pot contained a decoction made from a number of plants gathered and prepared under special magic conditions. He undressed, washed himself ritually with the water he had collected from the seven pots, and slipped on all his amulets, some around the waist, some on his arms and others bandoleerwise. He covered all this with his *sigi doloki*, which is a sort of magic shirt made of buffalo skin, usually worn by warriors and supposed to render one invulnerable.

He went out of the room the same way he had gone in and completed his attire with a field-service uniform.

Now he was ready. He went out to assume command of his battalion of fifteen *bons-tir*, chosen from the sixty security guards of the Diussola squad.

He met them at the appointed place.

Was it because he was wearing his field-service uniform, and he was surrounded by fifteen armed men? Be it as it may, a swelling of recollections from his time as infantry sergeant, former squadron-sergeant with the Spahis, and former lance-sergeant in the patrol units surged in his breast. He shouted: "At my command! Right dress! *Garda bou!*"[3]

The fifteen men lined up before their "captain," who thought it appropriate to harangue them in this way:

"Men! Let us be tough as hell! We're off to attack Wangrin—a most deadly panther armed with huge claws and sharp teeth. He is strong. There isn't an atom of fear in his heart. He is evil to the core. We must be prepared for some resistance. And let me warn you that he carries a gun and that he's swift as a bird of prey. As soon as we get to his house, surround the compound. Meanwhile, I will go in and proceed to arrest him. And now, fix bayonets! Shoulder arms, column of twos! By the right, quick march!" The tiny army carried out the captain's orders impeccably. They began marching, their bayonets flashing in the sun. At nine forty-five A.M. exactly, Romo and his men laid siege to Wangrin's house. When they had surrounded it, leaving no gap, Romo went on his triumphant way toward the main door. Meeting a servant who was just getting ready to go out, he shouted: "Where is Wangrin?"

"In the shop," she replied.

Changing course, Romo veered toward the shop, where he found Wangrin seated behind the counter busy inspecting a large ledger.

"Bad day to you Wangrin!" said Romo. "It would be in execrable taste to wish you a good day when in fact I'm here to arrest you, as I promised you long ago in Yaguwahi. I know that you haven't forgotten my words, but for my delight and your despair let me go over them once again. This is what I told you at the time: I swear to you that I shan't rest until I arrest you with my own hands and clap you in jail. . . .

"Well, Wangrin, get up now and follow me. I arrest you in the name of the law. And don't try any smart tricks on me. All exits are guarded by armed men, and they won't trifle with you. Get up off that chair and come along. Your confinement will be as painful as I promised it would be. I will see to it that you feed on your shit and drink your own piss. Come on now, before I take my butt to you!"

Wangrin, who as Romo was pouring out his spleen had been wearing a faraway look, now got up gently and pretending to tremble with fear replied:

"Oh! A true Fulbe, let him be light- or dark-skinned, will never really change. He'll always be either a magnanimous friend or a fearsome enemy. So, elder brother Romo, you have kept your promise and you're going to take me to jail. I am truly unhappy. If I'd been smarter I wouldn't have played quite so many dirty tricks on you, would I? And today I could appeal to your sense of compassion. Well, so much the worse for poor Wangrin! . . .

"However, brother Romo, your Commandant is committing an error in sending you to apprehend me, for you are an interpreter and not a representative of the local authority, a security man, or a member of the police force. Nevertheless I will let you arrest me, for I know that it means more to you than your own life. I must try and make up somehow for all I've made you suffer in the past by not depriving you of the glory and the immense pleasure that it will give you to arrest me. My action can be likened to a gift of soap with which to wash your face so besmirched by me in the last few years.

"But—there is a but—I hope you will consent to grant me a few minutes so that I can put away books in this cupboard here above the counter, against the wall. . . . I won't even need to step out of the shop."

"I am not worried, Wangrin. Even if you did step out of the shop you wouldn't be able to leave your premises. And as I have all the time in the world to prolong your agony, do by all means put your books away wherever and however you wish."

Wangrin climbed up to the counter and set about moving his books and papers into his tall cupboard. When everything was tidied, he said to his shop assistant: "Monsieur Gourbidan will be watching over our business until Fabukari arrives from the Ivory Coast."

Still standing on the counter, Wangrin turned to Romo: "There is only one book left to put away. But, now I think of it, you've forgotten to show me the warrant for my arrest! It's obvious that you are not familiar with the ways of the 'judiciary.' Otherwise, you'd know that I have every right to examine that document and ascertain that it is legal. I must ask you to show it to me, else I'll refuse to come along. It's the law and even if you are not knowledgeable in these matters, it so happens that I am."

Romo pulled the warrant out of his pocket. Extending it to Wangrin, he said: "Bend your warthog's head, accursed son of a desperate mother, and read the notice of your damnation with your own eyes!"

Wangrin bent over as if to read the paper which Romo was holding almost languidly in his left hand, accompanying his display with an air of mean sarcasm. Suddenly, Wangrin spat in Romo's eye a thick jet of kola which he had been chewing. Simultaneously, swift as a bird of prey, Wangrin tore the paper out of Romo's hand and applied a resounding slap to his right cheek, adding the comment: "And this is what Wangrin had promised you."

Before Romo, blinded as he was by the kola powder, had time to recover from his astonishment, Wangrin had already in a few bounding steps reached and opened his cupboard, which hid a door to a flight of stairs leading to a garage where the "torpedo" was parked.

Everything had been prepared in advance. Wangrin opened the garage door and jumped into his car, confounding the security men, who barely managed to jump out of the way to avoid being crushed to death. The car shot off like a rocket in the direction of Wagabilo.

For ten long minutes, oppressed by the weight of his unhappiness and incapacitated by his blindness, Romo was completely at a loss as to what to say or do. A slap across his face, some kola powder in his eyes, and the arrest warrant stolen! That was Wangrin's bequest to him.

In his desperation, Romo tried to kill himself by plunging a bayonet in his belly. Luckily, the weapon slipped in his hand, skirting all vital organs.

Meanwhile, the Commandant was in his office awaiting the outcome of the operation. But lo! Instead of a handcuffed Wangrin he saw his own interpreter being carried out on a stretcher!

As for Wangrin, within a few hours he had safely reached the frontier of the Gold Coast (now Ghana). There he sought shelter in the house of a fellow trader-friend who resided in that country.

Romo was taken to the Central Hospital in Gudugaua. Two months later, Wangrin sent off to Tronedon, whom he had engaged as his defense lawyer, a memo and the arrest warrant he had torn out of Romo's hand. Having studied the case, Tronedon advised him to give himself up in a neighboring territory.

Wangrin acted accordingly. He was transferred to the Diussola jail and his lawyer managed to get him released on bail. He returned home and took up where he had left off, waiting for his case to be heard.

Meanwhile, he had offered to a young schoolmaster of Senegalese extraction a return fare to his country, plus enough money for a month's stay, provided he tried to locate in the archives, either at Kuluba (now Bamako) or at Dakar, or at Saint-Louis, the official letter which proved that a certain gun had been presented as honorary gift to his uncle, a well-known provincial chief.

The grateful young schoolmaster, Mahibira Seri by name, felt extremely happy when he succeeded in tracking down at Kuluba, in the archives of the Bureau of Political Affairs—Firearms Department, both the letter and the original copy of a gun license made out to Tiemogofing Trearo, provincial chief. The letter of transference stipulated that this honorary gift could be inherited by Tiemogofing's descendants or by any other person who could lay legal claim to his property by right of succession.

Through official channels, Tronedon applied for a certified copy of the documents found by Mahibira Seri. At the same time, he wrote to the Commandant of Nubigu to request a document certifying Wangrin's right to the ownership of the incriminating gun.

The affair dragged on for six months. In the end it was brought before the French court and judgment given. It acquitted Wangrin, and laid down that he be granted a regular license for his rifle gun. While all this was going on, Romo had come out of hospital and was enjoying one month's convalescence in his own house at Diussola. He had lost face to so great an extent that he no longer dared appear anywhere. Nor was the news of Wangrin's acquittal calculated to make his life any the more bearable. So he asked for a transfer, and Chantalba sent off the application with a favorable recommendation.

27 A Souvenir "Crafted by Wangrin"

Now Wangrin was more prosperous than ever, and the risk of being frustrated by Romo had become a thing of the past.

His mind free of all worries, he decided to set to rights Tenin's ambiguous position and enable her to enjoy a happy future, for the young woman found it very painful to have to divide her attention between the Commandant and Burabura. Whereas she was genuinely in love with the young cook, she squeezed everything she could out of her gold-braided protector, who was positively demented with love.

One day, Wangrin asked her to come and see him:

"My daughter," he said, "you will remember that once I asked you never to mention my name to Jacques de Chantalba. Now at last I have triumphed, for Romo has left, and Chantalba has only six months left before repatriation. If he asks, and obtains, an extension, I will take the proper steps; I'll 'prescribe' an illness that will wear him out without killing him outright.

"I have no desire to have him stay on in Diussola, but before he leaves I want you to get out of him three quarters of his savings. Then you will be able to settle down and marry Burabura, who is your heart's choice. This is what you are going to do. You will hide for a fortnight in my house, where Burabura will be able to visit you to his heart's content. We will see how the Commandant reacts to the situation. I will plan my campaign accordingly.

"Don't forget that I have every right to revenge myself and make him feel how wrong he has been in trying to do me damage for no other reason than wanting to please his friends. He has failed in his duty as administrator by placing his authority at the service of his personal feelings. He deserves to have a souvenir 'crafted by Wangrin' tucked away in his memory-box! I count on your assistance as well as Burabura's."

Tenin agreed to the proposal, and so did Burabura.

Came the evening when Tenin was due to pay a visit to Jacques de Chantalba. She had got into the habit of arriving around 8:00. At 8:15 she still hadn't turned up. Chantalba sat down at table.

"The soup!" shouted Zumana, letting Burabura know that the master was ready. While the steward was waiting, Burabura quickly warmed the soup. As he was pouring it into the tureen, Zumana said: "Put in enough for one only; Tenin hasn't come yet."

"Where is she?" asked Burabura casually.

"It's you the Commandant is going to ask, since she is your cousin, and not mine," teased Zumana.

Zumana knew perfectly well what was going on between Burabura and Tenin, but being one of Burabura's sanankuns he could not have betrayed him without risking a curse from the gods and the spirits of his ancestors.

"If you don't beat it out of my kitchen fast, I'll give you a taste of my foot, you vicious little panther. Get out!" shouted Burabura.

"If you do that to me," replied Zumana laughingly, "I will play a 'Wangrinery' on you. I'll put some hot pepper in the Commandant's soup and set his tongue on fire. Then you'll have to explain. . . . "

"Go on, take the soup in at once, before it gets cold," advised Burabura.

The soup was served. The Commandant took no more than a ladleful, and only a couple of spoonfuls of the dishes that followed.

Eight thirty. Still no Tenin. Chantalba called in Burabura.

"I don't understand what is happening," he said. "Tenin hasn't come yet. Go to her house at once and ask her what is holding her up that she keeps me waiting so long."

There was no need for Burabura to go to Tenin's house. Instead, he went straight to Wangrin's and said to him: "The Commandant is very worried. He has sent me to find out what might have prevented Tenin from coming to see him. He has eaten virtually nothing. He is waiting for a reply or for Tenin herself."

"Go back to Chantalba and tell him this," replied Wangrin. "Tenin left home this morning around ten o'clock. She was seen in Wangrin's shop, but nobody has any idea where she might have gone from there. She has left no message."

Burabura returned to his master bearing a piece of news which was bound, if anything, to exacerbate his anxiety. Chantalba saw him and walked rapidly toward him: "What's the matter? Where is Tenin?" he asked.

"Nobody knows, Sir. She left home around ten o'clock this morning. She called at Wangrin's shop but hasn't been seen since. She hasn't left any message. Wangrin alone can help you. Tenin may have told him what she was going to do. . . . "

"Yes, I know. . . . I've been told, unfortunately too late, that Tenin keeps nothing secret from Wangrin. She considers him her adopted father. I must say that that doesn't improve matters where I'm concerned. . . . I care a great deal about finding Tenin, yet my position compels me to act with caution. I love Tenin as I've never loved any other woman, not even the one to whom I am legally married in my own country. . . . "

By so pouring out his sorrows into Burabura's ears, Chantalba was breaking his heart without realizing it. It was hard for the youth to listen impassively while another man proclaimed his love for Tenin. But what power had he against a white-White, especially when the white-White was a colonial administrator, on top of that his master, and, it is only fair to say, his benefactor?

So Burabura, with anguish in his heart, listened to the unbosoming of his master and unwitting rival. When the latter fell silent, Burabura said:

"If I were you, Sir, I would ask for Wangrin's help. If you don't want to ask him directly, I could easily speak to him on your behalf. I too am upset to see that my cousin has hopped it without providing any justification for her disappearance."

Chantalba had no desire to throw out to that roguish Wangrin a lasso which might give him a chance to strangle and annihilate him without leaving any trace of his crime.

Noticing his hesitation, Burabura continued:

"Sir, I suggest that you make haste before things deteriorate any further. You cannot possibly avoid one or the other of these alternatives: either you allow yourself to be lacerated by your love for Tenin, which has penetrated the innermost recesses of your heart and is likely to stifle you to the extent that you won't be able to do your work in peace—or you use Wangrin who, if you make him a few concessions, is bound to find a remedy for your sickness, and moreover will do so with the utmost discretion. Although Wangrin reigns supreme among practical jokers, he is also a man of his word, who, in a grave situation is capable of acting courageously and reliably. He always keeps his promises. I've heard Romo, his most lethal enemy, say as much before witnesses."

Chantalba seemed annoyed by the suggestion. He left his cook very abruptly and went to shut himself up in his study. He sent for his clerk, Tiombiano. As soon as they were face to face, he asked:

"Do you know Tenin Pretty Doe?"

"Yes, Sir," answered the clerk who, as you will recall, was one of Wangrin's men. "I know her extremely well. She originates from Leo, but has been living in Diussola since she was a child. Her father was an NCO in the colonial infantry. He died here after being discharged from service. He was extremely close to Wangrin, the former interpreter. I believe he entrusted his daughter to him, and Wangrin seems to have been an extremely good father to her."

"Well," rejoined the Commandant, "Tenin disappeared two days ago. Can you help me to find her? But I would prefer people in town not to know that I'm interested in her. The way to do it would be for somebody to inform me officially of her disappearance and ask the administration to help establish her whereabouts. I could give orders accordingly and see to it that they are carried out."

Tiombiano went to call on the provincial chief, Surako Nyami, and asked him to cooperate in the game proposed by the Commandant. Naturally, an indigenous chief who is keen to hold on to his turban wouldn't dream of refusing a favor to the administrative authority.

During the afternoon of the second day of Tenin's disappearance, Surako Nyami turned up at the district office and pleaded with the Commandant to help him trace Tenin, who had vanished from her house without a word of explanation.

Chantalba ordered the town-crier to announce Tenin's disappearance and to promise a handsome reward to anyone who could find her or give relevant information.

First a week, then ten whole days elapsed without anyone showing up. Jacques de Chantalba was positively ill. He could neither eat nor sleep, had become extremely short-tempered . . . he must have Tenin at all costs. As we know, love and hunger can demolish a man in no time at all and even push him to countenance the impossible. Chantalba had reached that point. He called Burabura. "You were right," he said. "I am going to use Wangrin's help to find Tenin. Go and see him tonight, after dinner, and bring him back here."

In the evening Burabura called on Wangrin to inform him of the Commandant's latest decision.

Wangrin considered for a few moments. "Tell the Commandant that it would be imprudent for a rascal like me to be seen lurking around the Residence in the middle of the night. If I were accused of having gone there to murder him, it would mean hard labor in Cayenne for me! I think there are enough varieties of spices in our country without my having to go and look for them in Guyane! I think it would be better if the Commandant sent me a regular summons. Then I will go to his office in the full light of day, and I promise to place myself entirely at his disposal."

Burabura related this proposal to the Commandant who, tortured by longing, was ready for anything. Accordingly, he prepared a summons and wrote Wangrin's name on it.

On the morning of the twelfth day of Tenin's disappearance, Wangrin turned up in Chantalba's office.

Without resorting to a lot of useless preambles, the Commandant offered him a chair.

"Wangrin," he said, "I admit that I have fought against you and attempted to do you damage. By now it's ancient history, and I am asking you to forget it.

"My reason for summoning you here is entirely personal. It's a thing of the heart. I am in love with Tenin Pretty Doe. Twelve days ago she suddenly vanished and I've been searching for her without success. I realize that it was foolish of me not to come to you from the very beginning. I am sorry for it now. I'd like you to help me find that girl. I can't live without her."

"If I consent to help you find Tenin, what will you do for me?"

"Anything you say, on condition that it does not entail disloyalty to my country and that it doesn't do violence to my oath as a high-ranking civil servant. I will be your friend, and as you know friends must help one another."

Wangrin promised to return the next day at the same time. At nightfall, Wangrin, Tenin, and Burabura met in Wangrin's house and held a veritable war council. In the end Tenin and Burabura said: "We are your children and we will follow your advice with blind faith."

On the morrow, Wangrin went to speak to the Commandant. "I bring you news," he said. "She is fine, but she tells me that she's been wasting her time with you. When in six months' time you return to France, she's going to find herself destitute. If you want her to resume relations with you, you will have to buy a plot of land measuring ten thousand square meters, and make her the legal owner. On that land, you will build houses and shops. You will also buy her a hundred heads of cattle and five hundred and fifty thousand francs' worth of jewelry."

"But where is she?" cried Jacques de Chantalba.

"She is staying with me," replied Wangrin.

"What do you mean, with you?"

"Well, it's the only place where Bodressoul, President of the Chamber of Commerce, who wanted to kidnap her exactly twelve days ago, couldn't reach her. She came to tell me of Bodressoul's designs, so I advised her to hide in my house and discover in that way whether you really cared for her before surrendering to Bodressoul, who is expected back in ten days' time."

"Thank you for your intervention, Wangrin!" exclaimed Chantalba, "from now on think of me as your friend. I will be only too glad to give Tenin anything she wishes."

Wangrin inclined his head towards Chantalba and whispered in his ear: "Not a word of this to anybody. If Bodressoul were to learn the truth, he could make things extremely awkward for you. He is the local large-man of both Chambers of Commerce in Marseille and Bordeaux. His protectors have the ear of the Prime Minister in Paris. Any order coming from that sphere could easily make short shrift of your career. . . . "

Thus Wangrin had managed to rid himself of Romo and to convert Jacques de Chantalba as well. How true that a beautiful woman is often more powerful than a well-equipped and well-trained army.

28 First Warning: The Hausa Geomancer

At this point, Wangrin had reached the zenith of his glory and the apex of his good fortune. No obstacle stood in his way. Now he was ready to enjoy his worldly possessions, the only goal he had set himself during his long money-making career.

He bought himself a vast piece of land and built a large restaurant on it, complete with esplanade. He called it "Come and Enjoy Yourselves." Before long, his restaurant had become a choice spot for rich merchants, white and black, who wanted to take refuge somewhere and forget their worries. The establishment included all amenities: a restaurant, a night-club, a casino, etc. . . .

Before leaving the territory, Chantalba had kept all his promises. Not only had he left a generous dowry for Tenin; he had also helped Wangrin to regularize all his documents. He had even proposed him for the Legion of Honor, in addition to the decorations he had already received: the Black Star of Benin, the *Mérite Agricole* (awarded to successful farmers by the Ministry of Agriculture), the Labor Gold Medal, and five other peppercorn awards. . . . Wangrin had accepted this honorary "kitchen battery" not so much for the pleasure of hearing a jingle on his chest but rather because, at that time, a few decorations conferred considerable status. Policemen stood to attention when he passed, and during official ceremonies he was permitted to sit on the podium.

It was then that Wangrin's behavior underwent a subtle change. Was he stunned, perhaps, by the extent of his immense fortune? Be it as it may, from then on he was never quite the same man. No longer so prodigal with the poor, he didn't of course refuse to give alms, but he was not as generous as he had been in former days and if he still clothed the widows and orphans who came to solicit his help, he no longer actually sought them out.

Suddenly he had become fond of hunting. At nightfall he would de-part in his new "torpedo" and quite often did not return till dawn. He killed for pleasure, drawing away yet a little further from pure African tradition, which demands that hunting be ritualistic and utilitarian rather than aimless and gratuitous.

One day, he was visited by an old Hausa geomancer. Wangrin asked him to set up a geomantic pattern and foretell his future.

The old man contemplated the patterns he had drawn on the sand for a very long time. Then he shook his head gently. . . .

"Why are you shaking your head?" asked Wangrin.

"Because I see nothing good," answered the old man. "I am going to start all over again. . . . "

He spread out his sand anew and traced a new pattern.

"Does it look any more promising?" asked Wangrin.

"No, it's worse than ever. And the most disquieting thing of all is that I can't envisage any sacrifice that might avert the catastrophe which appears with baffling consistency in all the main 'houses' of this design!"[1]

"Why don't you try again? What are you waiting for?"

"Your command to do it; as for myself I can see your sun moving toward a total eclipse and I don't need any complementary information."

"Have one last look."

The geomancer spread out his sand, traced his patterns, and remained bent over them for a long while. . . .

"Well, what does the oracle say?" asked Wangrin jokingly. "It looks extremely bad," replied the geomancer, now sweating profusely.

When he said that, Wangrin burst out laughing: "You need a little fresh air. You had better go outside and see whether a better disposed divinity won't speak to you a little more to the point. Here you are! Take this." And in so saying, he let drop a hundred-franc note, adding: "Use it to mop up your sweat, and then go quietly home without worrying your old head. But let me teach you something first: When the sun is at its zenith, it dazzles those who raise their eyes to it, and prevents them from seeing the truth. That is exactly what happened to you just now. But go in peace nevertheless, although to me you have promised no peace at all. I am Wangrin, whose power can alter fate. I will triumph over your hap-less predictions."

The old Hausa got ready to leave without picking up the hundred-franc note.

"What is it?" cried Wangrin. "Do you consider my gift too insignifi-cant to go to the trouble of picking it up?"

"On the contrary," answered the old man. "Far from it. But I won't take it—first of all because you haven't given it to me. You dropped it on the ground. It is to the ground, therefore, that it belongs. Besides, I am not in the habit of accepting payment when I am not sure that I can cure the sickness. And you are very sick indeed. . . . "

Once again, Wangrin burst out laughing.

Almost as if Wangrin's laughter had excited him, suddenly the old Hausa man burst out laughing too, but so boisterously that a band sprang loose from his huge turban and fell to the ground like a dangling tail.

Wangrin was intrigued by this unexpected manifestation of mirth in an old man who only a few seconds earlier had felt so anguished that his face had been covered in large beads of sweat. He stopped laughing and looked intently at the old man, seeing him now as a very mysterious figure. But before he could open his mouth, the old Hausa had already picked up the piece of turban that was trailing behind him and—head and back bent low—had quickly gone out and disappeared among the people crowding the little market not far from Wangrin's house.

Wangrin pondered the old geomancer's prophecy for a moment. He decided to call him back and consult him once more, but all his emissaries' enquiries proved fruitless. Finally, the innkeeper who had sheltered the old man told him that the latter had left Diussola for an unknown destination a week earlier.

This news caused Wangrin an abrupt and indefinable twinge. He shook his head, attempting to rid his mind of morbid thoughts. To chase away the feeling of apprehension which had somehow seized him, he began to hum:

> Koro Koonin, ohe! ohe! O elder,
> Go and rest in peace,
> You great valiant one.
> On the day of battle
> At Nonngon you died without shame,
> You great valiant one,
> Your death was noble.
> Go and rest in peace.
> You who never
> Ran from your enemy.

This tune was part of a ballad composed in honor of Koonin, a Bambara warrior who was killed at Nonngon[2] at the end of the nineteenth century. He had defended the town against an army ten times stronger than his own, killing fifty men and five great war chiefs before falling himself—wounded eight times—but never in his back.

Wangrin went to bed very late and slept fitfully. As a result the next day he got up very late and contrary to his habit didn't go to his office at all.

Toward five, Tronedon came to invite him to go on a little jaunt in his car. He found Wangrin very low-spirited.

"I've been feeling out of sorts these last few days," he said. "I can't imagine where the hell my 'double' has been roaming. The fact is, he's brought back a nagging feeling of anxiety that has spread throughout my consciousness and drained all my courage."

Tronedon patted him on the shoulder. "You're overtired," he said. "You go and rest for a few days at the seaside, in Dakar for example, or in the Futa Djallon mountains. If I were to choose, I would infinitely prefer the Futa Djallon area," added Tronedon, "especially Dalaba, a place full of beautiful women. . . . "

Wangrin followed his advice, but chose Dakar after all for a good rest and a change of air. But he didn't leave until three months later.

29   Madame White-White

Wangrin was positively rolling in money. Once in Dakar, he deprived himself of nothing, excluding from his holiday only the pious pilgrimages that would have cloistered him in one of the flourishing Kadri, Tidjani, or Mouride Zaooia[1] which were scattered all over Senegal.

One day, as he was finishing a meal in one of the restaurants of the famous Place Protet, rendezvous of all the most stylish women, unscrupulous businessmen, politicians, and bums of Dakar, Wangrin became aware of a woman who, he was told, had been nicknamed by the *habitués* of the place "Madame white-White." He found her looks absolutely riveting.

"Here is an artifact," he thought, "which the good Lord has sculpted slowly and lovingly. He has spared no effort in chiseling, filing, touching-up, and finally coloring, before delivering this masterpiece unto the gaze of the sons of Adam."

The "white madame" made her way toward the cloakroom, where she deposited her hat and coat. Then she began to walk from table to table, smiling to some, speaking to others, and sometimes sitting down for a while with the customers.

Wangrin asked the old sailor who was sitting next to him: "Who is that 'Madame'?"

"She is a hostess, my good friend," replied the sailor. "Her job is to encourage people to drink as much as possible and increase the takings of the joint."

"Is she married, this 'Madame'?"

"She lives with a handyman, a mechanic who at the moment is looking for a job. Nobody is quite sure whether they are actually married or just living together."

"But how can such a beautiful woman end up being hostess in a restaurant and companion to a mechanic who's out of work?"

"Search me!" replied the old sea-dog. "I'm just repeating what the town tittle-tattle relays free of charge. If you want to know more, address yourself to 'Madame' herself. She is neither prudish nor racist, and she always enjoys a chat."

Wangrin bought the old man a glass of Pernod and left.

Madame was no novice to café existence. She knew how to decipher conversations held a few tables away from hers by observing the speakers' eyes, hands, and lips. She had noticed, then, that Wangrin was interested in her.

Moving on to the table where the old sailor was sitting, she asked: "Who is that very well-dressed gentleman who was asking you about me?"

"Tell me, do you have antennae?" jested the old sailor. "And if you do, how come you didn't catch our conversation which, as a matter of fact, was about you?"

"The reception was bad," jested Madame in her turn, adding: "Tell me about it, and tomorrow I'll buy you an aperitif."

The old sailor had just emptied his glass. He raised it and looking at Madame declared: "I would prefer half a glass now to a whole bottle tomorrow."

The fine lady was curious. She ordered another glass of Pernod for the old tar. He took one gulp and then, laying down his glass:

"That gentleman's name is Wangrin," he said. "He is general manager of the Bani Import-Export Company. He's here to enjoy himself. He oozes money from every pore, but unfortunately he's a teetotaler."

Madame had heard a great deal about the CIEB and its prodigious capital of ten million francs. She expected to see Wangrin again, but as it happened he didn't show up for five whole days, for he had gone on a brief visit to Saint-Louis.

On his return, Wangrin went to sit in the café, where he met his old friend the sailor once again. The latter related word by word the conversation he'd had with "Madame."

Wangrin didn't have long to wait. Like a skiff maneuvering through a reef, Madame was steering a skillful course toward him among the tables.

"Good morning, Monsieur le Directeur Général," she greeted him. "I have come to offer you the apologies of my employers for not paying you the tribute due to all special customers the last time you were here. But your incognito is more to blame in this case than our lack of courtesy."

Madame clapped her hands, and an impeccable waiter brought a tray laden with bottles of aperitif and little cocktail snacks. Then she sat opposite Wangrin but was careful not to turn her back on his companion, and started to pour.

"Monsieur le Directeur," she said "this aperitif is on the house. Moreover, in the next half hour anyone among our old customers who may chance to come in will have a similar treat—in your honor. After that, we will give you an ovation by applauding you all together. You deserve only too well this acknowledgment, Monsieur le Directeur. If I weren't afraid to overdo it, I would go so far as to invite you to my house and introduce my husband to you."

Wangrin was at a loss as to how to reply. He began to thank Madame and the management. Within ten minutes, forty people were already drinking his health on the house.

The old mariner was in heaven. By himself, he had already drunk for five and more. When the time came for the ovation, he shouted louder than any of the others and clapped his hands with such vigor that he disturbed the rhythm of the applause.

Wangrin accepted Madame's invitation and then left, having made a deep bow to acknowledge the tribute he had been paid.

Back at his hotel, he threw himself on his bed, flat on his belly, without taking off his clothes. He spent a few moments in that position, lost in a wild daydream. As he got up, he saw his image reflected in a large mirror that hung on the wall at the foot of his bed. He looked at himself as if he were seeing his full image for the first time in his life. He blinked, stroked his chin, then, abruptly, burst out laughing, as if he'd been seized by a fit of madness. He started talking to himself, laughing hard enough to split his sides, and twisting as if his entrails were on fire.

"Ah Wangrin! O Wangrin! To think that you had stupidly believed that your fortune was on the wane and that you were stepping into the gloom of poverty just because that old rogue of a Hausa geomancer, toothless and hunched as he was, had foretold 'evil times' for you!

"You didn't realize that he was a short-sighted geomancer. Groping in an occult mist, the only events he could see were as deformed as images reflected in water. Look for that monumental liar and whisper—first in his right ear, and then in his left ear too—that your night star and your morning sun are now more than ever in the ascendant. And if he has any doubts, let him consult the citizens of Dakar, who will tell him: 'O mendacious geomancer! It's your downfall you have glimpsed in the sand, not Wangrin's, for the General Manager of CIEB is about to enter the life span in which white women are prepared to serve him drinks and high ranking white-Whites and Blacks are happy to give him an ovation!'"

Very pleased with himself, Wangrin started throwing sheets, pillows, and the bubus he'd taken off high up in the air. Then he began to dance the *tigi-naana*[2] with so much energy that the man in charge of room-service came to knock on his door:

"What is the matter, Sir?"

"The matter is that I'm giving you a hundred francs for your trouble!" replied Wangrin, handing him a banknote. At the sight of a sum equivalent to a month's salary, the man jumped for joy and began to dance the *tigi-naana* with Wangrin.

Two days after that memorable evening, Wangrin honored Madame's invitation to dinner. She introduced her companion, Monsieur Terreau, to him. "My husband," she said. Then, introducing Wangrin: "The General Manager of CIEB, who is spending a holiday here in Dakar."

"Delighted to meet you, Monsieur le Directeur."

"Same here," replied Wangrin.

The dinner, prepared by Fatu, Madame Terreau's Senegalese cook, was excellent. Wangrin ate with good appetite, Madame Terreau was all attention, and although she behaved almost coquettishly, Monsieur seemed to remain extremely aloof. Anyway the dinner ended happily.

Monsieur Terreau had spoken only a few words, but the little he had said revolved round the idea of opening a super garage.

Wangrin was thinking: "If I were to open a big garage, on top of my existing hotel/restaurant and my shops, I would become just as big as Scherek, Bouquet, and Archambeaud."[3] Leaning toward Madame Terreau, he asked casually:

"Are you satisfied with your work and with your life in Dakar?"

Before she had time to open her mouth, Monsieur Terreau was already saying: "My wife and I are living in Dakar because we have no alternative. We are waiting to find something better, where we can exploit our talents to the full. You see, Monsieur le Directeur, my wife leaves home at seven in the morning and doesn't get back till two in the afternoon—that is, when she manages to get back at all—and at four o'clock she must return to work and stay there, sometimes, until one in the morning.

"As for me, it's worse still. So long as there is an engine to be serviced, I can't leave the workshop. My life is spent between the deafening uproar of old machinery and the ravings of a boss who is both drunk on his success and neurotic from too long a stay in the tropics, where he lives totally without comfort in order to save money for the future. I feel that I am on the verge of a nervous breakdown.

"Are you kidding, Monsieur le Directeur Général? I wouldn't need to think twice before grabbing the first chance that comes my way to go and work elsewhere with my wife, in a place where we could use our own initiative and our skills, each in our field of competence. My wife has a diploma in commerce. For her, accountancy holds no secrets. She has accepted a hostess's job over here for a time because in France we suffered a setback and our luck hasn't turned since. We arrived here without recommendations, which is the surest way not to find a job or to be at the mercy of any old so-and-so."

"If I managed to get you a job with one of my friends, would you be prepared to move to my country?" asked Wangrin.

Now it was for Madame Terreau to reply. "It all depends on what guarantees we are offered," she said. "But we would be happy to leave this town where life is made very disagreeable by the Europeans' mentality, and the Africans' too, especially those from the four communes.⁴ The latter wouldn't hesitate to beat you up over the merest trifle, and moreover they'd take you to court and make life impossible for you before going on to ruin you altogether!"

"I can't promise you anything, but let us keep in touch," replied Wangrin. "If by any chance I come across something suitable I'll let you know."

Wangrin stayed in Dakar over three months, during which time Monsieur and Madame Terreau took tender care of him. Nor did he forget to pay a visit to the garage where Monsieur Terreau was employed, so that he could watch him at work. He saw that although irreproachably professional, he was unhappily at the mercy of a detestable man, whom drink and too long a stay in the colonies had made both rickety in health and churlish in temperament.

Eventually it was time for Wangrin to say good-bye to all the new friends he had made in Dakar, arid to board a train bound for Bamako, where his splendid sports car was awaiting him. After spending a week as a guest of his elder brother Dubie Trearo, quarryman, carrier, horse-trader with a reputation for tricky dealing, entrepreneur in contract work, and above all, the most feared litigant in the town of Bamako, Wangrin decided to visit his native village before returning to Diussola.

30 Second and Third Warnings: A Fatal Oversight and the Sacred Python

The day of Wangrin's reunion with his family was a day of great rejoicing. Everyone felt so elated that neither Wangrin nor his family remembered that on arriving, all members of the clan must offer sacrifices to the spirits of the ancestors who lie buried at the foot of the great baobab, deep in the sacred grove.

Wangrin was already sitting in the shade of the roof overhanging the house where his mother had given birth to him, when his little sister Nianamba came to kneel respectfully before him. Proffering a calabash full of cool water, she said: "Now that you have returned from the sacred wood, let me offer you the water of welcome that will refresh your spirit."

As if propelled by a spring, Wangrin jumped up and began to lament:

"O elders, we have both sinned. We have failed to observe our most important duty. Before sitting in the shade, before letting anything pass my lips, I should have gone to the sacred grove to offer sacrifices. And you, you should have reminded me of my duties. What will happen to us now? How are we going to right my wrongs?"

Old Sorimori, one of the masters of the knife,[1] asked:

"Which divinity were you accepted by at the time of your circumcision, Wangrin?"

"Gongoloma-Sooke," replied Wangrin.

"Well then! We can still offer a sacrifice to Gongoloma-Sooke. Are you carrying the pebble that symbolizes your link with the spirit of that god?"

Wangrin went into the room where his six suitcases had been set down. He opened one of them, thinking that he would find the little pebble in it. But the black catskin he was so sure he had packed was nowhere to be found. That meant that he had left it behind in Diussola, although he knew that wherever he slept the little bag must be there too.

"O Sorimori," he said, "I have left home without my *borofin*, my little black bag!"

Like the wise man he was, Sorimori refrained from expostulating, although he felt profound consternation. Now the damage was done. Why upset Wangrin any further . . . ? He looked intently at Wangrin and said:

"When a man leaves for a journey incognito so as to give his fate the slip, on arriving he will find that fate has preceded him and perhaps even booked accommodation for two. My poor little Wangrin, from now on you must prepare yourself for some terrible disasters. Be strong, unwavering. The weight of the greatest sorrow is alleviated if it is endured patiently. We will go to the sacred grove; we will offer a retrospective sacrifice to the spirits of our ancestors and attempt in this way to mitigate our offense."

Wangrin followed Sorimori to the sacred grove. Out of the three chickens and seven kola nuts that were ritually offered, the spirits of the ancestors accepted only half a kola nut.[2]

Sorimori poured three calabashes full of water on the large stone that served as altar. "We have a glimmer of hope," he said to Wangrin. "Sometimes an ember sparks off a raging fire. . . . "

Wangrin had been profoundly happy to see his native village and his family after such a long absence. Now, instead of being a source of pleasure, this touching reunion seemed to bode trouble, if not actual sorrow.

When it was time to part, Wangrin distributed fewer gifts than he would have done in more cheerful circumstances, when his heart throbbed with joy. He piled his suitcases in his "torpedo" and left for Diussola.

He traveled several hours, but in spite of driving extremely fast, he was caught by darkness when he was still halfway between Sokassi and Diussola.

As he cruised along, Wangrin let his mind wander—first from the old Hausa geomancer to Sorimori, and finally to the restaurant/café in the Place Protet, and to the great ovation he had received there.

He couldn't stop asking himself what obscure design of fate might have caused him to forget his *borofin*, with Gongoloma-Sooke's pebble, symbol of his divine protector, inside it. His "hopeful double" whispered to him: "Wangrin, don't worry. A man like you, upholstered with millions of francs and gold ingots, is usually spared all evils."

His "objective double" answered by insisting at his ear: "Wangrin, you have started on a slippery slope. Try to find some purchase. Instead

of nursing fond hopes, meditate the profound meaning of the little song
composed in honor of one of the emperors of Segu:

O king with the huge mouth
Drink your water
Your water that is kept
In a water cooler.
Whether the water cooler
Is wrought in gold
Or in silver
Remember, O King,
King with the huge mouth
That one king alone,
Cannot drain Eternity.

His head swimming in waves of contradictory opinions, Wangrin
pushed his needle to sixty, even to seventy miles an hour. In those days,
the road had already been well macadamized,[3] not by rollers, but rather
by thousands of toiling men, women, and children of all ages armed with
wooden mallets especially carved for that purpose. It was still the sad age
of forced labor, euphemistically called "payment in kind," which improved somewhat in 1936 under the Popular Front but did not really
come to an end until 1947 with the advent of the French Union.

Red as if it had been soaked in the blood of those who had built it,
the road unrolled like a ribbon which the sports car seemed to swallow
as it sped along.

The headlights were bright enough to prevent Wangrin from swerv-
ing off the road, but he was going too fast to be able to brake in time,
should the need arise. However, he wasn't worried. By now it was so late
that he couldn't possibly come across any living souls, whether human or
animal. His headlights could be seen from a great distance. It would have
been easy for anyone to keep out of the way and avoid being hit.

With his mind totally absorbed by the flow of ideas emanating from
his "two doubles," Wangrin didn't notice until too late a dark line stretched
across half the road. Thinking it was a shadow, and unable in any case to
come to a quick decision, he didn't bother to slow down. When he saw at
last that it was a python, the car had already run over the reptile and
broken several rings of his body. The car skidded with the impact, throwing
Wangrin and his luggage in a ditch.

His face bleeding and his body covered in scratches, and stiff all over
from the brutal shock, Wangrin picked himself up very painfully. He
went back to the spot where the python was lying dead on the ground.

Unwittingly, Wangrin had killed his "forbidden animal," the one which was at once a taboo for his clan and a protector of the country he was crossing. From now on, he might as well think of himself as an "involuntary suicide." As a matter of fact, a man's double is supposed to inhabit his *Tana*, or sacred animal, and this is why the man is forbidden from killing it. Owing to supernatural forces, a terrible fate is likely to befall those who happen to kill such an animal, whether they do so intentionally or not.

Wangrin remained on the spot the whole night. In the morning, some peasants found him lying on the edge of the road. He asked them to lead him to the nearest village, where he demanded to be taken to the "master of the knife." To him, he explained his sad adventure.

The master of the knife and eight men, all master hunters and therefore well-acquainted with the surrounding bush, identified the python. It was indeed the *dassiri*[4] of a vast sacred pond where all the wild animals of that region went to quench their thirst. The python went by the name of N'Tomikoro-Saa-ba.[5]

The master of the knife instructed Wangrin to offer a bull, a goat, a cock, and a cat, all of them black, to sacrifice to the pond so that a new *dassiri* might be made manifest by the genie who reigned over the entire region.

Wangrin gave the sum necessary for the purchase of those animals, as well as some kola nuts and millet for the preparation of a sacramental brew.

N'Tomikoro-Saa-ba was given a ritual burial at the foot of the tamarind tree that had been his dwelling place.

Only then did Wangrin understand how right his "objective double" had been in advising him to find a handhold before it was too late.

He returned to Diussola far more morose than he had left it.

31   Madame "Good Offices"

Once he had recovered from his wounds and his feelings of anxiety, Wangrin resumed his activities with a listlessness that couldn't help but be noticed by all who knew him well.

Jacques de Chantalba's stay was drawing to an end. In spite of many efforts, he had not been able to obtain an extension. If he left Diussola virtually empty-handed, at least Tenin's future had been taken care of properly. Burabura and Zumana he entrusted to Wangrin, asking him to find them more stable employment than the kind they had had up to then. As for Tenin, it was superfluous to ask Wangrin to take care of her He said quite simply: "I leave you your daughter. See that she marries as soon as possible."

After Chantalba's departure, Wangrin gave Tenin a very handsome dowry and made arrangements for her wedding with Burabura, who had opened a restaurant for Africans.

As the months went by, Wangrin noticed that his luck was breaking. He decided to seek the help of shrewd and experienced people, capable of dealing on equal terms with the local European merchants who were beginning to make life difficult for him. Accordingly, he wrote to Monsieur Terreau, proposing that he open and manage a sizeable garage, while Madame Terreau could be employed as his personal assistant in the management of the CIEB.

A month later, the couple were in Diussola with very favorable contracts in hand. They settled down most comfortably.

Surrounded by Madame Terreau's attentions, Wangrin gradually forgot the ill fortune that had been dogging his every step. As well as an excellent secretary, Madame Terreau showed herself to be a splendid deputy. Her husband opened the biggest private garage in the whole territory. He represented Wangrin most competently at meetings, was a hard bargainer, and always got the better of his business rivals.

Thanks to Madame Terreau's experience and knowledge, the restaurant/café/hotel grew to resemble a great palace. She engaged all the staff needed to run the restaurant, and clerks to keep accounts for the company as well.

Everything was going swimmingly—money was pouring in from all sides.

Wangrin's "hopeful double" recovered its supremacy over his "objective double," whose voice by now had become but a faint echo within the walls of his inner mind, further muffled by the rustling of large banknotes, and the chinking of silver coins which every evening fell into his immense safe, before finding their way into the current account that had been opened in the new bank at Diussola.

Life was wonderful . . . and Madame Terreau even more so!

Now Wangrin had plenty of free time. He could go wherever he wanted, whenever he chose. All he had to do was to append a few signatures. Madame Terreau got through more work alone than ten vigorous woodsmen felling trees in a virgin forest.

Wangrin was extremely satisfied. Everywhere he boasted that he had the best possible staff and that he was the first Sudanese ever to employ the services of two Europeans. The griots, modulating on their lutes, extolled his deeds in the refrains they sang to the accompaniment of other instruments in Wangrin's honor. Here, for example, is a praise song improvised by Dieli Madi, a song which had enjoyed great vogue for a number of years:

O Wangrin! O Wangrin! Wangrin oo!
Wangrin, you are the yardstick of unique worth.
So unique that when 'worth' sees you approach,
It draws away and says humbly:
This is my Master!
Whilst many of your rivals
Have only listened
With avid ears
To a description of the diamond,
O Wangrin! You own
A coffer full of such treasure.
You resemble a large jar
Full of cool water
Placed at a fork in the road
Under the tree of mercy

That poor thirsty wanderers
May quench their thirst.
Maa-Ngala has made of you
The only Black in the country
With two white-Whites in his employ.
When you hail them, they run,
And they say to you—"Master."

One fine day, Madame Terreau walked into Wangrin's office and found him in a state of deep depression. His wives had gone to spend a holiday with their families, one in Nubigu and the other in Diagaramba, and had been away two full months. Madame Terreau understood that Wangrin's manhood was complaining. She approached him with a letter, and bent over in such a way as to let him see the best part of her breasts, which were very beautiful indeed.

Wangrin, who for two years had been struggling against the charms of that lovely woman, felt that his strength was at last abandoning him. Overcoming his shyness, he said: "Madame Terreau, I have been very much in love with you ever since the day I saw you in that restaurant/café in Dakar. It is only because you are married that I have controlled my yearnings. You must know that my *borofin*, or fetish, forbids me from entertaining sexual relations with a married woman under penalty of the most complete moral and material abasement. Moreover, I don't like being turned down, nor do I want to provoke any scandal. . . . "

Madame Terreau burst out laughing. "One confidence for another," she said to him. "I am not Monsieur Terreau's legal wife. I am not married. In France, I was secretary to an important Cabinet Minister, as well as being his mistress. Then he got involved in a shady financial deal, his government fell and the police began to pry into my affairs.

"Fearing that I might talk, my lover and master advised me to disappear for a while. He entrusted me to the captain of a ship bound for Dakar, letting me understand that a job awaited me there. The job turned out to be what you saw me doing, in the restaurant/café. There, on top of entertaining the customers, I was forced to go upstairs with them whenever they felt like it.

"Exasperated by that kind of life, I agreed to live with Monsieur Terreau and to let him protect me. I was only waiting for my contract, which I had signed under duress, to expire. After that, I was going to leave. Your offer came just in time to save us both."

"And Monsieur Terreau, what sort of a past does he have?" asked Wangrin.

"I don't know too much about it, but I am under the impression that he too wants to be forgotten—or forgiven—or it could be that he had an unhappy love affair."

With such a vacant look on his face, Wangrin resembled a piece of calabash trailing in water. "Where will this false couple lead me?" he wondered. "But is it right for me to prevent their rehabilitation? Have they not shown an honorable amendment of their former ways by working so loyally for me and making my business prosper? In any case, what have I been in the past, if not an embezzler and—why not say it?—a lucky thief? Of course, I have never stolen from the poor, but I have stolen all the same. . . . "

As if he were surfacing from a great depth, Wangrin emptied his lungs with a great sigh. He looked at the woman: "Since before the world you are Madame Terreau, I will continue to call you by that name," he said. "But as any male animal is quick to feel jealousy when he sniffs another male on the tracks of the female he has been pursuing, I would ask you not to let Monsieur Terreau into the secret if anything takes place between us."

Wangrin, won over once more by his "hopeful double," stroked Madame Terreau's hand gently. By and by he patted her loins, saying, "Are there any limits, Madame Terreau to what you and I might achieve together?"

Thus, Madame Terreau became Wangrin's mistress. Was it out of admiration for that finely built descendant of the Bambaras, gifted with exceptional intelligence and courage? Was it a calculated move, prompted by the knowledge of his wealth and generosity? Or was it physical curiosity, a desire to discover the worth of an African male? Whatever the reason, certain now that no barrier stood in the way of his yearning for her, Wangrin decided not to deprive himself. In fact he prolonged his wives' absence, that he might have more freedom and no worries.

Yet, in spite of the pleasure he derived from his relationship with Madame Terreau, Wangrin was beset by a feeling of nagging apprehension, which at times turned into downright gloom. Then he would see everything in the darkest hues. He would exclaim: "Oh, I would much rather die than feel constantly anguished by my painful recollections!"

The image of the old Hausa, large beads of sweat falling from his brow into the sand, would rise before him. At such times, he also relived his arrival in his native village, his forgetfulness of the sacrifice owed to the spirit of his ancestors, and the fact that he had not placed his *borofin* in his luggage. Above all, he remembered the death of the python N'Tomikoro-Saa-ba, who was not only his "taboo" but also the *dassiri* of a vast sacred pond, under the wheels of his car.

One day, gripped by one of these violent crises, Wangrin pulled a gun out of his desk drawer and cried: "Since I am powerless against the evil fate that awaits me, I might as well put an end to this life, so determined to play on me all at once the tricks I have been playing on others."

And he was about to blow out his brains when Madame Terreau, who had heard him shout, rushed in just in time to tear the weapon— bravely—out of his hand. She spoke soothing words to him: "You are exhausted, my dear. You must take a tonic. You must rest."

Her idea of a tonic was a large cocktail of alcohol with aromatic flavorings. Without thinking of what he was doing Wangrin took the glass from her hand and drained it. A few minutes later, he felt immensely relaxed, his anguish relieved, and his spirit invaded by a feeling of contentment that quickly revived his languishing optimism.

That day he ate with a very good appetite.

He was now ready to surrender himself with thorough enjoyment to that first stage of drunkenness, taking regularly what he called with his customary wit, his digestive draft.

In less than four months, Wangrin had become totally converted to drink. His Bambara temperament, awakened and fed by Madame Terreau, had taken the upper hand and done away with his distaste for alcohol, inculcated by a Muslim environment.

Little by little, Madame Terreau had become the uncontested mistress of his life and his household. Everything went through her hands, both input and output, except the business that concerned Monsieur Terreau who was in sole charge of the garage.

Although things seemed to be arranged in the best possible way, Wangrin sank deeper every day in his addiction and all the more dangerously and swiftly, for his life had not prepared him for this eventuality.

32   An Irreparable Loss

One day, Madame Terreau arranged for Wangrin's apartment to be swept and for any old thing that might be found trailing round to be thrown out.

Drunk as a lord, Wangrin had no idea of what was going on. He was sleeping off the effects of drink in the wide and luxurious bed which Madame Terreau had had installed in a room contiguous with his spacious office.

As fate would have it, the day before, Wangrin had pulled out his *borofin* to sacrifice a few kola nuts to it. Then, instead of slipping it back into the small sack where it had always been carefully kept, he had left it trailing on the floor near his bed.

Sweeping the room, one of the stewards had happened on the little black catskin bag. Unsure of what ought to be done with it, he had taken it along to Madame Terreau, who had shouted: "Throw that rubbish in the dustbin!" Thus the *borofin* which contained the pebble symbolizing the alliance between Wangrin and Gongoloma-Sooke was thrown in the dustbin, then into the lorry which collected garbage, and finally in the oven where the town rubbish was incinerated.

Suddenly, five days later, Wangrin remembered that he had left his *borofin* at the foot of his bed. As he couldn't find it, he asked Madame Terreau whether the stewards hadn't seen a little black catskin bag while they were cleaning his room. "Indeed," replied Madame Terreau, "and it looked so disgusting that I told them to throw it in the dustbin."

"In what?" shouted Wangrin.

"In the dustbin."

Seized by a dizzy spell, Wangrin staggered and collapsed like a mud wall eroded by dampness. Then he began to lament:

"O mother! O father! Why does this implacable fate pursue your son?

"O great ancestors, come to my rescue!

"The white woman has committed an abominable sacrilege, but she is ignorant, it is as if she were sick. One must not torture the sick, one must take care of them. One must forgive. . . .

"It is I who am guilty. . . .

"It's my star that is waning. . . .

"It's my sun that is setting. . . .

"It's the night of sorrow that is engulfing me. . . .

"It's the moon of my ill fate that is climbing the horizon of my destiny.

"Is there a sun that has no sunset . . . ?"

Aware that something very serious had happened, Madame Terreau ran as if she had the devil at her heels all the way to Monsieur Tronedon's house, and asked him to intervene and protect her.

"But what have you done?" he asked.

"Out of sheer ignorance, I directed a servant to throw in the dustbin a bag of black catskin that was trailing under my boss's bed. It appears that that bag contained a very precious object, since its loss caused Wangrin such a shock that he crashed to the ground and started gibbering."

Tronedon went immediately to Wangrin's side. He found him in bed, shaking with ferocious fever. Even before Tronedon could open his mouth, Wangrin peeped out from under the blankets and said in a trembling voice:

"Don't worry, Madame Terreau has nothing to fear. The punitive forces have simply chosen to act through her agency. I must face my ill luck with courage. I have already been warned and given advice to that end."

Once he had recovered from his faintness, Wangrin decided to face adversity serenely. "At least," he thought, "let me enjoy life before being swallowed into the chasm that is opening under my feet. People will say: 'Wangrin had a good life!' And that will be my consolation."

In the hope of being forgiven, Madame Terreau exerted herself in every possible way and became more devoted than ever. As for Wangrin, he threw himself body and soul into a life of pleasure. The white woman was unable to dam the floodgates she had opened. Wangrin was drinking and spending money without restraint.

33 Last Warning: The Dove with a Black Ring Circling Half Her Neck

During a gathering at which the griots were improvising songs in his honor, Wangrin offered to regale them with the skin of a panther killed by himself. It was a truly exceptional present he had chosen to produce, one that only valiant men are able to place before the griots who sing their praises.

Having committed himself in public, Wangrin decided to send some professional game-trackers to locate the lair of a panther. They found one without difficulty and reported its whereabouts to Wangrin. Early the following morning he set off, accompanied by Zambila Wattara, ablest among all beaters in Diussola.

The two penetrated the bush, treading carefully and watching on all sides. Flowers were coming into bloom, the forest was green and fragrant.

Wangrin stopped a moment and said to Zambila:

"Hold my gun, I'm going to shed a little water."[1] He walked toward a cotton tree in full bloom and was about to relieve himself when he suddenly heard the clear, staccato cooing of a dove. The bird was perching on a dead branch of another cotton tree, also in front of Wangrin. Wangrin looked up and saw that the bird was flying away from her perch and coming to rest on the left side of the path. It was Ntubanin-kan-fin, the little dove with a slender black line circling half her neck.

Alas! This was the fateful bird which Wangrin should never have laid eyes on in such circumstances. Even less should he have heard her utter seven cries. All of a sudden he recalled the slender figure of Numu-Sama, the smith-initiate who had watched over him and taught him at the time of his circumcision—the very one who, bending over his geomantic pattern, had said to him: "You, my boy, will have a successful life if you can persuade Gongoloma-Sooke to accept you, and your luck will hold so long as you have in your safe-keeping the alliance pebble of that god. I do not know how you will die, but I can see that your star will begin to set the day Ntubanin-kan-fin, the dove with a black ring circling half her neck, comes to rest on the dead branch of a kapok tree in full bloom, cooing seven times distinctly, then leaves that branch and alights on the left-hand side of your path. From that moment you will become vulnerable. You will be at the mercy of your enemies and ill luck will dog your steps relentlessly. Guard against that moment, this is my advice to you."

He could still hear his voice, he even saw his profile take shape among the leaves of the cotton tree where the little dove had been perching.

Clammy, abundant sweat oozed from Wangrin's every pore. An involuntary contraction stiffened his body from head to foot.

Seeing him transfixed and motionless as a statue at the foot of the cotton tree, Zambila Wattara called on him: "Hey, Wangrin! What's the matter? What's happening?"

Wangrin neither replied nor moved.

Zambila ran toward him. He found him wide-eyed and open-mouthed. His mind had fled from his body. Zambila shook him, reciting the incantatory words which every initiate hunter knows by heart and uses as protection for himself or anyone else who might be endangered by the evil spirits who live in the bush.

Little by little, Wangrin's body regained its suppleness. Zambila caught him as he was falling and laid him down gently with his body stretched out to its full length.

An hour went by before Wangrin regained consciousness. He touched his forehead with one hand, then with both hands he rubbed his eyes vigorously, as if he wanted to remove the numbness from them. After a wide yawn, he said:

"Zambila, did you see Ntubanin-kan-fin?"

"Yes, I did."

"Did you count how many times she cooed before flying away?"

It was a rather superfluous question, for all initiate hunters know that the little dove is the messenger of the gods of the bush. Thus, as soon as she utters her first cry, hunters stop all their activities and lend a careful ear. Simultaneously, they try to see the bird, identify it, place it in space, get some idea of its size, its plumage, the nature of its perch, and the trajectory of its flight. They also attempt to appraise its color, which can vary from a bluish-gray variegated with black and white to a tawny cream variegated with brown. To arrive at a correct interpretation, this, plus the number of cries it utters, must be carefully noted.

Zambila knew all this, and had religiously fulfilled the duty which devolves on all hunters in pursuit of game. In answer to Wangrin's question, he limited himself to nodding gently in assent.

"How many times did she cry?" asked Wangrin.

"She let out seven very distinct cries," replied Zambila.

"Since you understand bird language, what message was the little dove trying to convey?"

"The little bird was perching on a dead branch of a cotton tree in full bloom. That portends that death is going to seep into a vigorous and flourishing existence, or else that ruin will drain an immense fortune.

"There were seven cries. That is an indication of the time lapse. It may mean seven days, seven weeks, seven months, but certainly no more than seven years.

"As it was a downwards trajectory, it infallibly signifies a downfall, especially as she landed on the left side of the path."

Wangrin got up. "This time I am for it!" he said. "I have seen and heard that which I was not supposed to see or hear. The white woman has incinerated my *borofin*, and Gongoloma-Sooke's alliance-pebble has been lost in a pile of filth. My hope has flown away like the little dove, and like her, it will come to rest on the left side of my life, which is the unlucky side of my destiny:

O destiny! You are a bizarre shadow.
When we want to kill you
You run away.
When we run away from you,
You follow us."

Zambila understood that Wangrin was by no means ignorant of the things of the bush. He said: "Wangrin, let's go back to town. You need to rest."

"I have no intention of going back without the skin I promised my griots before a large assembly," replied Wangrin. "Dieli Madi must sit on that skin to play the song he has composed in my honor before woe bursts my eardrums, depriving me of every chance to hear music and song, and all the words that will be spoken to exalt me or vilify me."

Wangrin picked up his gun and advanced steadily toward the leafiest part of the wood, where the panther had made his den.

Zambila followed in his footsteps. "Be careful," he said. "The panther is not only a courageous, ferocious, and strong beast. Often he lies in wait in the tree branches. . . . "

He hadn't quite finished speaking when he thought he heard a dull mewing sound which had nothing in common with that of a wild cat. Softly, he said: "Wait, Wangrin. Something is stirring over there, in the branches of that large tree in front of us."

Wangrin stopped. He asked: "On which side of the tree?"

Just then, a black panther, at least a hundred and thirty pounds in weight, and three feet high at the neck, appeared among two branches. Crouching and baring his fangs, he was obviously ready to leap.

"Careful! Careful, Wangrin! He's going to jump on you!" shouted Zambila, visibly anxious, if not altogether terrified.

Wangrin burst out laughing: "Poor black panther!" he exclaimed. "Your mother has given birth to a corpse." And so saying he advanced toward the beast.

Seeing him approach, the panther pounced on him. Fast as lighting, Wangrin took a wide leap to one side, landing into a thick patch of grass. The panther fell on the exact spot where he had been standing a second earlier. The animal rolled on his back and before he had time to get back on his feet Wangrin fired point-blank and shattered his skull with a well-placed bullet which lodged itself between his eyes.

Before so much courage, agility, and skill, Zambila found himself quite at a loss for words. He shouted: "Huwa-huwa-huwa! Wallay! Wallay! Wangrin, you are a master, both in the town and the bush! Billay-billay! Wangrin! You are worthy of the trousers you wear . . . !"

Wangrin arranged for his victim to be transported to Diussola, and skinned. Dieli Madi received his gift.

Thus Wangrin kept his promise, as he had always done throughout his life. Now his destiny was also beginning to keep its word—implacably.

34　Philosopher Tramp

Now Wangrin only went to the office one day out of three. He had become his favorite bar's most assiduous customer. He spent the best part of his days drinking and buying drinks for the local drunks, especially two of them who had been christened "dry throat" and "dry purse." These prodigious drinkers and snufflers had no other worry in the world than to find means of drinking, and plentifully so. To that end, they got into debt, they went begging; if necessary they even drained any glass that was left unattended within their reach. After they had drunk their fill, they improvised burlesque dances, singing in chorus the praises of *Koro-min-fen*, or Great-Sister-Drink.

Wangrin adopted all such fervent dramshop addicts, most of them former *tirailleurs* and now confirmed tramps. He too enjoyed singing the verses then in vogue in the taverns of Segu and Nubigu, especially:

> Let us drink. . . .
> Let us drink till our bellies are distended,
> Let us drink among spenders. . . .
> He who saves his money
> Deserts his friends.

> Now, he who deserts is a coward
> Who runs from General Vertigo.
> Let us drink till our bellies are distended. . . .
> We have no less inside us than a ruminant.

> Let us drink well, let us drink plenty,
> Let us drink the scum of liquor,
> So much the worse for those who are disgusted,

So much the worse for those who are finicky,
Real drinkers are never choosy. . . .

Who can tell me what liquor really is,
That most drinkable and hateful of things?
It gives one audacity
And the lofty fluency of a king.
It makes the visitor wander abroad
And sends his landlord in pursuit,
Which is both expensive and noxious to his work.

Let us drink well, let us drink plenty,
Let us drink till our bellies are distended,
We have no less inside us than a ruminant!

Wangrin's enemies, especially his rivals in business, were watching
his deterioration with the grim conviction that total bankruptcy was simply
a matter of time.

At first, Monsieur and Madame Terreau had had to endure jealousy,
then contempt, from the European, Lebanese, and Syrian merchants, who
referred to them freely as "nigger's menials." Now they attempted in
vain to steer their boss back onto the right path. It was too late. Wangrin
was deaf to all entreaties. He listened only to the gurgle of the bottle
which filled his glass with hot liquid.

Was it this lamentable situation, added to the contempt with which
they were treated by the Whites, that drove the couple to think of leaving
Diussola after having filled their pockets at the expense of a man they
had certainly served well but who had never shown himself stingy or
petty in the least?

Or did they harbor a latent dishonesty which only waited for a favorable opportunity to come to the surface? Be it as it may, one beautiful
morning the two left for a holiday, without saying good-bye to any of the
white-Whites and without leaving Wangrin their address. They promised
to get in touch later on.

Wangrin asked an accountant to check the records, with catastrophic
results. While Wangrin had been drinking and throwing money to the
four winds, the Terreaus had provided comfortably for themselves. Half
of Wangrin's fortune had found its way into their pockets and the pile of
bills they had left behind would barely be covered by the remaining half.
Wangrin was ruined.

The accountant, backed by Monsieur Tronedon, who had remained
a faithful friend, advised Wangrin to declare himself bankrupt. He filed
his petition.

The examining magistrate ordered the police to search for the Terreaus and issued a warrant for their arrest. But the year-long search proved fruitless.

When his property was auctioned, Wangrin astonished everyone by watching the proceeding with total indifference. He did nothing but joke and laugh; above all he spoke words of encouragement to the Africans who hesitated to buy property belonging to one of their brothers, and being sold now as the result of his ill fortune.

In this way, he was able to set his friends' minds at ease, while confounding his enemies, who would have rejoiced at seeing him sad, low-spirited, and disoriented. In the end, every item was sold. The operation had taken two whole weeks.

Fortunately, Wangrin had built a house for his two wives and only daughter still under age, and had registered it in their names. Thus, he was able to retain it and live in it with his family.

Burabura and Tenin, who on Wangrin's advice had long since retired to their country of origin, heard that their protector and benefactor had fallen on evil times. At once they ran to Diussola and, placing their property at his disposal, offered Wangrin the option to come and live with them together with his family.

"No restitution!" said Wangrin, teasing. "I have no intention, my dear children, to infect your house with the implacable ill luck that an even more implacable fate has offered me as a bride. It is a marriage I must consummate without any guest being present. Yes, I shall drain my new cup all alone, and I shall do it without batting an eye. Your father, Wangrin, is made of the same stuff as birds of prey. If necessary, he'll tear out a pittance with his own claws rather than beg for it. Tomorrow you shall go home. If you don't, I'll curse you before the rising sun and the setting moon. I'll call the morning clouds and the evening stars to witness. Come on! Forward, march. . . . Here are five francs; you can buy yourselves something to eat. Even when he's down and out, a father must give a little present to his children, and when he has nothing at all, he can always make them a present of his lice . . . !"

Burabura and Tenin were obliged to accept Wangrin's five francs. No one, however, could make him accept any offer of help, not even his wives, who managed to scrape together a little money by selling tidbits from a stall they had set up outside the entrance to their house.

With his destitution now complete, he decided to install himself outside the imposing building that housed the Post Office and write letters for the illiterate for a fee.

He shared half the small harvest he gathered from so uneven an employment among the blind who were in the habit of begging in that area, while the other half he squandered in the tavern, buying drinks for occasional customers, regardless of the fact that they might be more affluent than himself.

He enjoyed the company of idlers and children. To the latter he told fables and tales he had collected throughout his life. To the adults, he would say:

"Ask me some questions about life! I will be able to answer you, for I have been a great traveler. I have known highways, mountains, caves, forests, and deserts. I have also known towns, villages, and tiny hamlets, their streets, alleys, and paths. Take advantage of my experience and find out the answer while I'm still among you." It is a pity that it isn't possible to relate here all the questions put to Wangrin, and his answers to them which often bore the imprint of his numerous initiations. Some, however, have survived. They are as follows:

"What is life on earth?"

"It is a donkey without a mane who kicks and rears all at once. However able, his rider will be thrown in a ditch."

"It is anguish wedded with hope."

"It is falsehood mistaken for truth, although it plays one dirty trick after another on the living."

"Life is a neurotic old woman. She strikes with the same club—death—both the good and the evil, the pious and the unbelievers."

"What is man?"

"He is an ass who doesn't believe he's an ass, though he spends his life in the meadow of asininity."

"He is a mouse who comes in through one door crying and exits through another stinking."[1]

"He is a creature so pleased with himself that he can't smell his own stench, while he finds the least odor emanating from his fellow men repugnant."

"He is indulgent and tender toward himself, hard and pitiless toward others."

"What is fortune?"

"She is a brute force, who says to her master: 'Express your wishes and I will fulfill them in far greater measure than your asking.'"

"She is a superb mount who delivers her rider safely to any destination of his choice!"

"She is a bad horsewoman who ends up by killing her mount!"

"She is the truest mirror of a man's nature or state of mind."

Thus, Wangrin had become a perpetually semi-drunk storyteller and a public entertainer covered in rags who neither gloried in his past splendors nor reproached anyone for his dire fate.

But alcohol, that evil companion so inimical to man's nervous system, began to nibble at Wangrin's. His hands started trembling and very soon he became incapable of holding a pen. He could no longer earn the few francs that enabled him to drink, to buy drinks for others, or to distribute a few coins among the blind beggars who by now had become his protégés.

Unable to manage without this pittance, he decided to procure it instead at the expense of the rich women who shopped in the market, but like the dashing loser he had always been, he broadcast his resolve. He took a walk around town crying:

"I, Wangrin, formerly interpreter, capitalist, public scribe, now storyteller and public entertainer without a license, have decided that from today I shall post myself on the corners leading to the main market. From there, I'll swipe any money that women bedecked in gold display imprudently on the winnowing basket they hold shoulder high as they walk—an arrogant way of showing that they belong to well-to-do families!"[2]

The following day Wangrin posted himself on a corner, on the market road. A woman covered in gold jewelry and silver bracelets walked past, holding shoulder high a winnowing basket on which were displayed a few banknotes. Wangrin pretended to be passing by too. He caught up with the woman who, busy chatting with a friend, wasn't paying any attention to her winnowing basket. Now Wangrin bumped into her basket, sending her money flying on the ground. Then he shouted to three little boys he'd brought along: "Pick up those notes and give them to me!"

Caught unawares, the woman began to cry: "Wangrin! Kinakee! Wangrin, don't do it!"

In the same tone of voice, Wangrin replied: "*Nnynaa kee! Nnyaa kee!* I've done it! I've done it!"

Everyone burst out laughing. . . .

A man who was passing that way asked the woman:

"How much money did you have on you?" The woman told him. The man handed her a little over the amount, saying: "Wangrin, who is standing over there, has given me a hundred times more in the past!"

Meanwhile Wangrin was dividing his booty into two. One half he pocketed for a few rounds in the tavern, the other he shared among the children and the blind.

For eight months or so he lived on the proceeds of this lesser form of brigandage. Not only did no one ever think of telling the police; on the contrary, some good folks, who were unable to make him accept the least succor, used the ploy of carrying money on a winnowing basket to help him out in a tactful way.

35 The Three Bloods and Death

"The sun must set . . . " as Wangrin himself had been fond of saying. Alas, the hour of his own setting was fast approaching.

That evening, he had kept his audience longer than usual, as if he'd a presentiment that it would be his last. When he turned to his companions, saying as usual: "Ask me some questions!" someone ventured:

"How did the Terreaus manage to steal your money, Wangrin?" "It's a long story," he replied. "I'll just give you a summary. Personally, I find it very amusing. But you must try to draw a moral from it. Everything must be paid for, and in this case I have paid for you.

"'Madame White' was very beautiful, from whichever side you chose to look at her. She also had a very keen sense of hearing. She caught the rustle made by my large banknotes as they were gossiping in my safe, vast as a whole city. The notes were saying to one another: 'Good morning, Mister Thousand-Franc Note!' 'How are you, Madame Wad of Thousand-Franc Notes?' 'Have you any news of Mesdames Wads of Five-Hundred-Franc Notes?'

"She also heard the gold ingots and the huge diamonds say to one another: 'What are those miserable little coins up to, that they jingle day and night, preventing us from sleeping? They're having a good time before Wangrin, that old ogre, sends them off to be deep-fried and eats them up.'

"No doubt she spoke about it to her acting husband. Nothing surprising about that, for white-White women have no secrets from their men, and vice-versa.

"So Madame Terreau set about conquering me that she might also capture the gossips that were in the safe.

"For two years I remained as impregnable as the *Tata*[1] at Sikasso.

But a man can only resist a woman so long as a barrier divides him from her. Between Madame Terreau and myself, the barrier was her 'married' status. Now, through a piece of confidence that I'm very impudently going to pass on to you, I became aware that Monsieur Terreau had no more right than myself over the wagging of her hips, the sidelong glance, the ripples of laughter, and the caresses—with their inevitable outcome—of the self-styled Madame Terreau, who was simply allowing herself to be steered around by a temporary husband.

"When I became aware that no barrier existed between myself and Madame Terreau, I took the first step. That's exactly what I shouldn't have done. Madame Terreau extended a hand. Then she opened her beautiful arms. I rushed into them. Her scent filled my nostrils, her voice my ears, and her *je ne sais quoi* every single pore of my skin.

"Desire of her filled my mind, emptying it of all other desires. I lost my gravity and my gravity deserted me too. Madame vanquished me, with disastrous consequences for my purse. She placed a glass in my hand. It was filled with that loathsome substance which, however, some worship and others become wedded to. It is called 'Madame Drink.'

"Lamb's blood, lion's blood, and pig's blood—those are the three liquids that course in the veins and arteries of Madame Drink. Each blood symbolizes a degree of drunkenness, as the Muslim sages, enemies of alcohol, have told us.

"Oh, you who are bending your ear! Let me tell you, and never you forget it, that I was sadly cheated. . . . Madame Terreau drugged me with her *je ne sais quoi*, then she handed me the first glass of drink. I swallowed it. I saw a lamb who infected me with his gaiety. I followed him, gamboling into the plain of joy and healthy appetite.

"She handed me the second glass. Having drunk it, I stopped being a lamb, a mere neophyte. I came of age, for I had drunk the lion's blood. I no longer laughed—I roared; I no longer skipped happily—I leapt with fury, scattering the earth about me. I killed my honor, I tore at my money with fangs and claws. I was an angry king, like a black lion from Danfa Murga. Alas, like a choleric monarch, I shattered everything that came my way—even love and friendship. I listened to my own voice alone. I didn't tolerate any roars but my own.

"Then, of my own free will, I gulped the third glass of drink—the one filled with pig's blood, which is high-grade and topmost in the hierarchy of drunkenness. I downed that fatal glass and so became the stinking, grunting pig who is sitting before you now."

In a state of exaltation, Wangrin suddenly shouted:

"Lamb's blood! Lion's blood! Pig's blood! I am Wangrin, who drank all three. I, who was everything, whose life was laughter, was reduced to nothing, yet I go on laughing. I shall laugh at men and things. I shall laugh at those who neither know how to laugh nor how to make others laugh, for he who doesn't know how to laugh is either sick or evil. Now I, Wangrin, am neither!"

Suddenly, a whirlwind tore through the town without warning, sweeping away the echo of the laughter that had been Wangrin's applause. Everyone hastened home, battling against the wind that presaged a heavy downpour.

Wangrin refused to go home. Having drained the bottle he had been drinking, he decided to wait for the wind to subside. But as soon as it died down, the wind was replaced by a thick curtain of heavy rain that threatened to continue failing for the best part of the night.

Within minutes, the town was plunged in impenetrable darkness. The streets were converted into torrents. Wangrin, soaked to the marrow, attempted to escape the violence of the downpour by looking for a place where he might shelter. He walked unsteadily toward an entrance he had glimpsed about five hundred yards away during a burst of lightning that had rent a sky already darkened by rain and incipient shadows. Unfortunately, the streets of Diussola were very rough, with steep inclines, which became slippery as soon as the earth grew wet.

After falling twice (traces of his falls were found on the following day), Wangrin reached a ditch that had been dug very deep and was bridged only by a narrow wooden board.

In order to shelter under the porch he had glimpsed from a distance, Wangrin needed to cross it. Half-drunk and shivering with cold, he decided to try nevertheless. Did the board give way, or did Wangrin lose his balance? Be it as it may, our hero and the board found themselves in the ditch, which was over three feet deep and overflowing with tumultuous waters.

Neither screams nor cries for help were heard.

Wangrin fought alone. No doubt he died of exhaustion, or else he drowned in the ditch water, where his body was found the next morning, still clinging to the wooden board.

36 Adieu

The news spread like wildfire. Everyone felt genuine consternation. Wangrin's body was carried to his wives' house. Some kindly messengers undertook to walk about the town and announce the demise of Wangrin, "man of the people."

A few minutes later, a large crowd was flocking to the house of the deceased. On arriving, every woman threw herself on the ground and let out a lament, recalling a good deed, a kindly gesture, or a piece of advice Wangrin had given either to her or to her family.

The imam of Diussola came to inform the family: "According to our tradition, Wangrin's remains belong to those natives of Nubigu—the town where he was born—who happen to find themselves in Diussola at present. Before proceeding to prepare the body, we must look for the eldest member of Wangrin's community and announce his death to him."

Now, an ineffable fate decreed that Romo, Wangrin's sworn enemy but like him a native of Nubigu, should be on holiday in Diussola at that very moment, and that he should also be the eldest of Wangrin's fellow townsmen. It was to him, then, that Wangrin's death must be reported, and his too was the duty to preside over the funeral and lead the remains of the deceased to the cemetery.

Romo had been in Diussola two weeks only. Immobilized by an illness, he hadn't set foot out of the house ever since he had arrived.

When the messenger came in to announce the death of his old enemy, Romo got up, trembling with emotion, and said: "Oh, poor brother Wangrin! Death, who spares no one, has crushed you, as no doubt it will crush me, when my time comes. . . . "

Then he broke the sad news to his wives and children: "Go and mourn our brother,"[1] he said, "and keep his wives and daughter company." Dressed in subdued clothing, he started toward Wangrin's house. There he greeted the imam and all the customary chiefs present. Dieli Madi, Wangrin's griot, got up and said:

"O assembly of noblemen! O assembly of men of caste! O assembly of slaves! The imam asks me to announce that our relative Romo, elder of the people of Nubigu, has arrived. Wangrin's remains belong as of right to the people of Nubigu, and it falls to their elder to say whatever must be said and to decree whatever must be done."

Now, it was Romo's turn to speak:

"Let the imam lay out the corpse and lead us in prayer over the death of my brother Wangrin. Then we shall accompany the body to the place where all of us must be taken one day. Afterwards, everyone who wishes to speak shall do so, and then I too shall speak."

Wangrin's body was washed and clothed in seven lengths of white cloth. The ritual of prayer was celebrated, and his remains taken to the cemetery. A large crowd accompanied Wangrin on his last journey.

When they had returned from the cemetery, Romo told Dieli Madi that anyone who desired to speak was welcome to do so. Dieli Madi informed the assembly.

Over twenty people spoke, relating mostly how Wangrin had quietly got them out of one trouble and another.

A delegation of hunters had been present at the burial. Now they got up and began to dance, acting out the pursuit of a wild beast. Each dancer fired a shot in Wangrin's honor, for all initiate hunters had considered him one of them as well as a great master.

The blind beggars formed a chain by holding on to one another's stick. In this way, they filed past and expressed their grief at a loss which in their opinion left them more bereft than anyone else.

To cut short a performance that otherwise might have gone on several days, Romo now demanded silence from the crowd. He began to speak, thanking everybody first of all for participating in the funeral with so much fervor and good will. Then he said:

"O children of my mother![2]

"According to our tradition, death must put an end to all quarrels. It behooves the survivor to make sure that this really happens. My brother Wangrin and I were deadly enemies. My insane jealousy led me more than once to wish him dead and almost placed weapons in my hands that I might kill him.

"Now that he is no more, my deepest heartspring, hitherto held in check and silenced by my jealousy, begins to uncoil. Now I know that while I did call for his death, deep down I could not wish for it.

"My heart speaks truly, for Wangrin's death has perturbed me, aggrieved me, I would say even killed me a little. Yes, life on earth is a battlefield. Rivals challenge one another, sometimes with downright ferocity, yet always with enthusiasm and with a yearning for glory. But when one's most worthy opponent disappears, fighting ceases to be manly and loses its charm. That is exactly what will happen to me now, for that valorous adversary, whom I always struck but never felled—that adversary was Wangrin.

"Finally death has struck him down, as it will do to me; of that I am certain. Now that I can no longer fence with him, my limbs will grow stiff while I wait to join him in the eternity of the beyond.

"This I declare before God and the spirits of our ancestors: that I forgive the late Wangrin for anything he may have schemed or, indeed, wrought against me. I forgive him with my heart and with my mind. Besides, I beseech Wangrin's memory—before God and all of you, my brothers—to forgive me in my turn for any evil plot I may have fomented or thought of fomenting against him. I know that if I had been the first to die, Wangrin would have spoken in the same vein at my funeral.

"I have led my brother Wangrin's mourning as a sorrowing brother and I shall weep for the loss of our great departed as a contrite relative until the day I die.

"It is a comfort to me, as it will be an inspiring force until the end of my days, to know that Wangrin had remained a man of the highest quality to the very end,[3] a product of an extremely rare breed. For him, fortune and misfortune were but transitory conditions, which must never adulterate the fundamental human qualities of goodness, courage, and sincerity. . . . "

Suddenly overcome by a sense of grief which he found quite unbearable, Romo more or less collapsed into an armchair which happened to be nearby. With a voice that faltered with emotion, he said:

"Let anybody come forward, to whom Wangrin owed money!"

Nobody did, for the simple, yet almost incredible reason that Wangrin had never asked anyone for help in spite of his extreme poverty. Romo thanked God for this state of affairs, which enhanced yet again Wangrin's honor. Then he added:

"As for those who owed money to Wangrin and had not been able to pay their debts, I want them to know that Wangrin had already paid in their stead before declaring bankruptcy, destroying all promissory notes at the same time."

Upon which Romo signified his gratitude to the assembly and dismissed everyone.

Before dispersing, all the mourners said in chorus: "Peace be unto Wangrin's soul!"

Amadou Hampaté Bâ

AFTERWORD

Since the publication of this book in 1973, a few misunderstandings have arisen both on the true personality of the hero and the nature of the work. I don't know why, even in spite of the specific assertions contained in the Foreword, some people ask themselves whether this narrative is fiction, reality, or a clever mixture of both. Although the existence of the man who chose to call himself Wangrin is generally accepted as a historical fact, they think I "romanticized" his life somewhat and even added a subtle sprinkling of oral tradition and supernatural events of my own making in order to flesh out the story and give it a patina of symbolical significance.

I'll repeat once more, then, for anyone who might still be in doubt, that I heard everything relating to the life of the hero, from the account of his birth (a story told by his parents), through his relationship with the animist world, the various predictions, and so forth, all the way to the downfall caused by his commercial bankruptcy, from Wangrin himself, in a Bambara often poetic, full of verve, humor, and vigor, to the soft musical accompaniment of his griot Dieli Maadi. To this very day I recall with emotion Wangrin's voice against the background of a guitar.

When I met him again in Diussola, he had only just declared bankruptcy following the flight of the Terreau couple. Instead of complaining when faced with the collapse of everything that had been at the center of his life, he laughed. "A man is classified not according to his fortune, but rather to his birth and intrinsic worth," he said, quoting an African adage. "Wealth is like a nosebleed: nobody knows why it happens, nor why it disappears." He genuinely thought that the story of his life might serve "both as lesson and entertainment." He didn't know then that his last years would be even more meaningful.

As soon as my task had been accomplished, I left Diussola, never to see Wangrin again. Taking advantage of my various assignments in the area, I rounded off the information already at my disposal by visiting everyone who had frequented him: Romo and his son, Dumuma, who happened to put me up; the family of the Beule chief, Brildji; Count de Villermoz himself, under whom I later served. I have made up no event or circumstances whatsoever. Every single story was told by the people in question or by someone in their circle, either griot, houseboy, or friend.

In the hope that this matter has been settled once and for all, I turn now to the misunderstanding concerning Wangrin's personality. In the years following publication, several people approached me with proposals for filming or televising the text. For a number of reasons, I was obliged to refuse them in each case. To my utter astonishment, most of them had turned Wangrin into a vulgar scoundrel who had neither kindness nor scruples, someone with an almost total lack of human dimensions. Yet, had I not pointed out repeatedly (especially in my Foreword) that Wangrin had cheated only the rich and the powerful, at times with great panache, and on the other hand had acted with almost boundless generosity toward the poor and the needy in all walks of life?

I understood then that some rectification was necessary, and that I owed it to Wangrin's memory to enlighten the reader with the addition of further information. When Wangrin told me the story of his life, narrating with relish and a wealth of detail the outrageous tricks he had so enjoyed playing on the eminent and well-to-do people of that time, he was careful to abstain from alluding to his own good points or good deeds, while in fact the latter were worthy of great admiration as I learned in the course of further inquiries. This attitude is dictated by a rule central to traditional African decorum. Its nobility consists of never praising oneself or boasting about one's good deeds but rather in diminishing oneself while ascribing to oneself the worst faults, according to the proverb: "Self-aggrandizement is unbecoming in the mouth of the speaker." In other words, to praise oneself is in poor taste.

Noble by birth and in his behavior, Wangrin adhered rigorously to this rule. It is as well to remember that the worst epithets in the book, the severest judgments concerning his actions (in the unfolding of the conflict between his two consciences for example) come almost always from his own mouth. He was in no way compelled to do this and very probably out of a sort of inverted coquettishness he did exaggerate a little. On the other hand, no word was ever spoken about the help he had lavished on all the people who surrounded him. It was I who, later, making inquiries of my own in the towns he had visited, came upon traces of his mostly discreet, sometimes anonymous generosity. Although I have alluded to it here and there in the book, I have omitted the details, which is surely an error on my part.

Especially in Diagaramba, I witnessed some of the typical gestures that made him so lovable. He could not bear to see a blind man trying to find his way without going to his aid. He would take him by the hand and often accompany him to his destination, a most unusual attitude for someone as important as "the great Chiefs' interpreters" were in those days. Nor could he behold an old man sitting in the shade of a tree or a wall without handing him those little gifts which give pleasure to old men: a little money, tobacco, kola nuts. . . .

On the other hand, it is true to say that Wangrin was totally devoid of scruples toward the powerful and rich whom he duped shamelessly. The greater the risk, the more intense his pleasure. He was above all a gambler and a man who was afraid of nothing. He would risk anything, and the success of his cunning delighted him almost as much as the gain itself.

To restore the balance and render justice to Wangrin, today I will quote some of his remarkably good deeds:

In all the towns where he served as interpreter, people told me the same story over again: a poor man taken to court for debt or failure to pay taxes (which was frequent at the time) was never imprisoned on those grounds if Wangrin got to hear of it. He always found a way to help the person out of the predicament: either he influenced the Administrator so as to influence his judgment (if need be by deceiving him, which did not bother him in the least), or he paid the sum in question out of his own pocket. He would tell the Administrator that a distant relative of the defendant had sent him the required sum, and the person involved that the Administrator had gone back on his decision and the matter had been archived.

As soon as he arrived in a town, his first concern was to draw up a list of the needy. Old women, old men, those who had no one to provide for them, regularly received assistance from him through discreet emissaries who did not reveal his name. But in the long run, the truth came out. . . .

He was the first and probably the only person to support all the beggars, blind, and infirm of the town where he worked by means of regular allowances—and they were devoted to him. It is true to say that this helped him organize a vast network of information under the nose of the colonial administration, but this reason alone does not explain his generosity which, I repeat, was often anonymous. For example, when he was in "Diagaramba," he used to give his father-in-law everything required to prepare meals on his premises, which were distributed free of charge to the poor without his own name being mentioned. All the merit went to his father-in-law.

No traveler arrived in his town without being sent a gift of welcome or an invitation to be his guest. And often, when the day came for the foreigner to return to his own country, Wangrin gave him a little nest egg for the return journey. Nobody asked for his help in vain, as the speeches on the day of his funeral testified.

It should be remembered that, when he became bankrupt, he possessed "credit notes" in the name of many shopkeepers in town. Their value amounted to several hundred thousand francs, a large sum at that time, which would have allowed him to make a fresh start in life. Instead of claiming these sums, as advised by his accountant, he tore up the credit notes, declaring: "A noble Bambara lends, he does not ask for repayment."

So then, who was Wangrin? Certainly neither saint nor bandit. Like so many men, he was a blend of both virtues and faults, but perhaps more intensely so than others. A complex of contradictions, in the image of his patron god, Gongoloma-Sooke, he was a veritable confluence of opposites, both within himself and the society in which he lived, a forced intermediary between white and black worlds. In spite of everything, his nature was noble and good. This very nature enabled him to show his true grandeur at the time of his downfall. He possessed that exceedingly rare gift, the ability to laugh at himself in any circumstance whatever.

Around 1971–72, as I got down to writing this work, I had no idea whether one day I might be able to publish this work in book form. What mattered to me was to write it and in this way keep the promise I had made to Wangrin. Even if in the end only one human being were to have read this work, I would have felt satisfied. But friends of mine looked around for a publisher and when the book was given the Grand Prix Littéraire de l'Afrique Noire in 1974, I was indeed delighted. Yet, deep down, it is above all on behalf of Wangrin that I have rejoiced. And I like to think that perhaps, in his new abode, he too gets pleasure out of the new episode added to his other adventures. . . .

NOTES

Foreword

1. The term "Commandant" in the original French corresponds to "District Officer" in the British colonial administration in Nigeria, or "Commissioner" in other territories such as Sierra Leone. However, the French term has been retained here, in order to reflect the difference between the structure and the functioning of the British and French systems. As pointed out in Professor Irele's Introduction, the French colonial administration was initially set up by military officers, and its higher ranks continued to be occupied by individuals transferred from the army to the civilian administration. The term "Commandant," with its military resonance, is more suited to their status and function, which enabled them to wield considerable powers over their colonial subjects well beyond those of their British counterparts. (*tr.*)

2. He had been assigned the task of collecting African tales and fables by a colonial civil servant, Monsieur Equilibecq, who later published them (Maisonneuve-et-Larose, Paris, new ed., 1972).

3. I had been nicknamed Amkullel, which means "Little Kullel."

Overture

1. *Dan*, a sort of five-stringed lute made from one-half of a large calabash. Fodan Seni (whose name has also been changed) was a Bambara "knowledge man" in the area of Nubigu. A poet, a great "Master of Words," he was above all an eminent Master of the Komo initiation, hence his deep knowledge of all things traditional regarding his country. (For further information on this character, who so influenced A. H. Bâ's childhood, see *Amkoullel l'enfant peul*, second vol. of his Mémoires, pp. 152 ff.) (*tr.*)

Chapter 1

1. This exclamation signifies astonishment.

2. This exclamation expresses astonishment. The birth of twins is a happy surprise.

3. According to tradition, whenever a sorcerer stumbles into a *soma* (countersorcerer) he is said to lay a soft-shelled egg to signify submission.

4. The placenta is called "the little brothers" of the newly born baby.

5. In traditional Africa, this gesture indicates that someone wants to know something while experiencing a measure of anxiety.

6. The "man's hut" is a house reserved for the head of the family. No one can go there without being summoned. It is also used for storage and as an altar for the spirits of the ancestors.

7. Cowries are small shells which at that time were used as currency.

8. Komo, god of smiths, is the most important deity in the whole Mande

area. When the head smith, called Master of the Komo, dons his ritual garb and bears the ritual mask, he is considered the incarnation of the god. In this condition, and accompanied by ritual drums, he speaks words inspired by the god and is able to predict the future.

9. During that period the French authorities compelled all sons of chiefs and eminent citizens to attend the School for Hostages so as to ensure their fathers' allegiance. They were given the kind of education that enabled them to become servants, houseboys, cooks, or low-ranking civil servants such as copy clerks, telegraphists, or male nurses. The most intelligent of them became school instructors. The School for Hostages was given a number of names. It became "The School for Sons of Chiefs," "The Professional School," "The Advanced Elementary School," "The School Terrasson de Fougères" (named after an eminent Governor-General), and lastly "The Askya Secondary School."

10. When an eclipse occurs, Africans are wont to say that "a cat has caught the moon."

11. The Sema is the guardian of circumcised adolescents who presides over the ceremony of their initiation to Komo.

Chapter 2

1. Telegraph.

2. Red-tailed queleae are little birds which, when resting, warble as noisily as they possibly can without listening to one another.

3. A Sofa is a member of an African Royal Corps.

4. This prophecy came true, for he was obliged eventually to live in exile in a large neighboring kingdom.

5. If a man has been murdered, it is said of him that "he has been swallowed by the night."

6. Marabouts use a sharpened reed as a pen; therefore the expression "reed owner" came to be synonymous with literate, cultivated men.

7. The sheep in question is cherished like a pet and may only be slaughtered and consumed in exceptional circumstances.

8. The Jaawanndo (*plural* Jaawambe) are an ethnic group very close to the Fulbe. They are renowned for their intelligence and spitefulness.

9. A bubu is an ample overgarment.

10. A turti is a large undergarment worn with a bubu.

11. Fifteen francs is a sum equivalent to an African soldier's monthly pay.

12. This very strong perfume is sold by the Hausa of Nigeria. It was an item of great luxury reserved for marabouts, chiefs, and privileged people.

13. To "ask the way" is a conventional way of seeking permission to withdraw.

14. A "man's apartment" is reserved for the head of the family and is inaccessible to anyone who has not been invited.

15. To place something "between one's flesh and blood" is to grant it protection, at the cost of one's life if necessary.

16. "Marabout" paper is a thick, white paper with no lines, extremely costly and difficult to obtain at that time.

Chapter 3

1. *Katran-Zuliye* is "Quatorze Juillet," or July 14th, the French national holiday.

2. The Fantirimori were the colonial infantry.

3. The *alkati* were the district guard in charge of the police force in the town.

4. To "lend one's back" is to be in the wrong.

Chapter 4

1. This proverb means that no circumstances can be more favorable to a pre-established plan, for when a hyena falls into a well, she is rendered powerless; therefore, she cannot escape Death, who is lying in wait.

2. The "secret room" contains a man's fetishes, charms, and earthenware pots with filters, as well as objects used in occult rituals.

3. *Chef de Canton* and *Chef de Province* in the original. (*tr.*)

4. Musso literally means "female," and by analogy something that gives pleasure.

Chapter 5

1. Bintou-bala is a type of rice with a very rich flavor cultivated in the whole region along the vast loop described by the Niger as it traverses Mali.

2. Worwordu is the Fulbe equivalent of the Bambara *thieso*, or "man's apartment."

3. In one of the verses of the Koran, Jesus is referred to as Rouh Allah, that is, Spirit of God.

4. Like all other parts of the narrative, this conversation is authentic and reported accurately in all its details, just as it happened at the time.

Chapter 6

1. Jinjiber is a cool, sweet drink flavored with ginger.

2. "Waadu" is one of the names given to monkeys. It means literally "man look-alike."

3. A griot who is inept at playing his instrument loses all prestige, for it is through his music that he holds noblemen in thrall.

4. Dayemaatien, meaning literally "mouth ruins man," is the name of a celebrated orator who lived in Mali in the thirteenth century.

5. Translation of an African expression which means literally "a heap of garbage."

6. Valiant warriors whose courage and martial feats during the Battle of Woytala—a Bambara city conquered by El-Haji Omar's Tukulor and Fulbe army—became legendary. (*tr.*)

7. When one is not aware, or contemptuous of, the strength of one's enemy, one speaks to him recklessly. Thus, if one were to oppose Wangrin, either not knowing or making light of his true strength, he would meet his match.

8. Traditionally, in Africa, all rivals are called "cousins," that is, "brothers."

9. To have a "mouth that stretches from ear to ear" is to be impudent in the extreme.

10. This passage alludes to the sad end of a young European who in 1908 had trespassed in forbidden places.

11. This expression means that there are noblemen who are prepared to live on the fruits of their labor. Besides, *dé* is French for thimble, but the pun is lost in translation. (*tr.*)

Chapter 7

1. African politeness does not permit an older person to carry even the smallest amount of weight.

2. To "rip someone's mouth" means to punish someone cruelly for their insolence or indiscretion.

3. A *dyula* is a West African peddler.

Chapter 8

1. *Lassidan-Deelral* means literally "warrant-officer belly," a nickname given to the special agent in charge of cash in any given district.

2. *Neguediuru-tigui*, meaning "wire-master," is the nickname given to the postmaster.

3. See note 1 above. (*tr.*)

4. A "single eyeglass" is a monocle.

Chapter 9

1. In the sonsoron posture people, holding their torsos erect, kneel and sit on their heels, their feet resting vertically on their toes.

2. *Bamuso*, meaning "mother-woman," is a respectful term of address.

3. *Dutigui* refers to the head of the household.

4. The *Fantirimori* were the colonial infantry.

5. African soldiers were permitted to attain no rank higher than that of warrant officer, except in very exceptional cases.

6. District guards played the role of mounted police.

7. *Goujat* is the name given to people who followed the army and were employed as laborers for any kind of job that might be needed at the time.

8. "Zindinnguesse" means literally "camp and you'll see."

9. A *lougan* is a large stretch of cultivated land.

10. This proverb encourages people to be on their guard even if a really serious disturbance appears very unlikely.

11. A Fulbe may behave as if he'd forgotten, but in fact never forgets; a reputation which is not always justified. . . .

12. *Annassaara*, an Arabic word meaning "Christian," is used by the Fulbe to designate a European.

13. Soul and mind resemble flowers. The scent they release is called "obliging ways." (Fulbe adage.)

14. The expression "like an ear of corn" is used to describe one who is richly attired in several layers of clothing.

15. To be someone's mouth is to be someone's most precious and indispensable helper. Without a mouth, one could neither speak nor take nourishment.

16. *Mousse Gofornere* is Monsieur le Gouverneur.

17. A "smallboat" is a steamer.

18. Railway line.

19. "Terrestrial canoes" are trains.

20. In Fulfulde, *essi,* or mother-in-law (in French, *belle-mère*), is a term which may be used by extension to designate respectfully the mother of any beautiful woman.

21. "Visceral concretion" is an image frequently employed to describe amber.

22. This expression is used to depict extreme avarice.

23. Wangrin did in fact belong to a family of chiefs in the town of Nubigu.

24. See 12.

25. Yettoore is a specific name used to designate a man, or a clan, through which greetings, congratulations, and praises may be addressed to that man or that clan.

26. Literally "garbage heap." This expression signifies enormous poverty. Reenatu's recollections before her mirror were repeated to me by her griote, who was also her confidante.

27. With the exception of kola nuts, Fulbe custom does forbid eating in front of one's parents-in-law in sign of deference.

28. *Mechoui,* barbecue or whole lamb roasted on a spit.

29. Former wife of a white man.

30. Nickname given to white men.

31. Freshwater fish.

32. A woman of loose morals is often compared to a trough where all sorts of wandering animals come to quench their thirst.

Chapter 10

1. Within the framework of African tradition, all children of friends or companions who are one's contemporaries are considered equal to one's own.

2. Said of a man who feels a strong inclination towards women.

3. This ironical metaphor is a hint to Dumuma that his father, who was nicknamed "the red-eyed black bull" because of his imposing bulk, his black complexion, and his red eyes, is running the risk of being sacrificed as a result of Wangrin's discoveries.

4. Meaning ruthlessly.

5. Fulbe expression signifying prison cell.

6. *Mon capitaine.*

7. Clerk in charge of correspondence.

8. I heard this story from Dumuma himself. When I was serving in Gudugaua, I used to frequent his father's house.

9. The dead of night, when only rats, thieves, and womanizers are abroad.

10. "Black-White," that is, African civil servants and employees within the French administration. Europeans were called "white-Whites."

11. "Black man," or, by analogy, "black-Black."

Chapter 11

1. Greeting formula used by callers.

2. Conventional reply to the greeting formula above.

3. The milking of cows ends between seven and eight in the morning, and between six and seven in the evening.

4. In Fulfulde, *Lamido* means commander, or king.

5. In Fulfulde, *rimaybe* means former slaves, whose original condition cannot be retraced in time. By and by, they became servants attached to one particular house. Traditionally, their status grants them ample rights—namely, those of managing their masters' estates, of bringing up their children, etc. They are considered part of the family, to the extent of bearing the same name.

6. According to African tradition, the father's brother is considered a father. He has the same rights and the same responsibilities. In Fulbe tradition there is no paternal uncle. The father's brother is simply called father. Only the maternal uncle is an uncle. Similarly, the mother's sister is a mother, and only the father's sister is an aunt.

7. Auriferous zone situated in the Mande area, east of Bamako.

8. In Fulfulde, Gueno is the name of the supreme god.

9. In this case the turban represents the highest insignia of chieftaincy.

10. Maana was a powerful Fulbe monarch who in the course of a morning gave away a thousand lots of each item. This episode was referred to during his crowning ceremony, and the tune played on that occasion was called *Eerel-Maana*.

11. In West African savannah country, kola nuts play an important role in the reception of distinguished visitors. They are equivalent to flowers as used in Western etiquette.

12. Sheep fattened by women within the precincts of the household and offered up as sacrifices only in exceptional circumstances.

13. Affectionate expression meaning brother.

14. *Goforner-zenderal*—governor-general; *Franci*—France.

15. Word used to designate Europeans. *Toubab*, which is the plural of *Toubib*, means doctor in Arabic.

16. The expression "to drink water through one's nostrils" means "to be a perfect idiot."

17. *Dogotoro*—doctor.

18. This proverb means that when a man goes to meet some considerable danger with full awareness of what might await him, it is obvious that he has already taken all necessary precautions to ensure his safety.

Chapter 12

1. Magic words used by the Bambara magicians to wish sickness or violent death on their enemies.

2. These cabalistic verses belong in a recitative which Komo's praise-singer intones when the god's sacred mask, borne by a Master of the Komo, has ritualistically left its sacred retreat and been shown to the population. The diospiros is a sacred tree from which the Fulbe cut the stick they use in ritual ceremonies.

3. *Dimadjo* is the singular of *rimaybe*: "house-captives." Among the Fulbe

a *dimadjo* often has more authority over his master's family than his master's eldest son. Besides, he cannot be sold.

4. The cemetery.

5. Expression meaning the late hours.

6. Exclamation which prompts people to act.

7. *Varan* and *gueule-tapée* are saurian reptiles, or giant lizards.

8. This expression is used to describe men who are courageous, mature, and experienced.

9. If a man disappears without leaving a trace, he is said to have been swallowed by the night. Established authority is compared to a dark night that devours her enemies silently and inconspicuously.

10. "Praise be to God!" in Koranic language.

11. "Did you spend the night in peace?" is a customary Fulbe morning greeting.

12. "Entirely peaceful" is the traditional response to that greeting.

13. Men belonging to a noble caste, lords.

14. Exclamation which means "By God's truth!"

15. Quatorze juillet, July 14th, as above. This is sometimes also pronounced *Katos Suliye.*

Chapter 13

1. This expression means that Wangrin was in the habit of praying according to the Muslim rites, bending his body in the prescribed manner and reciting quotations from the Koran.

2. Sacramental greeting spoken by the visitor. The pronoun *you* is used instead of *thou*, to signify that man is supposed never to be alone, but rather in the company of his multiple inner beings as well as with other invisible beings.

3. A response which is traditional in the Bambara tongue. Etymologically, if spoken with emphasis, it means "O my mother!" and its meaning can be extended to "I owe my earthly existence to my mother. . . . "

4. Djenne and Timbuctoo are ancient, famous centers with a high reputation for artistic and scientific accomplishment. There, a special tobacco is cut, which is usually inhaled through the nostrils. In the Sudanese society of that time this tobacco tended to be sold to people favored by good fortune and to "big men." If it was said of a man that he was an *Almundialla*, it meant that he belonged in high places.

5. Since in Africa, slaves, and especially domestic slaves, were considered part of the family, according to their age they could claim the appellation of father, brother, etc.

6. According to Islam, this is the angel who will sound the trumpet on the day of judgment.

7. The Hausas of Nigeria are one of the most industrious ethnic groups in the whole of Africa, renowned for their predilection for fine musicians, eminent diplomats, and courtiers.

8. Supposedly an ancestor of the Fulbe.

9. July 14th.

10. German helmets. (*tr.*)

Chapter 14

1. The *balanza* and the cotton tree are among the most famous and largest trees of Africa. The cotton tree yields kapok, while the balanza fruit is fed to cattle. The timber is burned and the ash, mixed with water, is used to fix dyes on cloth.

2. "To have white teeth wedged in bloodshot gums" means to be a hypocrite.

3. Fearing that rumors on the subject of the exhumation might reach the Commandant, Wangrin decided to ensure himself against any unpleasantness by mentioning it first.

4. Absinthe.

Chapter 15

1. According to the proverb: "The snake is afraid of his killer and the snake killer is afraid of the snake!"

2. Of course it was one of Wangrin's schemes.

3. The adjective "red" is generally used by Bambaras and other ethnic groups to designate the Fulbe because of the particular color of their complexion. Here, it is used in another sense: by "red," the Fulbe allude to those among themselves who are nomadic shepherds and live in the "wooded highlands" with their herds, far from towns and cities. That was the case for the Thiala clan in ancient times, and this appellation has survived. (*tr.*)

4. Locally made millet beer, strong enough to inebriate even a consummate drinker.

Chapter 16

1. An ancestor of the Fulbe, believed to be Thianaba's twin. Thianaba is a mythical python, king of beasts; he rules especially over bovines, goats, and sheep.

2. Steamer.

3. Casse-Carreaux, literally "window-smasher," was a real name, whatever the reader may think of it!

4. The expression "transit house" is derived from African usage but applied in this case to a pavilion or suite of rooms reserved for civil servants or important guests who may have been passing through Dakar.

5. G.G.: Governor-General.

6. One of the most important among Fulbe warrant chiefs of that area.

7. Quatrebras, literally "four arms." Again, a real name.

8. This expression means being inexorably and inextricably locked in combat with one's enemy.

Chapter 17

1. Agents recruited among former African soldiers and administered on the same lines as a police force.

2. *Bons-tir*, literally "good shots." (*tr.*)

3. This piece of information came from Romo Sibedi himself. I served with him, at a time subsequent to these events, both in Gudugaua and Yaguwahi.

4. Mossi, Dogon, and Hausa healers know a number of recipes that are specially designed to catch out simpletons!

5. Having myself served under the Count, one day I heard him say of Wangrin: "He caused me no end of trouble, he betrayed my confidence, and I was ready to send him off to rot in jail. Yet, almost in spite of myself, somehow, I can't help liking him. There is no question that he was a scoundrel, but he had the grand manner and was also very human—always extremely generous with the poor, for example."

Chapter 18

1. Corneille, perched on the roots (Racine) of the heather (La Bruyère), drinks the water (Boileau) of the Molière fountain (La Fontaine). In translation, the rhythm of the rhyme is lost and the meaning of the phrase becomes less clear. (*tr.*)

2. Cap cut according to the Phrygian model, worn by boys who had come of age and had access to important secrets, such as the initiation into the rituals of the gods Komo and Nama, etc.

3. Name of the elder to whom were entrusted both the education and the care of the young boys who had been circumcised. *Se* means power, and *ma*, person; therefore, powerful master.

4. The last prayer before a Muslim retires for the night.

5. A deformation of the French word *représentants*, meaning representatives.

6. A vegetable butter extracted from karite nuts, and sold commercially.

Chapter 19

1. A Muslim mystic.

2. God of gold, to whom the gold mine workers habitually sacrifice.

Chapter 20

1. The White Fathers did often make things difficult for non-Christian administrators.

2. Nicknames given to the White Fathers who ran the Catholic missions.

3. In Africa, injurious words directed at somebody's mother are regarded as the worst possible insult.

4. See note 5, ch. 18. Representatives of warrant chiefs employed in colonial stations.

5. Only truly extraordinary deeds are celebrated by lute players with a song composed specially for the occasion.

6. Expression describing a dance acted out by people so insane that they go on killing until extermination is complete.

Chapter 21

1. This expression is used to describe big game, such as the hippopotamus, the rhinoceros, and above all, the elephant.

2. It must perhaps be explained why Romo had chosen to be paid this way. Being often rewarded with bribes, all interpreters from time to time would take this kind of precaution so that if an inquiry were to be opened, they could swear on what they held most sacred that no money had passed from hand to hand.

3. In order to keep drinking water cool, it is quite common practice in Africa to sink an earthenware pot in soil up to the neck in the shade of a tree.

Chapter 22

1. An allusion to the seven fundamental forces in African tradition which in sequence are generated and destroyed by one another: stone generates iron but is crushed by it; iron is melted by fire, which is put out by water, which is dried by the wind. Then comes man, the only living being who is able to walk against the wind, but drunkenness destroys him; sleep kills drunkenness, worry destroys sleep, death kills worries, and lastly afterlife destroys death. Five material forces begin at the mineral level, five immaterial forces end in the infinity of the beyond, and man is poised in the middle.

2. According to African belief, within one's physical body many others exist, called "doubles." Each one of them is more profound, or more subtle than the preceding one. Thus one has a physical body, a deep double, a deeper double, etc. Illnesses are supposed to result from a perturbation among these doubles. If the disorder doesn't manage to manifest itself in the shape of a physical illness, then it becomes a mental illness.

3. See note 3, ch. 12.

4. *Sanankunia* is a peculiar kind of relationship. Within that context, friends can mock one another and exchange home truths without any ill consequence or unpleasant reactions. This *Sanankunia* establishes among its members, or *sanankuns*, a duty of mutual assistance at all times. Called by some ethnologists "joking relationship" or "cathartic outlet," *Sanankunia* may exist between two individuals, two ethnic groups, or even two countries.

5. Savannah tribe, reputed for its deep knowledge of the occult.

Chapter 23

1. "Pretty Doe of the Markets" is a nickname generally given to beautiful girls who shine at the gatherings and assemblies that are usually held at crossroads or market places. "Egret of the Caravanserai" was another nickname given to Tenin to celebrate her great beauty and her competence in business matters, since caravanserai are places where merchants gather.

2. This expression means to make a deep cut when slashing the throat of an animal. Of course Wangrin never dreamt of cutting anyone's throat in his life. This was a matter of mere intimidation, for threats are extremely common in African parlance: "I will chop you into a thousand pieces. I'll slit your throat, etc. . . . " Although they are used as figures of speech, they represent nevertheless a serious warning for those to whom they are addressed.

3. African women's clothes have no pockets.

4. Bambara name for the supreme God.

Chapter 24

1. This nickname, "Touch-and-Perish Woman," in French "Femme-Toucher-Mourir," was given to any woman who was forbidden from being courted under penalty of death.

2. It was bound to happen, for all households without cesspools were obliged to throw their dirty water on the road, where it dried in the sun.

3. Words uttered by the god Komo, as Bambara tradition has it: "You are what you are, but you could turn into that which I would want you to be."

4. A Malian proverb commonly used by the Fulbe and Bambara people.

5. This tender gesture between man and woman, whether they be married or lovers, betokens intimacy and love. It corresponds to the Western embrace.

6. A boa constrictor who has swallowed a doe is totally at the hunter's mercy, since he can't budge until he's finished his digestion.

7. It is worth mentioning that at the time, it was almost impossible for an African woman to refuse the advances of a colonial big shot without risking endless embarrassment. Some women were even coerced into a temporary union, called "colonial marriage," as a result of the situation that obtained in those days.

8. Generally, civil servants were repatriated after a tour of two or three years.

9. This expression means that a woman is menstruating.

10. To send "someone roasting" means to wish him violent death.

Chapter 25

1. The bark of mahogany trees produces an extremely bitter decoction.

2. Department within a district which fulfilled the function of Treasury.

Chapter 26

1. In this case "sorcerer" refers to someone who is well versed in the occult.

2. Mahogany trees are inhabited by genies, fairies, spirits, etc.

3. "Garde à vous" (or "stand to attention" [tr.]), pronounced the *forofifon* way.

Chapter 28

1. A geomantic pattern is divided into sixteen sections, called "houses."

2. One of the ancient capitals of the Bambara kingdom of Beledugu, in Mali.

Chapter 29

1. A *Zaooia* is a place of meeting and prayer for members of Islamic congregations.

2. *Tigi-naana*, literally "the master has come." A dance which consists of upward leaps, with hands and feet following the same thrust, as in Russian dances.

3. The largest private business in existence at the time in French West Africa.

4. The Senegalese born in the four communes of Goree, Dakar, Rufisque, and Saint-Louis had French citizenship and came under the jurisdiction of French tribunals.

Chapter 30

1. Master of the knife: priest and chief sacrificer of a given village in the Animist tradition of West Africa.

2. A special divination process, based on the way victims and offerings fall back onto the ground. This enables the offerer to interpret the reply given him by his ancestors.

3. The road was not, in fact, tarred with macadam, but simply beaten until the surface became hard and flat. It was usually built out of pebbles and clay, often carried to the spot by men or donkeys. These roads lasted the length of a dry season. But at the time the expression "macadamized" was commonly used.

4. The *dassiri* (literally "mouth-seal") is a sacred animal, protector of a certain area, who must never be killed if the alliance concluded between the ancestor-founder of the village and the protecting animal is not to be terminated, and evil punishment loosed on the area.

5. Literally, "the great python of the old tamarind tree."

Chapter 33

1. Polite way of saying that one is going to urinate.

Chapter 34

1. The mother's genitals represent the "front door" leading to life, while the grave represents the back door or exit. Besides, a corpse stinks.

2. Some African women carry a winnowing fan flat on the palm of their hand, which they point backwards and hold level with their face.

Chapter 35

1. Enclosing wall (see ch. 2 [*tr.*]).

Chapter 36

1. In Africa, fellow townsmen, or countrymen, consider themselves brothers.

2. This expression means "O my brothers!"

3. Wangrin is referred to here as man in the fullest sense of the word, man unto himself as well as one who shapes other human beings. The term has knightly connotations as well. The French word used here is *étalon*, meaning "standard" or "quality" as well as "stallion." The pun is lost in translation. (*tr.*)

CPSIA information can be obtained at www.ICGtesting.com
Printed in the USA
LVOW08s2203141214

418841LV00001B/212/P

9 780253 212269